The Future
of the University
in a Polarizing World

The Glion Colloquium held its 11th meeting 15-18 June 2017 in Glion above Montreux, Switzerland. Founded in 1998 by Werner Hirsch and Luc Weber, the Colloquium's objective is to allow leaders of renowned universities to meet and discuss various questions related to the governance and leadership of research intensive universities — problems and solutions, strategies, special initiatives and failures — in an environment particularly favourable to open and frank exchanges of view. In order to launch the discussion, each participant is invited to write a contribution beforehand in relation with the general topic chosen for each meeting and to present it briefly. To secure a dissemination as broad as possible of the analysis and recommendations coming out of the contributions and discussions, the revised contributions are published 6-8 months later in a volume which is given to numerous university leaders worldwide and sold commercially. Up to last year, ten books have been published, nine of them by ECONOMICA in Paris. Searchable PDFs of the books and of each of their composing chapters are posted 1-2 years later on the Glion Colloquium's website www.glion.org and on the Open Archives of the University of Geneva https://archive-ouverte.unige.ch/. Altogether, more than 130 different leading figures, in particular active or recently retired university leaders, as well as a few politicians and business leaders, have participated in one or more Colloquiums. Participants considered topics such as the rapidly changing nature of research universities, university governance, the interaction between universities and society, collaboration between universities and business, the globalization of higher education, and how universities prepare to address the changes characterizing our times.

The first 10 books drawn from the Glion Colloquium have been traditionally released by a publisher, in particular ECONOMICA. But new technical editing solutions and new commercial channels have emerged. Considering the importance attached by the Glion Colloquium organizers to making the results of the meetings available to all those interested, we have opted for a new solution for editing and disseminating the book, that is self-publication and a print-on-demand. This allows us to make the book available worldwide at a cheaper price. We hope this solution will be well received.

The Glion Colloquium is organized by a small Association based in Geneva, Switzerland, and by an international planning Committee designated every other year to set up the program and invite participants. They have established a partnership with or are subsidized by the Swiss Government and Swiss universities and global corporations, as well as research and cultural foundations.

Volumes

1. *Challenges Facing Higher Education at the Millennium*, Werner Z. Hirsch and Luc E. Weber, eds, American Council on Education/Oryx Press, Phoenix and IAU Press/Pergamon, Paris and Oxford, (1999)

2. *Governance in Higher Education, The University in a State of Flux*, Werner Z. Hirsch and Luc E. Weber, eds, Economica, Paris, London, Geneva (2001)

3. *As the Walls of Academia are Tumbling Down*, Werner Z. Hirsch and Luc E. Weber, eds, Economica, Paris, London, Geneva (2002)

4. *Reinventing the Research University*, Luc E. Weber and James J. Duderstadt, eds, Economica, Paris, London, Geneva (2004)

5. *Universities and Business: Partnering for the Knowledge Economy*, Luc E. Weber and James J. Duderstadt, eds, Economica, Paris, London, Geneva (2006)

6. *The Globalization of Higher Education*, Luc E. Weber and James J. Duderstadt, eds, Economica, Paris, London, Geneva (2008)

7. *University Research for Innovation*, Luc E. Weber and James J. Duderstadt, eds, Economica, Paris, London, Geneva (2010)

8. *Global Sustainability and the Responsibilities of Universities*, Luc E. Weber and James J. Duderstadt, eds, Economica, Paris, London, Geneva (2012)

9. *Preparing Universities for an Era of Change*, Luc E. Weber and James J. Duderstadt, eds, Economica, Paris, London, Geneva (2014)

10. *University Priorities and Constraints*, Luc E. Weber and James J. Duderstadt, eds, Economica, Paris, London, Geneva (2016)

11. *The Future of the University in a Polarizing World*, Luc E. Weber and Howard Newby, eds, The Glion Colloquium, Geneva (2018)

Declarations

12. Rhodes, F. H. T. *The First Glion Declaration: The University at the Millennium*, The Glion Colloquium (1998)

13. Rhodes, F. H. T. *The Second Glion Declaration: Universities and the Innovation Spirit*, The Glion Colloquium (2009)

The Future of the University in a Polarizing World

Edited by

Luc E. Weber

Howard Newby

The Future of the Research University

Volume 11

Geneva

Published by the Association Glion Colloquium
6, Florissant
CH-1206 Geneva
Switzerland

© *Association Glion Colloquium, 2018*

All rights reserved
First published 2018

Printed in the United States

Luc E. Weber and Howard Newby (editors)
The Future of the University in a Polarizing World
ISBN 978-2-8399-2272-2

CONTENTS

PREFACE xiii

CONTRIBUTORS AND PARTICIPANTS xvii

Part I	**Missions and Responsibilities**	1
CHAPTER 1	Rethinking the Education Mission: teaching & learning in the next decade .... *Jean Chambaz*	3
CHAPTER 2	Discipline-based research and inter-/transdisciplinarity as mission .... *Bernhard Eitel*	13
CHAPTER 3	Universities as Curators of Knowledge .... *Lino Guzzella and Gerd Folkers*	19
CHAPTER 4	The Evolution and Missions of Universities in China .... *Jianhua Lin*	29
CHAPTER 5	University-based Innovation and Social Equity "Putting the moccasins back on the feet of our youth" .... *Tim Killeen*	35
Part II	**Resources**	43
CHAPTER 6	Campus Planning and the Future of the University: A perspective from Singapore .... *Chorh Chuan Tan*	45

Chapter 7	Global Research Collaboration: a Vital Resource in a Turbulent World...	57
	Meric S. Gertler	
Chapter 8	Open Science: A Global Enterprise	71
	Luc Henry and Martin Vetterli	
Chapter 9	Impact of Disruptive Technologies on Employment and the Role of Universities..	81
	Atsushi Seike	

Part III	**Leadership and Governance**	93
Chapter 10	Leadership for Change: Some Simple Lessons from the University of Sydney...	95
	Michael Spence	
Chapter 11	The Public–to–Private Shift in Universities: Consequences for Leadership...	105
	Patrick Prendergast	
Chapter 12	University Governance: More Complex than it Appears...	119
	Tony Chan	
Chapter 13	The Geneva-Tsinghua Initiative as a Test bench of the Future of Universities...	133
	Yves Flückiger and Pablo Achard	
Chapter 14	Leadership and Governance — How to 'Manage' Change in Universities?..	139
	Nicholas B. Dirks	
Chapter 15	Managing Change in Change-Resistant Universities	149
	Rebecca M. Blank	

Part IV	**The Future of the University in a Polarizing World**...	159
Chapter 16	The Future of the University — Preparing for Change: Building a Nimble and Responsive University..	161
	Thiam Soon Tan	

CHAPTER 17	National Strategy for Higher Education and Research: Challenges and Pitfalls from a French Perspective... *Alain Beretz*	173
CHAPTER 18	Beyond Brexit: the Road ahead for UK Universities. *Leszek Borysiewicz*	183
CHAPTER 19	Preparing the American University for 2030................. *James J. Duderstadt*	193
CHAPTER 20	The Story of the Cambridge Taxi Driver and the Future of the University.. *Bert van der Zwaan*	205
SOME CONCLUDING REMARKS		217

PREFACE

University leaders have clear responsibilities for addressing the needs of the moment, such as making key appointments, securing the resources required by their institution (not only financial, but also human in terms of faculty and students), and managing these unusually complex institutions. But they also have responsibilities for preparing their institutions for an increasingly challenging and uncertain future. Science and technology continue to advance at an accelerating pace across a broad front, e.g., artificial intelligence, big data, brain research, human gene editing, etc., with important implications for the fundamental missions of the university, learning and scholarship, as well as research. Modern transportation and communication are compelling universities to view their opportunities and responsibilities increasingly on a global level, particularly in scholarly activities. Rapidly changing demographics, associated with aging populations in developed economies and the needs and aspirations of young populations elsewhere, will challenge both the traditional missions and responsibilities of established institutions. Moreover, the rapid changes which are taking place are modifying the way people work, think, learn, communicate, exchange and/or trade, and are rewarded.

Although all the innovations we are witnessing are rooted in the results of the fundamental research done in Research Universities and independent research labs, Higher Education institutions do not adapt automatically to the profound changes brought by these innovations. They have to be responsive in acting intelligently and decisively to adapt the way they accomplish their missions to avoid becoming obsolete.

The changing environment of university action as succinctly described above, combined with the observation that Higher Education institutions are slow to change, motivated the planning committee to focus the Colloquium 2017 on "The Future of the University". To make these considerations more specific, 2030 was set as a target date, roughly a decade ahead.

The planning Committee invited more than 20 university leaders, the great majority of them at the helm of Institutions ranked among the 100 best of the World, located in North America, Western Europe, China, South-East Asia and Australia. High ranked representatives of two global industries, one traditional and one disruptive, also participated in the meeting to provide a different point of view and some input from the culture of business. Moreover, to clarify what is really going on in frontier research, the organizers invited two participants who are highly renowned specialists in their discipline to give in Glion for the Colloquium an introductory presentation of the breakthroughs taking place in artificial intelligence (language machine) and in life sciences.

Participants were invited to write a contribution related to the general theme and more specifically on the implications of scientific and technological progress for teaching and learning, research, governance and leadership. But, not very surprisingly, many papers prepared for the Colloquium and the discussion in Glion revealed that University presidents from the West are also very preoccupied by the fact that the changing world in which we live and where universities are active is suffering a deepening divide between those engaged and taking advantage of the modern world, and those who do not have access or reject these innovations and are, therefore, increasingly left out. If the regional disparities tend to diminish at world level thanks in particular to the rapid economic development of many Asian countries, social inequality is rapidly increasing, as well the feeling among the "have-nots" that they are victims of the new world and have nothing to say. A growing proportion of the population is unsatisfied and frustrated, and is increasingly inclined to blame the elites, leading political or economic organizations, the political and economic system, as well as higher education and research. This deepening social divide explains the rise of nationalistic and populist political parties, the growth of "fake news" and the growing difficulty of dialogue.

University leaders are becoming aware of these new developments, conscious that their institutions should not only be responsive to changes in society, but are also responsible for finding social as well as technical solutions to today's problems.

The 20 chapters assembled in this book clearly reflect this *prise de conscience* brought into the discussion in a couple of papers prepared for the Colloquium and by many participants in the discussion. The missions and responsibilities of Universities are becoming even more delicate and complex. Higher Education institutions have to prepare students for a world and a labour market which might well be very different in ten years' time and therefore will also have to retrain a much higher number of students all through their lives. They have also to continue performing in frontier research as it will remain the main source of innovation crucial for the competitiveness of national and regional economies. But they will have, more than before, to contribute to solving societal problems such as climate change, clean energy, peace, social cohesion, less unequal income and wealth distribution and the pre-eminence of truth and scientific methods. If universities are part of the problem, then these institutions are obviously in a key position to be part of the solution, providing they focus a greater part of their efforts on these threatening societal difficulties.

The chapters are arranged in four parts: missions and responsibilities, resources, leadership and governance and the Future of the University in a Polarising world. The conclusion will focus the attention on the necessary change of paradigm.

The XIth Glion Colloquium was arranged under the auspices of the University of Geneva and enabled thanks to the generous support of the Swiss State Secretariat for Education, Research and Innovation, the Swiss federal Institutes of Technology of Lausanne (EPFL) and Zurich (EPFZ), the University of Zurich and Nestlé to whom we are most thankful. We are also particularly grateful for the effort of those who contributed to the colloquium and to the production of this book, in particular Dr Gerlinde Kristahn, research fellow, and Natacha Durand, head of admissions at the University of Geneva, as well as Edmund Doogue in Perth, West Australia, who provided rigorous editorial assistance.

Luc E. Weber
University of Geneva

Howard Newby
University of Liverpool

CONTRIBUTORS AND PARTICIPANTS

Pablo ACHARD (Co-author of Yves Flückiger's contribution)
With a background in particle physics and computational neurosciences, Pablo Achard works at the University of Geneva Rectorate where he has been in charge, among other duties, of strategic planning and foresight. In this position, he developed the university MOOC program in 2013. He is currently senior advisor to the rector, and co-founder of the spin-off Ayaru.

Alain BERETZ
Pharmacologist (thrombosis & vascular pharmacology) Alain Beretz was president of the Louis Pasteur University in Strasbourg (2007-2008) and of the refounded University of Strasbourg (2009-2016). He has chaired the League of European Research Universities (LERU) (2014-2016). He is currently Director general for research and innovation at the French ministry for higher education and research.

Rebecca BLANK
Rebecca Blank is Chancellor of the University of Wisconsin in Madison. An economist, she served in both the Obama and Clinton Administrations. She was Dean of Gerald R. Ford School of Public Policy at the University of Michigan, and has been on the faculty at Northwestern and Princeton Universities and a fellow at the Brookings Institution. Her contributions to the academic and policy worlds have been recognized with numerous national and international awards, as well as honorary doctoral degrees.

Leszek BORYSIEWICZ
Leszek Borysiewicz was the 345th Vice-Chancellor of the University of Cambridge from 2010 to 2017. He is a Fellow of the Royal Society and a

founding Fellow of the Academy of Medical Sciences. In 2016, he was appointed Chair of Cancer Research UK. He was knighted in 2001 for services to medical research and education.

Stefan CATSICAS

Stefan Catsicas is Chief Technology Officer and member of the Executive Board of Nestlé S.A. After taking a PhD in neurosciences in Lausanne, he started his career as Head of Neurobiology at the Glaxo Institute for Molecular Biology in Geneva. He joined the University of Lausanne as Professor and Chairman of Cell Biology, and was later appointed Vice-President Research and Professor of Cellular Engineering at EPFL. He then co-founded a private group of biotechnology companies and came back to academia as Provost of the King Abdullah University of Science and Technology.

Jean CHAMBAZ

Jean Chambaz, president of Pierre & Marie Curie University since 2012, is a professor at the Faculty of Medicine and former head of the Biochemistry department. His research is in metabolism and intestinal differentiation. He founded the UPMC Doctoral Education Institute and was the first president of the Council for Doctoral Education at the European University Association (EUA). Since 2015, he has sat on the EUA board and chairs the Coordination of French Research-Intensive Universities.

Tony F. CHAN

Tony Chan became president in September 2009 of HKUST, where he is also Chair Professor of Mathematics and Computer Science. He was formerly Dean of Physical Sciences at UCLA and Assistant Director of the Mathematical and Physical Sciences Directorate at US NSF. He is an elected member of US NAE, Fellow of IEEE, SIAM and AAAS. He is Trustee of KAUST and Skoltech, and President's Advisory Council/Board of KAIST and U Vienna.

Nicholas DIRKS

Nicholas B. Dirks is the 10th Chancellor of the University of California, Berkeley, where he is also Professor of History and Anthropology. Before coming to Berkeley, Dirks was the executive vice president for the arts and sciences and dean of the faculty at Columbia University. He is the author of many works of scholarship, including *The Hollow Crown*, *Castes of Mind*, *Scandal of Empire* and *Autobiography of an Archive*.

James J. DUDERSTADT

James J. Duderstadt is President Emeritus and University Professor of Science and Engineering at the University of Michigan. A graduate of Yale and Caltech,

Dr Duderstadt's interests include nuclear science, applied physics, computer simulation, science policy and higher education. He currently teaches science and technology policy at Michigan, while chairing the National Academies Division on Policy and Global Affairs and directing the Millennium Project, a research centre concerned with the impact of over-the-horizon technologies on society.

Bernhard EITEL

Bernhard Eitel is full professor for Physical Geography at Heidelberg University with special focus on dryland research, particularly in Africa, South America and China. After serving as Dean of the Faculty of Chemistry and Earth Sciences, he was elected President of Heidelberg University in 2007. Bernhard Eitel is involved in various scientific institutions, including as member of the German National Academies of Science and Engineering Acatech and of Deutsche Akademie der Naturforscher Leopoldina.

Yves FLÜCKIGER

Since 1992 Yves Flückiger has been a full professor at the Department of Economics of the University of Geneva. Vice-rector of this institution for eight years, in July 2015, he was appointed Rector. His scientific interests include international, education and labour economics and more specifically unemployment analysis, migration policies, income inequality and discrimination and working conditions in diverse labour markets. He has authored many books and more than 120 publications in international scientific journals.

Gerd FOLKERS (Co-author of Lino Guzzella's contribution)

Gerd Folkers is Professor for Science Studies in Chemistry and Pharmaceutical Sciences at the ETH Zurich, where he has been Professor for Pharmaceutical Chemistry since 1991. His research focused on the molecular design of bioactive compounds for personalized therapy of tumors and diseases of the immune system. He served at the Swiss National Science Foundation from 2003 to 2011. He has been a member of the Swiss Science and Innovation Council since 2012, serving as its President since 2015.

Meric GERTLER

Meric S. Gertler has been President of the University of Toronto since 2013. A professor of urban and economic geography, he is widely known for his research on the geographical dimensions of the innovation economy. He is the recipient of many international accolades, including the Distinguished Scholarship Honors of the Association of American Geographers, an appointment as a Corresponding Fellow of the British Academy, and honorary degrees from Lund University and Shanghai Jiao Tong University.

Lino GUZZELLA

Lino Guzzella has been President of ETH Zurich since 2015 and professor of Thermotronics since 1999. From mid-2012 until 2014, he was Rector of ETH. Lino Guzzella studied mechanical engineering at ETH Zurich where he took his doctoral degree. He has held several positions in industry. His research focuses on novel approaches in system dynamics and control of energy conversion systems. Prof. Guzzella is still involved in various international and national research bodies.

Michael HENGARTNER

Michael O. Hengartner is currently President of the University of Zurich (UZH) and President of Swissuniversities. He studied biochemistry at the Université Laval and earned his PhD at MIT. From 1994 to 2001, he was head of a research group at the Cold Spring Harbor Laboratory, US. In 2001, he was appointed professor for molecular biology at the Institute of Molecular Life Sciences at UZH. Between 2009 and 2014, he was dean of the Faculty of Science at the University of Zurich. Professor Hengartner is internationally renowned for his groundbreaking research on the molecular basis of apoptosis.

Luc HENRY (Co-author of Martin Vetterli's contribution)

Luc Henry holds a DPhil in Chemical Biology from the University of Oxford. He completed his doctoral degree in 2011 and was awarded a Marie Curie postdoctoral fellowship at EPFL, Switzerland. He became Managing Editor of the science magazine *Technologist* in 2014 and later held an advisory position at the Swiss National Science Foundation. He was appointed to his role as advisor to the President of EPFL in January 2017.

Tim KILLEEN

Timothy L. Killeen has been president of the University of Illinois System since 2015. As a space physicist, he earlier served as vice chancellor for research and president of the Research Foundation of the State University of New York, assistant director for geosciences at the National Science Foundation, and as a faculty member and administrator at the University of Michigan. He is a member of the National Academy of Engineering and earned his bachelor's degree and PhD at University College London.

Jianhua LIN

LIN Jianhua is the President of Peking University (PKU), with his presidential term starting in February 2015. Born in Inner Mongolia, China, Professor Lin received his PhD in Chemistry from PKU in 1986 and thereafter joined the University as an academic faculty member. He is a professor in solid chemistry, and has published over 140 journal articles. Professor Lin successively held positions including Dean of the College of Chemistry, Executive Vice President and Provost at PKU from 1998 to 2010. He served as President of Chongqing University (2010-2013) and President of Zhejiang University (2013-2015).

Emmanuel MOGENET

Emmanuel Mogenet leads the Zurich-based Google Research European. Prior to his current role, he led a team of 200+ engineers focused on improving Google's search engine. Before joining Google, he spent most of his career working on solving 3D computer graphics and image processing problems for the film special effects industry, in particular at Apple Computers. Born in a small town in the south-east of France, he earned his Master's degree in Computer Science and Artificial Intelligence in 1990 at the School of Mines of St-Etienne.

Howard NEWBY

Howard Newby is Vice-Chancellor Emeritus at the University of Liverpool, UK. He has been Vice-Chancellor of two other universities (Southampton and West of England), head of the UK Economic and Social Research Council and CEO of the Higher Education Funding Council for England. He was formerly professor of Sociology at the University of Essex and the University of Wisconsin-Madison. He was knighted in 2000 for services to higher education.

Patrick PRENDERGAST

Patrick Prendergast was elected as the 44th President/Provost of Trinity College Dublin, the University of Dublin in 2011, for a 10-year term. Coming into office in a period of economic austerity, he brought forward strategies in global relations, commercialization and research engagement. Under his presidency, Trinity has become a member of LERU, advanced a new Trinity Business School and an Engineering, Energy, and Environment Institute (E3). In 2016, a Provost's Council was created as an external leadership group for the university.

Atsushi SEIKE

Atsushi Seike is President (until May 2017) and a professor of labour economics at Keio University. He was a Visiting Scholar at UCLA and Consultant at the RAND Corporation. Currently he is a member of the ILO Global Commission on the Future of Work. He holds Honorary Degrees of Doctor from Ecole Centrale de Nantes and Yonsei University and the title of Chevalier de l'Ordre National de la Légion d'Honneur of France.

Michael SPENCE

After graduating from the University of Sydney with first-class honours in English, Italian and law, Michael Spence lectured in law and worked for the Australian Copyright Council. He obtained a PhD and a Postgraduate Diploma in Theology at Oxford, and headed the law faculty and Social Sciences. He became Vice-Chancellor of the University of Sydney in 2008 and was appointed a Companion of the Order of Australia in 2017.

Chorh Chuan TAN

Tan Chorh Chuan is President of the National University of Singapore; Chairman of National University Health System; Deputy Chairman of Singapore's Agency for Science, Technology and Research; Director of the Monetary Authority of Singapore; Director of Mandai Park Holdings Pte. Ltd; International Member of US National Academy of Medicine; and former Chair of the World Economic Forum's Global University Leaders Forum.

Thiam Soon TAN

Tan Thiam Soon is the President of Singapore Institute of Technology (SIT). He graduated from Caltech and worked in the National University of Singapore before joining SIT in 2012. Professor Tan's main research interests are in land reclamation and soil improvement. In Singapore, he sits on the Board of SkillsFuture, the Land Transport Authority and is a member of the Future Economy Council.

Martin VETTERLI

Martin Vetterli became President of EPFL in January 2017. He received a Dipl.Ing degree from ETHZ in 1981, an MS from Stanford in 1982, and a Doctorate from EPFL in 1986. He has held faculty positions at Columbia University, UC Berkeley and EPFL, where he has been a Professor since 1995. From 2013 to 2016, he was President of the Swiss National Science Foundation. He is an expert in the areas of electrical engineering, computer sciences and applied mathematics.

Luc E. WEBER

Professor of public economics at the University of Geneva, Luc Weber served for more than 30 years in Higher Education and Research in Switzerland, Europe and the wider world. Rector of his University and President of the Swiss Rectors' Conference, he then served numerous international university organizations, governmental and non-governmental. His excellent knowledge of the sector inspired him to create and conduct the Glion Colloquium.

Bert van der ZWAAN

Bert van der Zwaan is the 333rd Rector Magnificus of Utrecht University. Trained as a paleontologist, he has been professor of Biogeology at Utrecht and Nijmegen Universities, Director of the national Darwin Center for Biogeology (2004-2008), dean of the faculty of Geosciences at Utrecht University (2006-2010), and scientific leader and first CEO of Climate-KIC (2009-2010). He is president of the League of European Research Universities (LERU). He has held numerous positions outside academia. He is author of the book *Higher Education in 2040: a global approach* (2017).

PART I

Missions and Responsibilities

CHAPTER 1

Rethinking the Education Mission: teaching & learning in the next decade

Jean Chambaz

UNIVERSITIES ARE OBSOLETE? NOT SO FAST!

Some experts argue that the university model, if it exists, is out of date. It no longer responds to the needs of society or the economy. They say it is obsolete and must be put aside for the new opportunities to access, transmit and participate in the information available through digital technologies.

Facing an increasing flood of students coming to universities, we hear that the institutional capability to accommodate these students is past the breaking point. Our critics emphasize that universities can no longer guarantee that students will successfully complete their degrees nor that they will find a job when they go out into the world.

These same critics also claim that the diplomas we offer are losing their value — often too specialized, too restrictive in scope. Alternative methods of teaching and learning are springing up around us that will be much faster, more effective and less expensive! MOOCs and "fast-food" learning institutions will replace universities! Our institutions move slowly, while the digital revolution is accelerating the pace every day.

Their position is reinforced by the fact that the general public no longer feels restricted to receiving education and knowledge from the traditional providers, while part of the academic community with a nostalgic view of the golden age (which never existed) complains about the constant decline in students' capabilities.

In short, universities are an old-world construction that are doomed to extinction. Much has been said. But I believe this deserves at least some discussion.

IT'S TRUE, THE WORLD IS CHANGING

The world is undergoing a profound societal change. Globalization, as the word indicates, has affected every part of the globe. It has shifted economies and industries toward new sectors and new continents, putting societies in crisis, which must now learn to adapt.

Time seems to move faster. The digital revolution is transforming all activities and processes, including how individuals relate to each other. This represents a true change in civilization. Never before have so many people had access to such an overwhelming quantity of information.

These changes are also transforming professions in the span of a single lifetime. There are new demands on our professions, which are being overhauled and change the way we work. The relationships between generations, particularly in the professional environment, have brought about a reorganization of work, a shift in the norms of networking and a complete integration of an international outlook.

Globalization means enormous challenges; our very successes place a great burden on the wellbeing of our planet in terms of global warming and the scarcity of water and energy resources. This transformation spreads as a market-led organization of the world whose benefits are unevenly distributed in terms of wealth, health and access to knowledge for some, and hunger, poverty and infectious diseases for others.

As a result, globalization is today perceived by populations as more of a threat than an opportunity. It has brought about a loss of confidence in technology and science, and in the role of the "elites" in society. This is a far cry from the world's faith in science and in the relentless technological progress which were the hallmarks of the 1950s, 60s and 70s. The world is now messy and unstable, its cohesion and that of our societies are jeopardized.

The digital revolution has also shaken society, offering an avalanche of information to each individual to deal with in their own way. Our news cycles give the public at most 24 hours to process events happening all around the world; in parallel, social media are very quickly disseminating information to comfort a pre-established vision of the world; we have the ability to "individualize" the information that we receive, so we only hear the ideas that agree with our personal world view.

This new situation raises a critical question to an unprecedented level of importance: how can we verify, evaluate and make sense of the overwhelming mass of information that is available, in a world focused on immediacy and where everything happens so quickly?

THE POST-FACTUAL WORLD

In addition, it is not only the sheer volume of information that is problematic in this post-factual world in which we find ourselves today. As the public tries to inform itself, conflicting information from diverse sources is offered, but without confirmation of the reliability or veracity of each source. How else can we explain the debate on whether mankind has caused climate change when there is 97% consensus on the research among climate scientists? In a survey conducted in 2007-2008, barely half of the US population believed that climate change is caused by human activity (Gallup, 2009). In France, it was 63%, while in Japan, it was more than 90%. Why have some countries been more effective in informing their populations than others? Another example is the proper use of vaccines. Today, more and more people believe that vaccines are unsafe and this compromises the efficiency of public health policies again epidemics. More generally, what will this mean for the introduction of new treatments for diseases, or the ability of the public to intelligently discuss the endorsement or rejection of these policies?

The rise of fake news sites, and particularly the recent meddling in the US, German and French elections — and prominent leaders proposing "alternative facts" — have brought to the forefront the essential need for citizens to have the ability to evaluate and verify that their media sources are trustworthy and independent. Our fellow citizens cruelly lack the tools to sort out this onslaught of false or misleading news. They urgently need to be effectively equipped with the autonomous capacity for analysis.

This cannot happen by sitting alone in front of a screen, with no guidance in how to judge, sort and verify information from disparate sources. Learning this critical approach takes time, and must be reinforced throughout education cycles, from primary school to higher education. It is the underlying requirement for any quality learning and an essential role of universities.

THE VERY HEART OF THE UNIVERSITY EDUCATION MISSION

More than ever, the responsibility of universities is to educate the population to become informed and concerned citizens, as well as experts and leaders for society. In this post-factual world, there is a greater need to offer higher education to a much broader public. However, the resulting diversification of students of all ages and backgrounds (particularly in countries where the selective recruiting of students at the entry of university is not allowed), makes our work more difficult and questionably worthwhile. At the same time, this is a fantastic opportunity to disseminate rational thinking in larger sectors of the society.

Of course, we have to adapt to changes in society and transform our vision of teaching and learning. But we must not compromise on the essence of academic education, that which makes our distinctive contribution essential and also explains the longevity of these institutions and their successes when they are adapted to their time.

While the exponential development of different sciences during the 20th century yielded to hyper-specialization, and sometimes education in silos, today we need to encourage a comprehensive approach to complex issues on a global scale. At the same time, we have to contribute to building a framework of confidence, openness, creativity and responsibility that is necessary for a successful transition.

In research, a university's responsibility is to ensure a critical mass and a critical diversity to confront the evolving challenges, to build transdisciplinary teams of top-notch researchers in their disciplines, and to create an innovation-friendly ecosystem to facilitate the transfer of knowledge when appropriate.

In education, the priority is to equip graduates with conceptual skills and processes, rigorous methodologically-based foundations in disciplines, experience of real-life problems through a research-based approach in a broader interdisciplinary context and the mastery of generic skills in practice rather than through specific courses on "transferable skills".

While this educational role must be reinvented for the current context, it remains vital for the future of our society that universities focus on developing critical thinking and creativity in our students today and in future generations.

The permanence of this essential mission encourages certain sectors of the university — a conservative group, as mentioned above — to resist any changes to the established processes of knowledge transmission. However, there are also large sectors that are engaged in this transformation.

The Bologna process, these last 20 years, has been the occasion for European universities to re-focus on their education mission. While we can ask ourselves whether the European system hasn't become even more heterogeneous over this same period, the Bologna process has accomplished two major successes: the facilitation of student mobility; and the dissemination of the three-cycle degree structure accompanied by the subsequent work on the bulk of knowledge and competences corresponding to each cycle. Rather than slicing up each degree program into credits, which sometimes becomes too bureaucratic, the most promising trend is the reassessment of teaching and learning methods to enable the acquisition of knowledge and competences.

FACING THE CHALLENGES

The most difficult question that universities are facing is how to accommodate masses of students while still ensuring the development of critical thinking.

From 1999 to 2005, enrolment in higher education worldwide increased by 45 million students to 138 million (Britannica, n.d.) (and the share of the student-age population at university went from 14% to 32% in the two decades to 2012 [Economist, 2015]). How can we successfully tackle this challenge of a massive increase in students combined with a regularly reduced governmental investment in universities?

Obviously, in the age of the knowledge society, the Humboldt model — which was conceived for small, privileged classes of students — is still inspiring, but meeting the needs of society requires contemporary solutions.

This massive increase in demand is also accompanied by a large diversification of student populations and their various backgrounds, which in turn implies a larger number of students that need personal mentoring.

ARE DIGITAL COURSES THE MIRACLE SOLUTION?

The rise of MOOCs has been hailed as the education of the future and the demise of universities. Who needs classrooms when we can all take classes from the comfort of our homes? Beyond their initial, impressive success, their business model has so far proven to be questionable. MOOCs have also been known to have very low completion rates, in part because many of the people who sign up for them do not necessarily plan to finish the course. For undergraduates, MOOCs have not been particularly successful, since most students are still at the beginning of their academic journey. At this part of the educational cycle, students usually need more personal interaction and support.

But there have been a number of benefits from MOOCs. Some small, self-selected and therefore homogenous colleges have benefitted from having the participation of international students and others from very different backgrounds because they bring a new perspective to an otherwise fairly closed system. Well-structured students, and particularly graduate students, sometimes use MOOCs produced at other institutions to add content and another teaching point of view to the coursework at their home institution. They are also used by educated adults to complement or update their skill set, making MOOCs a good addition to lifelong learning programs.

TAKING THE DIGITAL AND DATA REVOLUTION FULLY INTO ACCOUNT

Universities are now dealing with generations that have been raised with information technology. This brings its own paradoxes. On the one hand, today's students — and those of the future — consider it a given to have access to an almost infinite amount of information. So they are therefore accustomed to looking for their own answers. University professors now find themselves challenged with competing ideas drawn from the Internet by their students. The ivory tower is open to all winds and universities must now function in the context of a much broader information base.

Much more than a technology shift, the digital and data revolution changes the student's relationship to knowledge, since while it is easy to get, it is difficult to master. The irruption of massive data sets has profoundly transformed research practices in most scientific fields and calls for new ways of teaching & learning. Teaching is no longer the transmission of the state-of-art of knowledge, and learning is no longer just a thorough exploration of a single discipline. The accumulated waves of new knowledge will quickly reshape the state of art, and, at the same time, unverified non-scientific information will challenge this knowledge. In this context, the major function of higher education becomes teaching how to learn and discern.

This requires a re-examination of the learning process. The challenge now is to make our students build their own overall capacity of critical thinking that they will exert throughout their professional and civic life. They need to learn how to label, sort, search, evaluate and analyse data.

The digital world has also brought students the capability to access much more information within the university structure, to review videos of lectures and receive documentation electronically. This change affects how we think and express ourselves, and how we structure information and integrate ideas.

The educational innovation needed is much more than just the integration of digital technology. We must reimagine the role of the professor, one-on-one tutoring, classroom interaction and the best way to support each student using whichever tools they are most comfortable with. This means redesigned teaching methods to give more space to the development of skills and creativity that are in line with a methodological acquisition of knowledge. This would ensure student autonomy. An appropriate balance of distance learning options, learning through case studies, personal or collective research projects, as well as direct teaching and mentoring, are needed to accompany student growth and maturity.

Overall, e-learning technologies bring additional flexibility and alternate learning behaviour. Currently they are more often seen as a supplement rather than a replacement of classes, and e-learning is currently run at the faculty level, offering students blended-learning opportunities. While these programs take time and money to put in place, universities have generally found that they not only change students' approach to learning, but it also can improve the quality of knowledge acquisition. The possibilities offered to personalize the learning experience and to measure performance through e-learning analytics indicate that these tools will see a broader implementation in the future.

MEETING THE NEEDS OF THE SOCIETY

This expected transformation of teaching and learning consumes considerable time and resources, and yet still does not solve the dilemma of how to accommodate the massive increase in the number of students, given their extremely varied backgrounds.

In addition, the job market is constantly changing and there are high unemployment levels for young adults, which puts into question the efficiency of the education system. The demand for skills is continually evolving and the population must therefore adapt to career paths that incorporate changing companies and changing the job types several times during one's life. The job market for executives now functions at a global level, as companies and graduates are automatically referencing an international context.

Encouraging a much larger proportion of the population to attend higher education is as much the current demand of society as an attempt by governments to mask the large numbers of unemployed youth. In France, the recent rise in the number of students at universities is mostly due to a constant increase in the number of students that have passed their vocational and technological baccalaureate (the final exam of secondary schools). Nevertheless, due to the lack of places in higher education vocational curricula, these students enter university to attend general bachelor's programs, for which they do not have the prerequisite skills. This is an important contributor to the high attrition and low success rates found at the bachelor's level in France.

Perhaps we should not be surprised to find that many economic actors now favour "practical" education programs so that graduates are immediately productive in their job. But there are serious drawbacks to market-based educational programs. While it has always been important for universities to prepare students with the knowledge and skills needed for employment, the constantly evolving job market means that the most effective graduates will be those who can adapt.

There is now another stakeholder in higher education that is taking a market-based approach, and strangely enough, it's the students themselves, particularly in countries where the rising costs of higher education have transformed their perspective from student to consumers who are buying a "service". A recent study that surveyed 608 undergraduates in England showed that this consumer orientation was associated with lower academic performance (Bunce, 2016).

A global answer to youth unemployment is to offer more vocational higher education curricula and to fully embed the initial university education into a broader approach of lifelong learning. The degrees earned in initial education are just the first phase of an individual's career path. The Bologna structure of higher education is an opportunity to articulate the acquisition of blocks of knowledge and competences along with professional experience during the span of a career. It facilitates the ability of individuals to return to higher education throughout their lives, at the same institution or a different one — even in another country.

Happily, today's students, who have grown up with ubiquitous access to information, are used to being actors in their own knowledge acquisition, either through online classes to improve a skill set, returning to university for an advanced degree, or anything in between. The idea of circulating between education and professional activity would be reassuring to the individual and reduce the demographic pressure that universities are currently experiencing.

The definition and development of each student's professional project are the driving force for their educational orientation. Universities now multiply student experiences to help guide this orientation, through immersive internships in companies, apprenticeships, research-based projects, working in FabLabs, international student exchanges and accrediting non-university learning. The goal is to enable a student in the first step in the direction they choose: becoming a researcher, integrating the workforce, becoming an entrepreneur, or creating a startup.

Naturally, some university programs are designed for graduates to enter the workforce sooner than others, and as noted above, this workforce should also be able to continue lifelong learning to augment or hone their abilities. Other university programs demand longer studies and teach concepts that require high-level abstract thinking. The graduates from these types of programs will require an adaptation period to their work position — but the payoff is bigger. When education is informed by research techniques, associating a deep understanding of a subject and a broader interdisciplinary context, it pushes students to be more curious, creative and to think outside the box. Executives have been trained to adapt, think of the bigger picture and synthesize diverse information, so that in the five to ten years while rising into their positions of management, they are building on their educational base. The experience these executives gain during their career will equip them to respond to a different, future context.

BEING AGILE WHILE STANDING BY OUR FUNDAMENTALS

Knowledge is expanding at such a rate that it has become difficult to define the parameters of an education in just a few years of study. Progress in science and technology is so fast and so disruptive that it will difficult to predict what graduates should know ten years from now. Universities must be in the business of anticipating the future — in the research they do, and in the knowledge they transmit to the next generation.

It is also essential that students be active participants in their educational plan. In addition to identifying their professional project to define their course of study, this and future generations are more flexible in their approach to learning how to learn — and are more ready to come back for courses as needed.

The acceleration in technical advances has also pointed to a growing need for lifelong learning. Universities are already anticipating the need to work closely with the private sector to ensure that the workforce has access to regular courses to update their skills and take on new abilities. This is an essential support for the transformation to a knowledge-based society.

Finally, we anticipate the importance of internationalization to increase in the future. A university education must enable students to have not only a basic understanding of disciplines other than their major area of study, but to be able to think globally and work in multidisciplinary teams. In a society where globalization is now a given, students must be open to other cultures, where the student body includes people from all over the world and where student mobility programs enable every student to experience life in another country, another language and another culture, since upon graduation, they may find themselves working anywhere in the world.

We can no longer afford to have students graduating without having experienced another way of looking at the world. Their increased access to information around the globe must be accompanied by an enrichment from other cultures and other ways of thinking, leading to a wider and deeper understanding of contexts other than their own. This overall need to ensure student diversity through international mobility is a direct contributor to improving the quality of teaching and learning, enhancing international cooperation and increasing international awareness, which will offer new perspectives and ways of viewing the world.

INFORMATION IS NOT KNOWLEDGE

There is no easy solution, no silver bullet and no magic fix. But for centuries, there has been a reason why our societies have turned to learning centres — to universities — as sources of knowledge and reason. And it is our responsibility to rise to these expectations, to meet today's challenges, and to ensure society's evolution to the benefit of all. Our ability to fulfil our education mission requires regular experimentation, renewal and transformation. However, this can only be accomplished with more openness and the mobilization of our communities, increased university autonomy, the removal of bureaucratic constraints and the sustained support from public sources and other stakeholders.

REFERENCES

Britannica (n.d.). "Global Trends in Education". https://www.britannica.com/topic/education/Global-trends-in-education

Bunce, L. (2016). "The student-as-consumer approach in higher education and its effects on academic performance". *Studies in Higher Education*. Taylor and Francis Online. http://www.tandfonline.com/doi/full/10.1080/03075079.2015.1127908

Gallup (2009). "Awareness, Opinions About Global Warming Vary Worldwide". http://www.gallup.com/poll/117772/Awareness-Opinions-Global-Warming-Vary-Worldwide.aspx

The Economist (2015). "The world is going to university". http://www.economist.com/news/leaders/21647285-more-and-more-money-being-spent-higher-education-too-little-known-about-whether-it is worth it?

CHAPTER 2

Discipline-based research and inter-/transdisciplinarity as mission

Bernhard Eitel

FOREWORD

Disciplinarity and interdisciplinarity are no contradiction. Both are interconnected pillars of outstanding research and the related infrastructures, and both belong to the essentials of research universities. In order to strengthen the university's impact, it is necessary to foster awareness for the potential of multidisciplinarity under one institutional roof in contrast to program-oriented research institutions.

Research profiles the research university. It is central part of their mission. Providing new knowledge, they contribute to an outstanding education and training of the next generation of researchers, to the welfare of humans and societies, and supply insights into the complexity of so called global "grand challenges" as prerequisite for the successful tackling of problems we face. In most countries on Earth, Research Universities in particular are the backbone of the academic system due to the symbiosis between research and academic teaching. Discussing strategies on "research" needs a common ground of what we call research. Therefore some brief remarks about that.

BRIEF DEFINITIONS

We call an academic process "research" if it is the search of unknown knowledge (in German: *Erkenntnis-geleitet*). We see that this process is in general curiosity driven. In contrast to so called applied research, which is rather "processing" on the basis of consolidated knowledge, fundamental research is not assessable, it is a product of creativity. And creativity needs freedom and an environment that supports pollination of open-minded individuals by new ideas, questions or challenges.

An academic discipline is at least defined by a special topic with a corona of challenging questions. Disciplinary research is like drilling into well-defined ground in order to explore the unknown depth. The new knowledge itself profiles again the discipline, provides new special questions and justifies the status of the research field as its own discipline. Thus history teaches us how new disciplines emerged in particular by extremely increased and expanded research activities in the past two centuries.

The attractiveness of disciplinary knowledge for intramural and external third parties is bound to irreplaceable disciplinary expertise. This expertise is generated and further developed by on-going discipline-based research. It is obvious that at the disciplinary rims in contact with other disciplines the integration of adjacent expertise (a) can foster or enable own disciplinary research, or (b) can be used for interdisciplinary research, which is often of more complex character. Just to supplement: we often hear of trans-disciplinary research. We want to stress, that we understand transdisciplinary research as an interdisciplinary research process encompassing expertise of different institutions.

What we see is that two things are necessary: Interdisciplinary research depends on disciplinary expertise and therefore on disciplinary research. And more: Interdisciplinary research cannot substitute disciplinary research, and disciplinary research cannot tackle cross cutting issues of high complexity. So, what we learn is that a research university must provide excellent conditions for doing both to fulfil its obligations, or: to follow its mission!

CHALLENGE FOR RESEARCH UNIVERSITIES: STRENGTHENING DISCIPLINE-BASED RESEARCH WHICH IS CHARACTERIZED BY INTERDISCIPLINARY AND INTERGENERATIONAL BRIDGES

Following the research mission, it is necessary to strengthen monoclinal disciplinary research and disciplinary teaching, on one side, and to foster the mechanisms to entangle them under the institutional roof facing higher complexity on the other. At first that sounds contradictory, but taking a second look we see that its realization requires different measures and instruments.

Particularly in a globalized world with increasing amounts of research outputs and the danger of data jungles, research quality becomes more and more important. Often measuring or quantifying research quality is misunderstood. This becomes obvious if we look at approaches to evaluate and compare the individual quality of the research of our academics. Such attempts are highly difficult because of different disciplinary backgrounds and possible long-term effects of the research, regardless of them being published in prominent journals or not. And, more and more research is not done by individuals, but by teams of outstanding experts.

In our discussion to increase "research quality", and this includes output quality of research and teaching, as well as time-relevant productivity, it is the obligation of the university government to provide best conditions for research by excellent creative milieus and infrastructures. This is of increasing importance if we consider the increasing complexity of research topics and the growing size and diversity of data. Therefore we have to focus on the quality of creative milieus and the technical and administrative facilities available. That is what should be (re-)evaluated in order to make research in our universities even better.

In order to realize the potentials given by the multidisciplinary comprehensiveness of a research university, creative milieus should get optimized in a discipline-based environment, as well as in interdisciplinary contexts. It is to emphasize that the allocation of such creative milieus, as well as a competitive infrastructure, belongs to the tasks of a university government. But how to do that better in the future, that means more consciously and planned, rather than the way it was done more intuitively as in the past? With regard to the increasing research complexity and to the globally accelerating speed of generating research results, academic institutions must provide spaces and institutional structures to make it possible or more efficient to filter, to exchange, to recombine and to generate information, data and new knowledge across the disciplines.

What we learn by studies of creative academic milieus, knowledge spaces, geographies of sciences etc. (e.g. Meusburger & Schuch, 2012; Malecki, 2013; Gregory *et al.*, 2015) is that creativity needs not only time and research shelters, but also spaces to communicate, to meet, to discuss and dispute very different topics informally. In such situations, it becomes easy to entangle the disciplinary expertise intra-institutionally. Our academics get acquainted with their colleagues, they learn about their thinking and language, and they make contact with new ideas and emerging research fields earlier and often more sophisticated than in other places. For about ten years Heidelberg University strategically has been using a set of tools and measures to foster intramural exchange in order to realize the potentials of its comprehensiveness. A selection of some exemplary and successful measures should be briefly illuminated.

Since 2007 Heidelberg University has been following the concept of "Bridge-Professorships". Such professorships are disciplinarily bound, but additionally and reliably financed by two or more so-called Budgetary Units with their own endowment (different institutes, centres or faculties of the university). It is clear, that, as a side effect, this model also supports the university's recruitment by providing additional equipment. Meanwhile more than 10% of the full professorships form such bridges between the disciplines. On one side, they are well rooted in their discipline, develop and create disciplinary expertise, but, on the other side, they contribute to cross cutting issues by maintaining staff and infrastructure in other university subunits. This guarantees sustainable collaboration across disciplinary borders, adds adjacent expertise to institutes and makes them fitter for the competition to contribute to new or emerging research topics. Such bridging structures also support students and young researchers, helping them to discover new fields and to realize the potential of a comprehensive university.

Ten years ago in Germany, we took the risk of requiring, by law, that professors aged 65 or over retire. The mainstream agenda was to focus on young researchers and to offer job positions at professor level earlier than before. We combined the training of young academics with the introduction of strategic Senior Professorships in order to strengthen inter-generational exchange in research and teaching. A Heidelberg senior professor gets equipment and an additional salary generally in arrangements of up to three years (renewable depending on quality and efficiency of the arrangement). The idea itself is not new, but was new for Germany where we have used only traditional Emeritus status. We combined our support for the young with the experience of the well-established. This led to an increase of research performance and optimized processes in the competition for third-party funds. An added value is given for a globally acting institution because it opens up opportunities of informal/collegial mentorships for incoming foreign researchers to socialize into the academic community and to get familiar, faster than before, with the university mission and instruments to entangle disciplines. Again, this supports the research efficiency of the university as a whole.

An important tool to generate and handle data across disciplinary borders are core facilities. Often, and in particular during recruitment negotiations, researchers ask for their "own", exclusively available instrumentation or data access. From a bird's eye perspective, this is inefficient, expensive and supports ivory towers. The implementation of core facilities admits access to top infrastructures to every university member with costs, opens the awareness of interdependencies between shared expertise, creates space to meet and to communicate and reduces the costs. Such core facilities though should not become too big, because they should provide appropriate research-oriented services and should not mute into a simply administered, but instrumentally very complex service unit. This seems to be optimized if the facility is driven with scientific/disciplinary competence and in economic responsibility by a university Budgetary Unit or as a lean central institution endowed with own finances.

Another tool to solve the possible conflict between discipline-based research and interdisciplinarity is our Marsilius Kolleg (Marsilius was the first rector of Heidelberg University in 1386). Here we bring strongly selected groups of outstanding experts of the university and its extra-mural Heidelberg partner institutions together in order to discuss and develop new emerging interdisciplinary issues. The researchers get an extra sabbatical for that, but they do not leave the university. The university fellows stay in their research environment at Heidelberg and get additional time to develop new ideas and to filter and select information and knowledge while the research routine is ongoing. So, the university has no loss in research efficiency, on the contrary, we support research quality, and the best researchers stay in contact with the young academics in their departments.

Past topics were, for example, Climate Engineering, Human Dignity or EURAT, which is a codex developed by lawyers, ethicists, computer scientists and physicians for the use of human genome data in clinics and elsewhere. In a stimulating new building the Kolleg provides a creative milieu for research. Meanwhile a lot of research projects have come out of the Kolleg's debates.

Besides the traditional Studium Generale, the Kolleg is very attractive even for the students. They suggested the so-called Marsilius Studies, lectures given by Marsilius fellows on their interdisciplinary topics, which can be integrated in the individual disciplinary curricula. Again, this makes it obvious how research and teaching form a unit, not only as a propagated purpose but in real life.

It is to emphasize that the added value of this type of intra-mural centre for advanced studies is that more and more colleagues know each other, take notice of research in their neighbourhood and are more open for interdisciplinarity without losing their disciplinary expertise. And, from the rectorate's perspective, an important side effect is diagnosable: the Kolleg works as an engine to integrate newly recruited colleagues in the academic community. The internal cross-disciplinary exchange in the Kolleg, in concert with other measures, fosters the corporate spirit, supports a more coherent university self-understanding and strengthens identification with the university's mission, its strategic goals and ambitions.

CONCLUDING REMARKS

Universities are complex and they face more and more complex situations in our times: ongoing globalization with more and more glocalized identities, the acceleration of research speed and resulting obsolescence, and increasing numbers of students of very diverse origins are major challenges in modern, knowledge-based societies. Given their multidisciplinary character, comprehensive research universities are the backbone to tackle the challenges and to permanently renovate our societies. Therefore we have to realize the potential of our institutions. With regard to the challenging questions we face and the complex data sets we generate, we must avoid universal dilettantism in research and teaching programs by continuously strengthening disciplinary strengths, but we also have to entangle disciplinary expertise in view of the general complexity the modern globalized society faces.

Our mission is to optimize research and research-oriented teaching quality, an increasing field of activity for a modern university, and this field is linked with disciplinary competence and interdisciplinary orientation. It becomes more and more an academic obligation to filter the reliable and case-dependent suitable knowledge and information out of the pure data. And it will not become better by citizen science approaches! Again, this knowledge and information assessment should be better done by interdisciplinary collaborations than with mono-disciplinary view, because, in a complex world, simple answers do not consider feedback-impacts which are not limited by disciplinary borders. This counts not only for basic research but also for transformative and applied research in order to translate research and find innovations for the benefit of humans and society, which remain a central part of the mission and a noble obligation of a research university.

REFERENCES

Gregory, D., Meusburger, P. & Suarsana, L. (2015). "Power, Knowledge, and Space: A Geographical Introduction", in Meusburger, P. et al. (eds.): *Geographies of Knowledge and Power. Knowledge and Space* Vol. 7: 1-18, Heidelberg, Berlin, New York, Springer.

Malecki, E. J. (2013). "Creativity: Who, How, Where?" in Meusburger, P. et al. (eds.): *Knowledge and the Economy. Knowledge and Space* Vol. 5: 79-93, Heidelberg, Berlin, New York, Springer.

Meusburger, P. & Schuch, T. (eds.) (2012). *Wissenschaftsatlas of Heidelberg University. Spatio-temporal relations of academic knowledge production*. Knittlingen, Germany: Bibliotheca Palatina.

CHAPTER 3

Universities as Curators of Knowledge

Lino Guzzella and Gerd Folkers

Every society relies on some form of knowledge, which tends to be organized differently depending on the cultural and historical context. Curating knowledge was once the preserve of mediaeval monasteries and their libraries. This function passed to universities as they were established across Europe. At the same time, these institutions provided a home for thinkers who questioned received wisdom, effectively clearing a path for scientific progress. Modern and open democratic societies need a body of knowledge that is at once individual, collective and socially relevant. The following piece looks at how the Digital Era affects the interplay between knowledge and critical thinking, and the role currently played by universities.

SANCTUARIES OF KNOWLEDGE

In describing the rediscovery of the Roman philosopher Lucretius's work on atomic theory, *De Rerum Natura*, Stephen Greenblatt (2011) takes us back to the monastic world of the Middle Ages. We picture the monasteries as guardians and sanctuaries of knowledge, in keeping with the mediaeval tradition. This was often literally the case: their huge collections of manuscripts form the foundation of current knowledge. The Abbey of St Gall, whose architecture, administration, school and herb garden served as a blueprint for many monastic communities, not only saved lives, but also fostered learning. The role of abbey libraries was to take care of the knowledge they held: to curate it, in other words.

While the monks working in the scriptorium copied time-honoured Christian texts, with some scribes barely able to understand their content, the revolutionary ideas recorded in Roman manuscripts (such as Lucretius's tract) rotted in the cellars of abbey libraries — until Poggio, an "enlightened" former papal secretary roaming the country on a donkey no less, came across the treasure trove. This tale of discovery is told with great flair by the historian Stephen Greenblatt.

Then came Gutenberg and the flourishing riverside print and paper industry. Amsterdam, Mainz, Frankfurt and Basel used the Rhine to produce, clean and transport the new media. Suddenly information and knowledge became inexpensive and much more accessible. Libraries evolved into sanctuaries of knowledge for secular and private use. Although the collections included theological works, many of the earliest books printed had a more practical use: dictionaries, commercial and legal guides, as well as every conceivable tract on medical and herbal remedies.

A FORUM FOR COLLECTIONS AND DISCOURSE

Libraries soon came to house grand collections. In the baroque era — a period of revolutionary advances in optics, medicine and mechanics — library shelves were filled not only with books, but also mineral collections, exotic snail shells from across the globe, geometric models made of wood and wire, herbaria, skeletons and all sorts of mummified specimens.

The collectors, who gradually became highly qualified experts in their specialist fields, started to argue among themselves about the ordering and categorization of individual species. These discussions were formalized into regular meetings of "learned societies and colleges", which eventually evolved into our current academic system. It was common for collectors to be appointed professors at the new universities, which developed from these collegiate (in some cases monastic) communities, or were established by federal or regional rulers for their own utilitarian ends.

ENLIGHTENMENT THROUGH ORDER

The collections, and books describing and interpreting them, attempted to establish a new world order through empiricism. They therefore stood in stark contrast to most of the works held in libraries at the time, which still focused on religion and stayed faithful to biblical traditions. The university collections contained a mass of conflicting ideas — as they still do today. After all, the task of science is to continuously question itself. The American pathologist Theobald Smith (1929) formulated this task in the 20th century as follows:

Research is fundamentally a state of mind involving continual re-examination of doctrines and axioms upon which current thought and action are based. It is, therefore, critical of existing practices.

New (empirical) knowledge is usually needed to create a new order. Such knowledge offers new perspectives on the existing arrangement of the collection, and encourages its re-interpretation. One characteristic of a new order is that is embraces more elements in a categorization system than its predecessor. The new world view becomes more complete, its representation more comprehensive and its explanatory model simpler and more consistent.

PRESERVING THE OLD, FOSTERING THE NEW

Science and technology have helped to create an unprecedented quality of life for many people. Engaging in science involves the research and creation of new scientific knowledge through subjective experience. The tasks can be summed up as follows (Abel, n.d.):

    a) Posing of the "Why?"
    b) Searching for systematically ordered answers
    c) Taking a methodical approach
    d) Validating claims through reasoning and evidence
    e) Breaking the strangleholds of ideology and false authority.

All these five points require a suitable environment. Initially only a human brain is needed to ask questions. But when it comes to questions of chemistry, for example, a laboratory is needed, while any exploration of historical events requires a library or a collection of relevant objects, whether it be churches, paintings, ossified seed pods or sundials. Exploring the "Why?" of the universe requires modern audio-visual aids, along with sophisticated technology such as satellites and spacecraft.

Systematizing these bodies of knowledge by bringing them together in the institutions we now know as universities and research institutes has proved to be a rational approach. As well as imposing a strict methodology, they provide something even more important: the schooling of the next generation of thinkers who will critically engage with and augment our established knowledge, and enrich our scientific understanding. The existing order is not only taught, but at the same time continuously reformulated and questioned. This is only possible if these universities can exist within a democratic system that allows unrestricted freedom of expression.

The key element is therefore to ensure knowledge dissemination. Teaching at universities is thus a crucial element, along with the publication of research and debating its social relevance. As with the advent of the printing press 600 years ago, digitalization and the Internet play a revolutionary role in the dissemination of knowledge, as well as placing it in a critical and social context. And this knowledge is now being cultivated, processed, digested, questioned, refuted, believed and understood through these new media, exactly as it was six centuries ago. Now, just as then, we need places where these processes are transparent and accessible. The current situation is not straightforward — nor was it back then. There are many obstacles to overcome before a scientific discovery can be (provisionally) validated and incorporated into the repository of knowledge for society to draw upon.

Galileo incurred the wrath of the cardinals not because he placed the sun at the centre of our planetary system, but because he wanted to publish his work in Italian, in other words for the benefit of the "common people". True to Galileo's ideal, universities must make all their knowledge available to the public and be prepared to challenge the prevailing world view. Knowledge, and the ability to process it, is the capital of universities. Only by continuously nurturing this capital and putting it to good use can we increase the prosperity of an open society and its fitness in competition with other societal forms (Hanushek & Wössmann, 2015.)

TRANSLATION AND INTERPRETATION (NEW CONTEXTS)

Knowledge exists only with the context from which it was derived and in which it can be applied. A discovery such as the second law of thermodynamics, which defines entropy and posits that the universe evolves along an arrow of time, is not a fundamental law of nature, but has never yet been empirically disproven in our experiential world. Such principles, laws and empirical rules hold true over long periods, possibly for ever. The end goal was thought to have been reached on many occasions. When Max Planck began his studies, physics was assumed to be a closed book. During his lifetime (1858–1947) the formulation of quantum mechanics created an environment in which statistical relationships dominate, a series of traditional physical concepts makes no sense, and established laws cease to be valid.

Such contexts are so alien that they require not only a new order, but first a translation. As the term implies, this means crossing over to a different world, where another language is usually spoken and must be learned to find one's way around. On returning, the task is to tell others who were unwilling to make the journey about the world on the other side: to convince them of the realities over there, to come up with metaphors and comparisons that illustrate arcane relationships. These translation processes are fundamentally important for ordering knowledge and the associated world models. Universities should ideally be institutions that foster an exchange between different worlds, languages, models and ways of thinking. For this to happen, the barriers of a particular discipline need to be overcome, but not torn down entirely. Ordering principles can also be transferred to other contexts. Experiments can be conducted to show whether the new principle holds up. As David Wotton (2016) wryly remarks, it was the view through a telescope that put an end to Ptolemy's geocentric model of the solar system, not Copernicus' theory.

ENRICHING KNOWLEDGE AND MAKING DISCOVERIES

Every "Why?" question challenges the established view of the world. Like young children, science never seems to stop asking questions. It is precisely this childlike curiosity and positive naivety that creates a thirst for knowledge and continuously questions the existing world view. As already emphasized, this does not overthrow this world view, but rather enriches it, because questions inevitably inspire reflection. They enhance our knowledge of the world. They not only help us understand it better, but also — through technology — allow us to find our way around it more easily. These knowledge-based advances have eliminated diseases such as smallpox and polio, democratized mass communication to an unimaginable degree and revolutionized our mobility to such an extent that they have "shrunk the world" for many. Facilitating personal experience through first-hand encounters — the pyramids can be visited at reasonable cost and are no longer the preserve of a tiny intellectual and financial elite — has to be one of the biggest achievements of modern, knowledge-based technology.

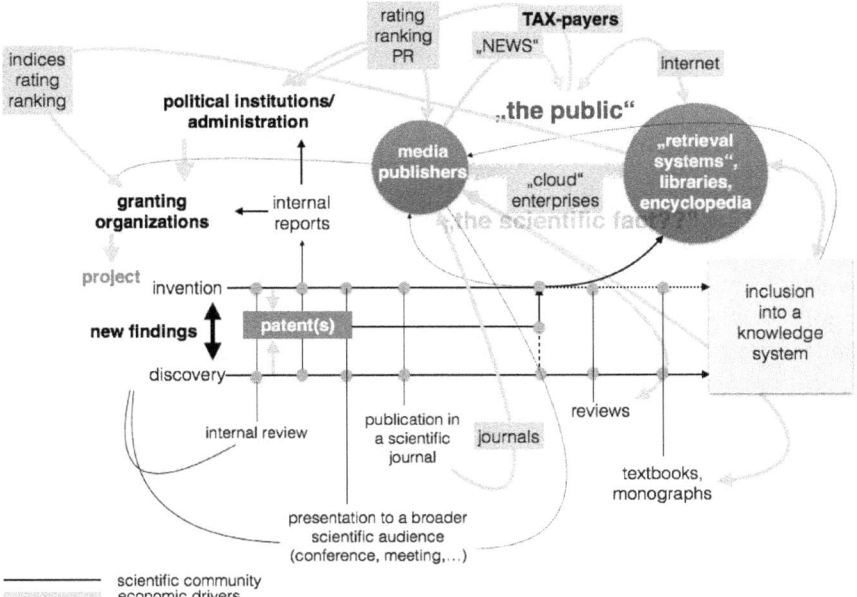

After *The Public Life of Scientific Fact*. See Gerd Folkers & Valdimir Pliska (presented at the 8th Villa Lana Meeting, Prague, 13 January 2006).

The process of enriching knowledge through curating is anything but trivial. The chart on page 23 schematically illustrates the "public life of scientific facts". The inclusion of acquired knowledge in the form of facts and their preservation as universally valid findings, as well as their public perception, has to overcome many hurdles. That is intentional. Every hurdle, or to take an analogy from the field of chemistry, every stage in a distillation column, represents a purification or clarification step. The illustrated system for arriving at a new observation — as the result of a "Why?" question — is the "engine room" for the examination of knowledge through academic processes as called for in the previous section.

Be it a discovery or an invention: it is first allocated to the "new" category and initially evades classification — except to the "new" category itself, of course. In contrast to the categories in everyday use, however, the "new" category is completely undefined and is not used or arranged within our normal scheme of thought and action.

Before a new idea can be released to the public, it must first be validated by one or more experts. This validation may involve the drafting of a research proposal, open discussion in a research seminar, the selection of a keynote speech for a conference or indeed be the subject of dialogue with one's research supervisor. Here "the new" throws up problems that fall within the domain of experts. So, what makes someone an expert? Their ability to categorize. However, experts have their own selves to contend with: it is virtually impossible for them to make an objective judgement that is not influenced by their emotional attachment to their expert knowledge. Objectivity requires a willingness to exclude certain experiences, opinions and views, and therefore draws on the same emotional power that the expert is trying to escape from. Absolute objectivity would be inhuman in the truest sense of the word. This implies that the expert attempts, in a kind of pendulum action, to bring the new (which is potentially beyond the scope of their expertise) into the centre of their knowledge and experience. This is a fundamental mechanism that evolves from a structure that Ludvik Fleck (Rheinberger, 1929) characterized as follows in an essay back in 1929: "*Natural science is the art of shaping a democratic reality and then being directed by it — thus being reshaped by it. It is an eternal, synthetic rather than analytic never-ending labour. Eternal, because it resembles that of a river that is forever forging its own bed. That is the true, living natural science. One must not be oblivious to its creative-synthetic and social-historical elements.*"

Science itself shapes its exponents, and they in turn shape science. Self-referential, autopoietic processes such as these are key aspects of chaotic, non-linear behaviour and allow an ambivalent picture — as Fleck goes on to conclude — of science to be projected "in public": a scientific activity that is clearly ordered and directed by logical conclusions and subsequent actions, as well as a contrasting attitude of an initially loosely oriented, experimental, probing and even playful approach (Folkers, 2013).

However, scientific knowledge must be "trans-subjectively valid" if it is to survive (Janich, 1997). This allows it to transcend the subjectivity which the individual scientist inevitably has, as a result of their personal experience of scientific experiment and through reflection on the question to which they have found the answer. Not until the findings have been generalized by formulating a new theory, or have been adapted to an existing theory that can be defined as meeting the criteria of "valid" or "correct", can there be any talk of science.

At the same time, the entire process is influenced by a vast number of economic and consequently also political factors. The higher the public profile of the newly established knowledge, the more likely its value is to be realized. New values — in the true sense of the word — are thereby created. New technologies and their commercialization happen more rapidly in the case of more prominent "publications". Findings overshadowed by the higher-profile scientific journals take longer to be recognized by the market, but their economic potential is nevertheless powerful. The new gene-editing technology CRISPR-Cas9 is a case in point. After years of attracting minimal publicity, prestigious universities are now squabbling over patents. The prominence of the discovery's publication and its potential (or actual) successful commercialization in turn serve as an important medium for universities, by attracting investors.

If a university can demonstrate that its research results are instantly marketable, this tends to enhance its reputation among taxpayers, and ultimately among politicians as well. As some universities are more successful at this than others, resourceful entrepreneurs, primarily publishers, have built up a rating system based on the number of publications, and in so doing have produced controversial rankings for universities. Any refinement of this system is of course permitted, allowing these rankings to be broken down into individual authors and even main authors, co-authors, lead authors, "responsible" authors and other permutations. As expected, this ranking is broadly reflected in the allocation of research grants as well, which in turn serve to finance new discoveries. Thus, the circle is completed. Universities' most important task is to make sure this knowledge production does not create a vicious circle. Any type of economic, political and ideological influence poses a potential threat to the creation of knowledge and to universities' role as its curators.

RESISTING IDEOLOGICAL STRANGLEHOLDS

In his seminal work on the development of a scientific fact, Ludwik Fleck characterizes such "thought-inhibiting" phenomena as the expression of "thought style" and "thought collective". No one disputes the fact that science and its many disciplines are built on a fixed structure of axioms, laws and theories. Not a random, but rather a methodical approach is the core of scientific investigation. The "scientific method" is the doctrine. And this very approach must be formulated in such a way that the actual scientific task — critical questioning of the prevailing world model — is not only allowed, but held up as a guiding principle.

There is still much room for improvement here. We have certainly moved on from institutional or state ideologies, such as the Stalinist biology of Lysenko, the Nazi ban on Fleck's writing, or the trial of Galileo. But today's ranking hype is an ideology in itself. It reduces scientific achievements to allegedly quantifiable parameters such as the number of publications, their regularity and their citation frequency. The ratings credited to the authors influence their standing in their own "thought collective" and within their institutions.

There is a strong temptation here to look for affirmation rather than disagreement, to form a citation cartel, to mention exclusively positive results in the manuscript and to narrow perspectives instead of trying to break free from the constraints of a single discipline. This problematic attitude gives rise to publication bias and potential misrepresentation and, at worst, "alternative facts", although it inevitably boosts the author's own academic standing and furthers their career.

The nature of science after the Enlightenment offers all the tools needed to combat these negative influences. The purpose of peer-review processes is to prevent such excesses, as the knowledge itself would otherwise seem barely credible, and with it the science as well. It is the duty of all scientists and their institutions, universities and research institutes, to continuously review and improve the peer-review process. The anonymity of this process is quite understandable and desirable, but — dominated by the thought collective — it can often block new ways of thinking for years. For a university's quality management to be effective, compliance, space and time are needed to configure these review processes and establish a strong style of governance.

Moreover, self-correction processes often fail to have an effect where the genesis of the data is simple, but their measurement generates a lot of noise and often occurs in small sample sizes (Holcombe, 2015). To counter this, a form of "social control" is common in a number of specialist areas, where manuscripts are passed around and discussed in small groups as working papers before being submitted to an academic journal. On the other hand, modern media allow comments to be made as soon as an article is published with global access. Some scientific institutions managing large publication databases promote these opportunities.

UNIVERSITIES: CURATORS OF KNOWLEDGE IN THE DIGITAL ERA

There is good reason why university structures have held up so well on the knowledge market for around 1,000 years, if we take the founding of the University of Bologna ("independent of the Pope and the Holy Roman Emperor") as a starting point. Processing knowledge — its reflection and transformation, and creating new perspectives from an empirical method as an integral component of teaching — seems to have proven itself as an effective approach, both in terms of effort and reward, for making massive improvements to our quality of life. Education and prosperity appear to be closely linked to one another (Abel, 2009).

Curating — literally caring for — knowledge was one of the maxims of the monastic libraries and still holds true. But the technical advances of the digital era have fundamentally altered the way in which knowledge is created and disseminated. This inevitably has consequences for universities, which have lost their once dominant role and now find themselves in competition with a host of other knowledge providers. As knowledge is democratized and made accessible 24/7 and worldwide through online platforms, encouraging value-based critical and creative thinking is becoming an educational USP for universities.

However, there are also significant changes ahead for the knowledge business as a whole. Certain concentrations of power in the publishing industry and the resulting criticism of a one-sided measurement of scientific achievements have released forces of reform that culminated in the Open Science movement. Questions of cross-disciplinary management of research data, from methods of assessing scientific achievements to the establishment of new publication channels, are now being discussed. New Open Access platforms have been announced by the medical research foundations the Wellcome Trust and the Bill & Melinda Gates Foundation. A third major player has now entered the arena, with the European Commission launching its own publishing platform (Enserink, 2017) to add momentum to the renewal process.

The new media and artificial intelligence are prompting a fundamental change in education and research. It may take a while, but machines may eventually be capable of asking "Why?" questions, searching for systematically ordered answers and adopting a methodical approach in doing so. Even so, the task of validating the findings of artificial intelligence through reasoning and evidence will remain an essential part of our culture of discourse. Humans will also continue to set themselves apart from intelligent machines in terms of their capacity for empathy, intuition and abstraction. We have a wealth of emotional intelligence that will prevent us from ever being replaced by robots.

Just as when book printing with movable type was introduced, the digital revolution will undoubtedly bring radical changes to our society. Luther's pamphlet is being nailed to the portals of the digital world, so to speak. Digital illiteracy is synonymous with social decline. The curators of knowledge are responsible for ensuring that this knowledge remains accessible under all circumstances, and that it can be continuously renewed and improved.

REFERENCES

Abel, G. (2009) "Die Transformation der Wissensordnungen und die Herausforderungen der Philosophie". *Allgem. Zeitschr. f. Philosophie*, 34: pp. 5-28.

Enserink, M. (2017). in: European Commission considering leap into open-access publishing, http://www.sciencemag.org/news/2017/03/european-commission-considering-leap-open-access-publishing [accessed: 29.03.2017]

Folkers, G. (2013). "Freiheit der Forschung", *Pharmazie* 68: 506–520.

Greenblatt, S. (2011). *The Swerve: How the World Became Modern*, New York, W. W. Norton & Company.

Günter A. (2009). Die Transformation der Wissensordnungen und die Herausforderungen der Philosophie. Allgem. Zeitschr. f. Philosophie, 34: pp. 5-28.

Hanushek, E. A. & Wössmann, L. (2015). *The Knowledge Capital of Nations*, MIT Press.

Holcombe, A. (2015). "Science is Self-correcting", in: Brockman, J., *This Idea Must Die*, Harper Perennial, New York, pp. 369–372.

Janich, P. (1997). *Kleine Philosophie der Naturwissenschaften*, Beck, Munich, p. 40f.

Rheinberger, H.-J. (1929). "Ludvik Fleck und die Historizität wissenschaftlichen Wissens", *Collegium-Helveticum-Hefte*, Vol 1. 2005 p. 30, with quotations from: Ludvik Fleck, "Zur Krise der Wirklichkeit", *Die Naturwissenschaften*, 17, p. 426.

Smith, T. (1929). "The Influence of Research in Bringing into Closer Relationship the Practice of Medicine and Public Health Activities". *American Journal of Medical Sciences*, p. 19.

Wotton, D. (2016). *The Invention of Science*, London, Penguin, p. 246.

CHAPTER 4

The Evolution and Missions of Universities in China

Jianhua Lin

THE EVOLUTION OF CHINA'S HIGHER EDUCATION

The past four decades have witnessed three major development phases of higher education in China.

- **Phase 1: 1980s** — recovery period. During this period, the national entrance examination for college studies was resumed and universities returned to normal operation, after more than ten chaotic years. In spite of the poor conditions back then and the longtime isolation from academic frontiers, faculty members and students were eager to learn everything new and they were all highly motivated for research and studies.
- **Phase 2: 1990s.** China was transforming to a market economy, with an orderly market yet to be put in place. It was a difficult time for Chinese universities. Scholars were confused and lost between pure academic careers and the reality of survival. University education suffered a heavy blow as teachers wanted to do business, students sought to go abroad and many universities began to set up companies for profits.
- **Phase 3: Since the end of 1990s,** China has been more confident for its development path and future directions, enjoying rapid social and economic development and a stable international political landscape. On the occasion of Peking University's centenary in 1998, the central government of China put forward the vision of building world-class universities, which marked an important turning point of higher education in China. Since then, higher education in China has entered a fast-developing stage.

The past two decades have seen drastic changes in China's higher education.

- The **first** change is the merger and expansion of universities. Through mergers, comprehensive universities came into shape. And the expansion and building of new branch campuses have been strongly supported by the central and local governments. Currently, the number of College students has grown from 875,000 in 1978 to 37 million, with the gross enrolment rate reaching 42%, enabling wider access to higher education.
- **Secondly**, efforts have been made to implement the plan of building world-class universities for enhanced competitiveness. The "Project 985", a project by the Chinese government, was launched in May 1998 to provide special support for the development of some major universities. Plans have been formulated at both national and university levels to attract top-notch talents, and science and technology investment has been increased to improve infrastructure and to enhance academic competitiveness.
- **Thirdly**, more inputs have been contributed to education reform. The resources for education in China have maintained continued growth and the input in 2012 reached 4% of GDP. Universities were encouraged to actively explore ways for education reform and enhance the qualification of talents.
- **Fourthly**, reform of management systems has been advanced to set up a modern university system. Extensive exchanges on managements have been carried out between universities from both home and abroad so as to draw on the governance experience of developed countries. In addition, universities have drafted their constitutions for governance in accordance with laws and regulations.

The past two decades have witnessed rapid development and much progress in China's higher education. Yet overall, the development of universities in China still follows an extensive model, as evidenced by more focus on immediate development instead of long-term strategic layout, more attention on academic research and less improvement in education, more input for infrastructure and less progress in institutional building. Obviously, such a model is not sustainable and that's why we need to step up the building of systems and mechanisms and enrich the underlying core values of universities.

THE COMPREHENSIVE REFORM OF CHINA'S HIGHER EDUCATION

From the perspective of serving a county and the public, higher education shoulders two responsibilities:

- **Firstly**, enhancing the quality of higher education so as to provide stronger intellectual and academic support for social and economic development; Secondly, promoting equal opportunities for education and, in particular, focusing more attention on western China and poor families, so as to promote upward social mobility through access to higher education.
- To **further** boost the development of higher education, the central government has taken measures to facilitate the comprehensive reform of universities. On one hand, efforts have been made to streamline government administration and delegate power, reduce administrative interventions and mobilize the initiatives of universities. On the other hand, universities have been encouraged to speed up comprehensive reform and institutional building for more efficient operation. In this context, the central government has designated Peking University, Tsinghua University and Shanghai Municipality as pilot project bases.

For comprehensive reform, efforts are being made to formulate integrated plans based on the analysis of various development bottlenecks and institutional constraints, and to resolve problems in a phased manner. The aim is to unleash the potential for creativity of both organizations and individuals, enhance the utilization of resources, and realize the missions and development goals of universities. Therefore, we should identify, first and foremost, the missions and tasks.

The mission of Peking University is to nurture individuals who lead the future, and to develop new thoughts, to frontier science and future technology. Built on that, our university should serve national development and social progress, which represent effective ways to pool social resources and enhance our core competitiveness. Comprehensive reform will centre on the university's core mission, identify bottlenecks for development and seek solutions.

In this connection, Peking University's plan for comprehensive reform includes the following four aspects: education reform, personnel system reform, reform of the governance system as well as of the system of resource allocation.

- **Education reform** holds the key for comprehensive reform, and it aims to develop a talent cultivation system which combines both specialized and general education. The reform of specialized education focuses on making cultivation plans more diverse and providing more options for students; whereas the reform of general education emphasizes efforts to enable students to have a deeper and genuine understanding of themselves, of society, of China and of the world. To keep a sound balance between teaching and research, and mobilize teachers' initiatives is a challenge facing all research universities, yet the situations are more severe for universities in China. In this regard, we have provided students the space to change majors within the same faculty and the freedom to choose university-wide optional courses. We also linked resources allocation of schools and colleges with teaching/learning, and steered more focus towards teaching and students. Meanwhile, we have launched reforms of teaching methodologies and performance assessment systems.

- The purpose of **personnel system reform** is to foster a sound institutional and cultural atmosphere. During the past decade, to attract top-notch scholars, we have put in place tenure track and annual salary systems, contributing to notable enhancement in competitiveness of Peking University. However, this has also led to a problem with current parallel implementation of both "old" and "new" systems. Therefore, the key to personnel system reform lies in reforming recruitment, compensation and promotion systems of faculty members. Since 2014, the new recruits have all been covered by the tenure track system. In 2016, Peking University adjusted its compensation system, increased benefits for faculty members and conducted tenure assessment for faculty members under the old system so as to facilitate their transition to the new system.

- **Reform of the governance system** mainly involves the academic governance system and the administration system. The goal of the academic governance system is to enable scholars to participate more in academic issues and even play a dominant role. In the past, Peking University practised a "university-schools/departments" two-tier management, which tilted more towards administration. Now we have implemented a "university-faculty-schools/departments" three-tier management, strengthening academic management as the directors of various faculties will be scholars. Currently, Peking University has six faculties in total: humanities, social sciences, economics and management, science, engineering, and medicine, shaping a more rational management structure. At the same time, measures have been taken to develop various types of committees consisting of scholars, especially the set-up of an academic planning committee to oversee the adjustment of academic structure. The focus of

administration system reform is to give schools/departments more autonomy. Moreover, Peking University is planning to make its management team more professional and more service-oriented so as to provide facilities for academic activities and convenience for faculty members and students.
- **Resource allocation** is an important means for universities to adjust the interests of various parties. At Peking University, the resource allocation still mainly follows the principle of centralized management. We will phase in the practice of budgetary management by faculties and schools/departments, and form a more open and sustainable management model.

DEVELOPMENT TREND OF CHINA'S HIGHER EDUCATION

The survival, development and progress of a nation depend on its capacity for innovation; whereas education serves as a bridge for the future as it enlightens people's mind. In a country with as large a population as China's, the abundant human resources will only turn into an advantage with high-quality education. To further deepen reform of higher education and improve education quality, China has introduced a series of new plans and measures, and universities are also stepping up with internal building for addressing future challenges.

One of the major measures is a new plan for "building world-class universities and disciplines", which will soon be put into practice. The new plan has several features: firstly, more focus on education and talent cultivation; secondly, introducing third-party evaluation and competition to break rigidity for dynamic adjustment of extra investment; thirdly, stress on Chinese characteristics to solve China's issues based on national conditions and enhance the international standing of Chinese universities; fourthly, attention to regional layout and special national demands. In addition, the input for the plan this time will see a large rise, twice the amount of the last round of plan, i.e. 100 billion RMB to be provided in the next five years.

Furthermore, the Chinese government has also rolled out new policies for higher education, including streamlining administration, delegating more power to various localities and universities and optimizing services. Covering a wide range of areas such as major setting, personnel system, compensation system, the use of research funds and governance of universities, the new policies are significant in developing modern university systems, removing institutional barriers for higher education development, further unleashing the creativity of universities and scholars, and enhancing the overall competitiveness of China's higher education.

The input for education and science and technology are on a continuous rise. According to the 13th Five Year Plan, the Chinese government and the public will further increase science and technology input, develop major science projects and infrastructure, and strengthen support for scientific research; build national laboratories to increase academic and research capacities that can better serve national strategies in fields of priorities; and education expenditure of 4% of GDP will be maintained to further enhance the quality and level of basic and higher education.

In the information era, education needs to make the best of information technology and promote sharing of high-quality education resources. In this regard, Peking University is leading a nation-wide alliance for sharing on-line credit courses and working together with Wisdomtree, an education service company. Last year, we offered 265 MOOC courses on the platform of treenity.com, with over 1,700 universities joining in course-sharing and 6.5 million students choosing credit courses through the network. The co-sharing of high-quality education resources has particularly helped universities in western China to enhance their teaching quality, thus effectively contributing to equity of education.

What makes a great university with Chinese characteristics is a fundamental issue and a profound challenge for Chinese universities. Modern universities were all originated from and based on western culture. Eastern countries and nations, in spite of their time-honoured history and glorious civilizations, failed to breed higher education in the modern context. In addition to those elements (such as academic excellence, good governance...) requested for a great modern university, an ideal Chinese university of world class shall be deep-rooted in Chinese culture and civilizations and able to tackle China's problems based on its own national conditions. This makes Chinese universities with Chinese characteristics. We are not going back to the old times or old-style schools. Instead, we are trying to explore ways to develop new types of universities in China.

I think, in the drastically changing world today, eastern wisdom may provide us with a unique perspective to observe the world. Eastern culture shall be an inclusive and organic system combining traditional Chinese culture, science and rational culture of the western world, Marxism as well as China's practice. This is actually how Chinese culture has evolved over thousands of years. Likewise, China's universities in the future shall also absorb the essence of all kinds of great cultures and build into world-class universities with Chinese characteristics in a genuine manner.

CHAPTER 5

University-based Innovation and Social Equity
"Putting the moccasins back on the feet of our youth"

Tim Killeen

INTRODUCTION

The dizzying rise of social media, new technologies and globalization over the past 25 years have had a profound impact on the world, raising standards of living to unprecedented levels, but also creating ever more sharply distinctive classes of "haves" and "have nots". This growing social inequity has, in turn, led to enhanced political and societal tensions. We see this clearly playing out in recent elections around the world, as well as within institutions of higher learning. Much of the relevant debate on college campuses in the United States, for example, has become far too acrimonious. Rather than openly seeking larger-scale and more effective solutions to deal with these rising tensions, we have tended to struggle defensively with managing the processes of the divisive discussion itself. Code words and code phrases are regularly used to polemicize and polarize the debate, with proponents often talking over or past each other. Fundamental societal co-benefits, such as student safety and freedom of expression, are often pitted against one another fruitlessly. This is an essentially modern conundrum that we are dealing with almost daily in academic leadership in the US.

This contribution is intended to be a modest thought piece on how large, research-intensive universities such as the University of Illinois System might better deal with the underlying disease at play here (i.e., widening societal inequities), while still accelerating the benefits of an increasingly technological and global society. How should we frame our response to this challenge? I believe that it comes down, at least in part, to the development of a new model of university-based technological innovation — one that has an explicit "full-cost accounting" standard for assessing the benefits of such innovation, moving beyond the more limited standard that is too often the entire focus: enhancing wealth creation by pointing to successful lucrative university spin-offs and/or more simply counting patents and disclosures.

MOTIVATING BACKGROUND

I recall participating in a broadcast debate at the time of a NASA satellite launch event I attended in the 1990s between myself and a very distinguished Native American elder. As the Principal Investigator for an instrument on the spacecraft, I suspect I was there to represent "high technology", and my interlocutor was there to represent his tribal community and its cultural underpinnings. I recall being bemused the first time he told me that "we must put the moccasins back on the feet of our youth". But, after hearing him repeat this statement several times over the course of our conversation, I finally realized that he was espousing a complete return to a more harmonious and humanistic "pre-technological" existence. I responded that I personally believed that — realistically — there were simply no places left on our planet that were sufficiently pristine to which such a retreat could be made, and that we were stuck with science and technology (S&T), for good and/or ill, into the foreseeable future. I suggested that the path forward to address the acknowledged negative effects of modern science and technology could only be found through exploring yet new layers and applications of S&T, making sure to design these new layers for direct public benefit and human welfare. Looking back, I do not believe that I prevailed in this debate — this gentleman was incredibly impressive!

Ever since that experience, however, I have used the moccasin metaphor in talks I have given. I have become firmly of the opinion that we must indeed return these moccasins, albeit only symbolically, by purposefully supporting the optimal and equitable application of knowledge and technology to expand human welfare for the many, not just for the few. For me, the expression now means intentionally reducing the number of "have-nots" while also increasing the number of "haves" — to reach that more harmonious place where human wellbeing writ large and wealth generation go together hand-in-hand.

This will be a massive task. Just one sobering statistic from my own experience will illustrate just how far away we are from investing adequately in social-equity-building S&T research and development. It comes from analysis of our response to the climate change challenge, which is clearly one of the most important ones that we face. Human-induced climate change is already disproportionately harming enormous numbers of people living in socio-economically disadvantaged regions. One would think that, as such, there would be a strong priority given to research and development (R&D) designed to mitigate (or create adaptation strategies for) the worst effects of climate change — a field sometimes called "global change research". As vice chair for strategic planning for the US Global Change Research program in 2012 and as a founder of the international collaborative global change research effort known as the Belmont Forum (n.d.), I was in a position to estimate with some accuracy the total world-wide governmental investment in research associated with global environmental change. The number at the time was somewhere between $10 billion and $15 billion annually, with the US still acting as the most significant funder of global change research in dollar terms, primarily due to its significant space sector. This number can be readily compared with the approximately $50 billion in harmful effects of Super Storm Sandy on the US Eastern Seaboard on one day in October 2012. The cost of damage from this major storm, quite possibly related to climate change, is seen here to dwarf the entire global change research budget for our planet! The dollars lost during this one day, with one storm event, occurring in one region, would have been sufficient to fund the entire global change research program around the world for more than three years! Certainly, and in hindsight, some of these damages could have been mitigated through steps taken to increase the resiliency of the Eastern Seaboard to such events — which are now predicted to occur with increasing regularity and/or ferocity into the future.

It follows that, if we are to find a way to make appropriately robust investments in new knowledge creation and innovation to extend and preserve prosperity and safety, available governmental and federal dollars are probably and will remain insufficient. We must, therefore, find a way to harness private resources together with governmental and public resources to attack the major problems of our time. The facilitating role of large public research universities in all this will be pivotal.

At a land-grant university system such as the University of Illinois, the two sides of this particular public-private coin are both elements of the mission and date back to the very essence of the idea that emanated from the 1860s. The originating impetus "To promote the liberal and practical education of the industrial classes in the several pursuits and professions in life" was a wonderful, principled and ultimately wildly successful idea. It provided an affordable, high-quality education for the many, while also creating new knowledge and disseminating ideas that have, over time, built prosperity and, indisputably, transformed global society.

This land-grant model is still very successful today. In a brief example from my own university system, we calculate that just 25 of the many companies founded by U of I (University of Illinois) alumni are today worth over $75 billion and employ over 220,000 people! And we have a tremendous list of legacy contributions — my current favourite example being the development of indoor air conditioning — think for a moment of the impact that has had on people living in the southern part of the US and therefore the population density in that region!

We now need to "turbo-charge" this successful land-grant model and bring it to bear on the critical socio-technical problems of our time by connecting university-based research yet more vigorously with commercial activities in support of the public good. The balance of this paper describes some of the elements of an approach to do this, based on our work at the U of I System.

A NEW MODEL OF UNIVERSITY-BASED INNOVATION?

A re-energized model of university-based Innovation can perhaps begin to address these questions. In fact, one could posit that large, research-intensive university communities, with their commanding interdisciplinary reach and access to both talent and capital, are possibly the only places where such a modern model can emerge rapidly. It is only at large research universities that the intellectual adjacency exists to enable the full span of disciplinary knowledge to be activated synergistically (i.e., the biophysical sciences and engineering, the social sciences and, most importantly, the arts and humanities).

Firstly, then, we should understand what there is to learn from the current "best of breed" models of innovation.

Classic and successful innovation ecosystems that one can study from around the world are typically closely associated with research universities. Examples most often cited in the United States include Silicon Valley, Research Triangle Park and the Kendall Square developments in Massachusetts. The reasons for these successes are fairly obvious. The access to talent and talent mobility, the ability to experiment rapidly and extend new technologies, and the ability to attract sustained venture capital are all factors providing some of the built-in advantages. These and other global models (e.g., Singapore's innovation system driven by its semi-public entity A*Star, the Fraunhofer Institute in Germany, and models in Finland, Japan, Israel, etc.) all show the importance and relevance of a well-regulated and vibrant innovation sector to national prosperity.

Singapore provides perhaps the most compelling example of the connection of innovation to human wellbeing. In this small country, per capita income has increased fourfold from $20,000 in 1980 to more than $80,000 today. And over the same time period, the life expectancy of the population has increased from 71 to 82 years, a gain of more than a full decade in roughly 40 years!

Common elements can be discerned among these successful models of innovation. In addition to the proximity of research-intensive universities, diverse commercial interests and financial capital, we see a strong connection to urban settings. Access to amenities and job mobility are important characteristics, as well as the presence of the more youthful "creative classes". Younger people are known to be more willing to take on challenging entrepreneurial activities with energy without being inhibited by the personal financial or reputational risks involved. For example, a plot of total entrepreneurial activity measure is seen to peak in the 24-35 age range (Sasaki, Global Entrepreneurship Monitor, n.d.)

So what does this mean for our plans and attempts to drive innovation forward in the context of a modern version of the land-grant movement? A comprehensive Venn diagram comes to mind: with specific petals related to: interdisciplinary research-intensive universities; multi-sector (small, medium and large) industrial firms; high-capability and readily-accessible computational and networking systems; rapid-prototyping possibilities with access to larger-scale markets; access to sustained capital; urban settings; access to pleasant amenities and housing catering to younger adults; and affordable living arrangements, enabling job mobility and regular skill-set renewal. An innovation ecosystem — taking advantage of the sweet spot in this (or similar) Venn diagram(s) — should be the intentional goal for the next-generation land-grant developments.

Such an optimized innovation ecosystem, at least in part, must also be driven by a more broadly-based articulation of what constitutes success in university-based innovation — co-designed from the very beginning with the explicit goal of raising social equity through job and education pathway creation. It cannot be merely about wealth creation any more, but the development of lasting — and more pervasive — prosperity and social equity, as well. By co-design, I mean the joining forces of public and private stakeholders in the formulation of both the success metrics and strategy to create full-scope innovation.

TOWARDS A CO-DESIGNED UNIVERSITY-BASED INNOVATION ECOSYSTEM

Next, I sketch out the recent progress made by the 81,000-plus student University of Illinois System — comprised of the University of Illinois at Urbana-Champaign (UIUC), the University of Illinois at Chicago (UIC) and the

University of Illinois at Springfield (UIS) — towards building out an urban and statewide regional innovation ecosystem designed to lift the social equity of the state while simultaneously building prosperity and creating jobs.

A critical requirement for this type of co-design is an extremely close relationship or explicit partnership between academia and industry — in fact usually between specific companies and specific university colleges and/or departments. This must extend well beyond the existence of a simple funding relationship into a parameter space where the mutually-acceptable and essential ingredients are: 1) achievable gains to the bottom line "share-holder value proposition" on the part of the industrial partner; and 2) rich sets of student opportunities for internships, references and jobs on the part of the academic partner. Without this pair of attributes being jointly and simultaneously met, the relationship often degrades into a much more restricted formula for disconnected research funding and talent recruitment. Importantly, if authentic commercial gains are in fact realizable on a timely basis for the industry partner and if authentic student enrichment opportunities are realizable for students (and faculty), then the partnership is particularly well founded. Often, this means that the university side must be prepared to sign non-disclosures and admit liberal intellectual property policies perhaps without immediate expectation of financial return. In turn, the industry side must invest in the educational experiential mission of university students and graduates, and be open to sharing goals for collaborative projects and products and services with commercial potential.

To foster these kinds of relationships, the University of Illinois System has developed an active "CEO Round Table" entity to discuss how to best develop a co-designed and scaled-up innovation ecosystem appropriate for Illinois and the Midwest. The Round Table is co-chaired by the University of Illinois System president and the chief executive officer (CEO) of a leading Fortune 200 company. The group is comprised of approximately 12-15 (typically Fortune 200) CEOs from various sectors, including manufacturing, health care, financial services and information technologies. It meets approximately three times a year and normally invites a leading official from a well-known innovation system (e.g., Research Triangle Park) to describe and present findings from their related work, or alternatively a regional thought-leader (e.g., the governor of Illinois attended the most recent gathering). The Round Table action agenda focuses on multi-variate approaches, including talent development, recruitment options, job creation (including both high- and low-tech employment opportunities), technology transfer and targeted research and development.

One of the Round Table's first projects was to create an action template for an intensive university-industry collaborative platform, based on a detailed prototype generously developed and shared by Caterpillar Inc., working with U of I leadership. The template describes a process for an in-depth university-industry executive exchange — basically a half-day intensive interaction between the commercial enterprise senior leadership (CEO, chief information officer, chief financial officer, chief technology officer, chief strategy officer, etc.) and appropriate senior leadership from the university (president, chancellors, deans, key faculty, etc.). The purpose of the executive exchange is to share and discuss industry needs and university capabilities in a "rapid dating" approach, leading to the identification of several work streams for promising follow-up by key experts from both sides. Our experience to date through five such executive exchanges with different corporations has been that it is always possible to identify exciting low-hanging fruit in these kinds of interactions suitable for intensive follow-up activity.

In addition to the work of the CEO Round Table to build the needed public-private partnering, the fundamental principles for such a co-designed innovation ecosystem must build from the public academic values of access, affordability, credential completion and success in civil society.

For the University of Illinois System, access is a key component, helping to enable promising students from many disparate backgrounds to gain a world-class education no matter their family financial circumstances. Specifically, the U of I System has committed institutional funding that more than doubles combined resources from federal (Pell grants) and state (Monitory Assistance Program) funds to provide additional financial aid to socio-economically disadvantaged students. In 2016, for example, the U of I System provided more than $65 million in such additional financial aid, enabling a historically high level of racial diversity among the student body, both enriching the student experience for all students while providing important opportunities for diverse participation.

College affordability and a vigorous degree completion agenda are also key principles for this work. With the growing national concerns in the US related to student debt, the U of I System has frozen tuition for in-state students for three years in a row to ensure that average debt levels remain well below national averages. Also, with high degree completion rates — both 4- and 6-year baccalaureate completion rates are well above national averages — the U of I System boasts of graduating large numbers of students with relatively low student debt. There is more to do on this agenda, but an important start has been made.

The success agenda requires that the university work hard beyond graduation — not only for alumni fund-raising purposes but also to provide opportunities for graduating students to engage directly with private companies and find satisfying jobs, enabling strong upward social mobility, not just for the students themselves, but for their families and communities. With more than 20,000 graduating students per year, the U of I System provides a rich resource for private sector recruitment in all fields and for all possible interests.

Finally, the co-design requires rethinking the role and nature of a university campus — or more precisely perhaps what might be called an innovation district — in an urban setting. We have developed conceptual plans for what we now call a "live, work, play, study, prosper" innovation district, located near downtown Chicago. Such a campus would need to have "open walls" to surrounding communities for job creation and full community participation. Amenities and affordable housing would be needed, co-located near appropriately outfitted laboratories and offices, all fully network-enabled and supporting a mix of public and private activities. Faculty and students would work together with experts from commercial companies (small, medium, and large), as well as teachers from the public-school system to enable a diverse family of rich experiential learning opportunities settings designed for and conducive to vibrant innovation.

In closing, it is my belief that the large, public, research-intensive university of the future must go well beyond its traditional mission of providing world-class educational and research outcomes. It also must also link — significantly more effectively than in the past — with communities and private sector partners to build the societal equity that is becoming such an urgent issue in modern times. Putting these moccasins back on the feet of our youth is both part of our public responsibility and in our own pragmatic interest.

REFERENCES

Belmont Forum (n.d.). http://www.belmontforum.org
Sasaki Global Entrepreneurship Monitor (n.d.). http://www.gemconsortium.org

PART II

Resources

CHAPTER 6

Campus Planning and the Future of the University: A perspective from Singapore

Chorh Chuan Tan

University campus planning and design have changed significantly over the last 10 to 15 years. The digital revolution has disrupted traditional approaches to learning in universities, and promoted new modes of education based on greater on-line delivery, diversity and intensified interaction. It has also driven a much stronger focus on experiential and "out of the classroom" learning in many campuses, as there is increasing recognition of the importance of personal and interpersonal skills in a future where technology will fundamentally change the nature of work. Research too is moving towards much greater trans-disciplinary collaborations, co-location of programs with synergistic adjacencies and the establishment of shared core facilities. In many countries, and universities, there is a growing expectation of entrepreneurship and collaborative research with industry.

All these call for fresh approaches to design and new types of spaces that facilitate and enable these activities flexibly and at scale. New infrastructure development models also have to factor in the desire for greater eco-sustainability, quality of work and living environment, and health promotion.

These changing requirements pose substantial challenges, but also offer exciting opportunities to innovate, and bring together, research, educational and entrepreneurial activities in new ways to nurture an enabling and stimulating environment that supports creativity and diversity.

This paper summarizes key lessons which NUS (National University of Singapore) has learnt in its journey in re-developing and implementing new campus infrastructure over the past decade as we evolved to meet the challenges of the future. The specific focus is on the period following NUS' corporatization in 2006 from a statutory Board to a not-for-profit company, and how the resulting increased autonomy allowed the University the flexibility to execute a series of infrastructural projects that promoted our vision of a diverse and immersive learning environment, integrated research clusters and a vibrant and innovative enterprise ecosystem.

TRENDS IN CAMPUS DESIGN AND PLANNING

Historically, university education was the preserve of a segment of the population who could realistically access a higher centre of learning (Crawford, 2014). Mass expansion of higher education opportunities became widespread in the 20th century: in Europe and the US, it was the period following WWII; and, in Asia, post-colonialism, independence and subsequent rapid industrialization became critical drivers for massification. Universities played a critical role in producing skilled manpower, while simultaneously supporting national economic growth and competiveness, often through applied research endeavours.

This period of growth and development saw the expansion of university campuses and a significant build-up of physical infrastructure and facilities.

The 21st century has brought dramatic paradigm shifts in the nature of knowledge curation, production and utilization, and this has substantive bearing on how spaces, buildings and facilities should be designed, configured and repurposed to meet "changing technology, pedagogy and instrumentation" (Crawford, 2014).

Technology, particularly digital, wireless and mobile technology, has become a powerful change agent in knowledge usage and creation, and in how students and researchers learn, live, communicate and interact (O'Neil, 2013). Seamless connectivity to online resources and interaction has blurred the once sharp distinctions between formal and informal learning spaces and, consequently, universities have to consider the re-configuration and adaptation of the physical learning environment to access learning networks and resources, both physical and digital. The sharp rise of blended, flipped and technology-augmented classroom modules supports the extension of what constitutes a learning space, to a "learn anywhere, anytime" model (O'Neil, 2013).

At the same time, the impact of digital disruption has counter-intuitively reaffirmed the enduring value of community learning and face-to-face interaction, of learning with a sense of place. A vibrant learning community is characterized by its diversity and its high rate of social exchange with peers, experts and resources. Community also provides a sense of context and imparts meaning and direction to learning activities (Long, 2016).

Static and specific spaces are being re-designed to become spaces that are more flexible, modular and technology-enabled to nurture these new learning modes of collaboration, interaction and connectivity. These more generalized spaces are designed to promote interaction and exchange, as well as cater to learners with diverse needs and learning styles.

A conducive environment helps build a community of learners, promotes a common culture and shared ethos, and strengthens local context, while providing global reach and connectivity.

The changing nature of work has also influenced campus planning and development. Employers are increasingly seeking graduates who are future-ready, with strong leadership skills and critical thinking and communication skills (Vel & Higa, 2016). The increased focus on employability, entrepreneurship and student innovation, and the shift from a narrow focus on discipline specific to general adaptive skills (Rytkönen, E., Nenonen, S., Österlund, E., & Kojo, I., 2015), also entail new spaces and facilities to accommodate new curriculum experiences such as project work, capstone programs and student enterprises.

Eco-sustainability has emerged as a major driver of change and innovation in the master-planning of campus infrastructure. As existing buildings and facilities age, operating and maintenance costs will rise, and there is the need to retrofit and repurpose, while carefully weighing up the cost-benefit. Universities also have to maximize their land use, as land banks become limited, and continuous expansion becomes unfeasible, particularly in dense, urbanized communities (Gorgati & Savid-Buteler, 2016). New projects will need to adhere to more rigorous building codes and meet stringent criteria for energy efficiency and sustainability.

But eco-sustainability goes beyond prudent estate management and the technical benefits of green architecture. Universities, as thought leaders and preparatory training grounds for future leaders, are expected to promote a culture of responsible environmental stewardship within their communities. Beyond formal curricular modules, the most holistic approach to raising sustainability awareness would be immersion in a culture of sustainability that is evident and integrated campus-wide, and includes the participation and engagement of students, faculty, staff and partners (Cox, 2015).

Moving forward, a similar strong focus on health-promoting campuses would become more prominent in the face of high and rising prevalences of obesity and chronic diseases in most countries. This would require much greater walkability and ample sports and recreational facilities to promote active lifestyles, as well as healthy eating options.

NUS' INFRASTRUCTURAL DEVELOPMENT OVER THE PAST DECADE

NUS is currently spread over three sites, with the largest by far being at the Kent Ridge campus. The majority of NUS' Schools and Faculties are located at Kent Ridge, and it has seen the bulk of development efforts. The approximate distribution of space allocation within NUS is: teaching (30%); research (30%); housing (20%); and support 20% (includes recreation, library, study spaces, etc); 55% of the Kent Ridge campus, which is located on hilly terrain, remains as green spaces, which adds a tropical lushness and visual aesthetic that defines the campus.

The scale and pace of development over the last 10 years following corporatization have been extensive. The total Gross Floor Area (GFA) of built space is currently 1.46 million m^2, an increase of 67% over the 870,000 m^2 in 2006, at the inception of corporatization. Virtually 100% of the older buildings in NUS have also being regularized over the past decade to meet new building and safety code requirements, and facilities upgraded and renewed.

Collectively, these development projects have reshaped the NUS campus. They have allowed the University opportunities to innovate and experiment, incorporate new technologies and ideas, enhanced the dynamism and vibrancy of our learning and social interactions, and provided new and diverse facilities for a thriving community of 38,000 students and more than 11,000 faculty, researchers and staff.

Campus development in NUS has been guided by a sequence of Master Plans. The First Master Plan, conceived in the 1970s, saw the proposal which led to the establishment of the Kent Ridge campus, and the consolidation of the bulk of NUS' faculties and schools at one main site. The planning at that time called for a linear campus, with the building of low-rise buildings to facilitate movement and a sense of community. Subsequent Master Plans, in particular the Precinct Master Plans from 2009 to the present, became springboards to fundamentally re-evaluate the planning and development basis of land use and campus infrastructure. The recent Precinct Master Plans have five main areas of focus, namely: (a) creating new, state-of-the-art education and research buildings and facilities to rejuvenate the campus; (b) decongest very crowded precincts such as the Medicine-Science precinct by identifying old buildings which would be demolished once new, much higher-rise buildings were completed; (c) clustering of laboratories involved with more hazardous forms of research; (d) enabling greater pedestrian and cycling connectivity in a hilly terrain; and (e) increasing interactions and the sense of place.

KEY LESSONS LEARNT

The transformation of NUS' physical campus over the past decade has yielded many important learning points, of which 5 key ones are outlined in this paper.

1. **The most critical enabler was the major change in the funding for infrastructural development** following NUS' corporatization in 2006. Prior to this, such funding was provided on a project-by-project basis which constrained planning and construction to single buildings and was not conducive to longer-term planning. With corporatization, the government converted the episodic funding it would have provided for cyclical maintenance and facility renewal into a predictable annual stream. A portion of this funding is given in the form of a grant and the rest is to be raised as debt with government provisions to assist with the debt repayment. At the same time, the university could now top up the funding of its new construction from its own internal sources. NUS has used this flexibility to build additional shelled spaces that serve as a valuable space bank for future demand. This financing framework has stimulated and enabled the long-term planning necessary for a holistic and future-facing transformation of the campus infrastructure. These were manifested, in particular in the Precinct Master Plans developed from 2009, which divided the Kent Ridge Campus into five precincts which were planned in much greater detail.
2. The successful planning and construction of an entire new University Town (UTown) from scratch based on a single academic vision, defined valuable principles which have informed and underpinned NUS' approach to the transformation of the other precincts of the campus. UTown comprises 26 buildings with a total GFA of 292,500 m^2. The 19-hectare plot also holds the National Research Foundation's research campus, as well as the campus of the Yale-NUS College.

Seven key design principles were applied in the conceptualization and planning of UTown.

    a) Integrate learning, living and discovery (including sports, culture and arts).
    b) Blur in- and out-of-classroom learning based on "my classroom is everywhere" concept.
    c) Diversity of dining and other amenities.
    d) Pedestrian-centric and wet weather mobility (as heavy rainstorms are common).
    e) Visual connectivity and memorable spaces.
    f) Sustainable precinct and buildings.
    g) Well connected to the main Kent Ridge Campus.

UTown provided the physical facilities that enabled NUS to pioneer a new model of residential college living, which emphasized a multi-disciplinary approach, small class sizes and a diverse student body. It is also a complete educational hub with student residences, teaching facilities and open study and social spaces that blur the line between in-classroom and out-of-classroom learning. The wide range of facilities, ranging from dance studios and music practice rooms to sports competition halls and gymnasium, further increases the opportunities for different student groups to mingle and interact. With good provisions for wet-weather mobility and extensive pedestrian walkways, UTown has promoted a lively intellectual, social and cultural environment. Some distinctive features include the Education Resource Centre and the Stephen Riady Centre — the first 24/7 mixed-use academic buildings in Singapore's higher education landscape.

Careful attention was paid to environmental sustainability — 40% of buildings space are naturally ventilated and buildings were built around lush greenery and existing heritage trees. Numerical simulation of air flow and ventilation have ensured that the site is walkable even during the heat of the tropical midday. A central district cooling plant efficiently provides chilled water for the air conditioning of buildings in the entire site. In 2009, UTown was among two recipients of the inaugural national Green Mark for sustainable development on a precinct level, and a number of its buildings have won prestigious architectural awards (figure 1 below).

Figure 1

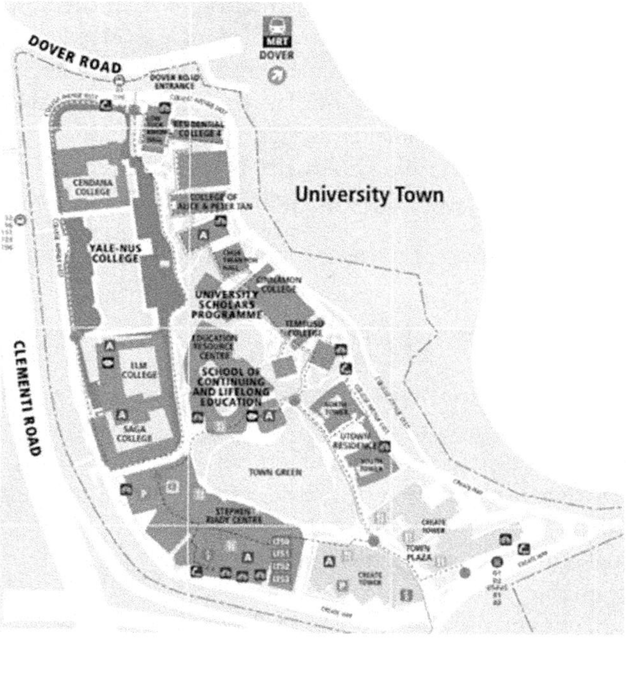

Chapter 6: Campus Planning and the Future of the University

UTown has been extremely well received particularly by the approximately 10,000 students who use it each week. The siting of NUS new School of Continuing and Lifelong Education (SCALE) at UTown in 2016 has also opened up the use of its facilities to a much broader and diverse group of students from the wider community. Based on NUS' analysis, the following factors have contributed significantly to the effectiveness and positive impact of the space.

  a) a highly distinctive district place-making concept supporting one over-arching academic vision.
  b) the rich mix of academic, cultural, research and social programs that are stacked or in close proximity, creates a density and variety of activities throughout the day and night.
  c) effective and experiential shade and shelter, pedestrian-focused, car-lite strategy.
  d) flexible master-plan strategy that is able to absorb a diverse range of building types and usage.
  e) sufficient number and range of spaces and facilities which different student and staff groups could adapt for different uses.

3. The remodelling of the densely packed Science and Medicine precinct over a 10-year period demonstrated that these principles could be usefully applied to transform and refresh existing built environments. (figures 2 and 3).

Figure 2 – Medical Precinct before development

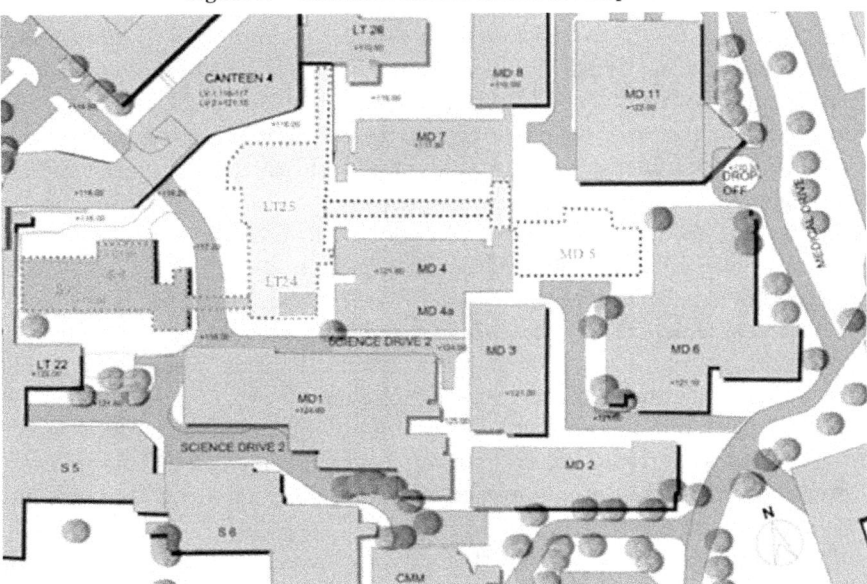

Figure 3 – Medical Precinct post re-development and including Academic Green

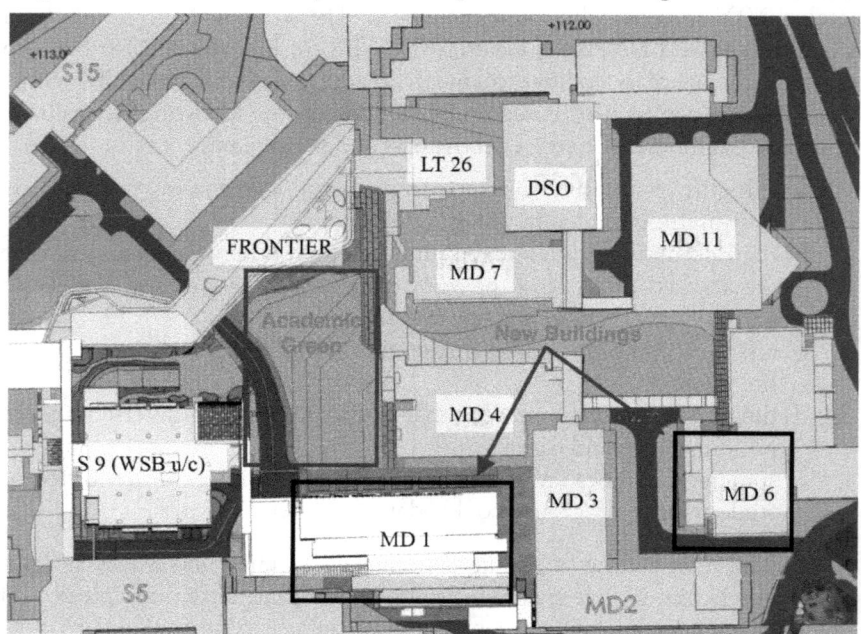

This journey started with the construction of two new high-rise research and education blocks (MD6 and MD1), and the extensive renovation of a third building (MD2) to house wet-lab research in the NUS Yong Loo Lin School of Medicine. These provided leading-edge facilities that have enabled new training modes such as Collaborative Learning Cases (CLCs), an innovative educational strategy to enhance constructive, collaborative and contextual learning for students, and the Centre for Healthcare Simulation, which is the biggest and most comprehensive facility in Asia that utilizes computerized manikins and advanced simulation technology to provide inter-disciplinary training of medical and health professional students, as well as junior doctors. MD6, otherwise called the Centre for Translational Medicine, is a 15-storey complex, which also houses research centres such as the Cancer Science Institute of Singapore and a range of clinical translational research programs focused on human health, and the Asian phenotype.

These new buildings replaced old buildings that were no longer functional. Furthermore, with the additional space, another old building (MD5) could be demolished so as to create a large green space which connects the new and existing buildings.

In similar fashion, a new, high-rise, wet-science building is currently being constructed in the adjacent Science Faculty. This entailed the demolition of two existing old buildings (S9 and S9A), as well as two lecture theatres. When this work is finished in 2019, the resultant cleared space would become a large academic green which would provide a pleasant central heart for the precinct, enlivened at the ground level by a mix of dining facilities, students' spaces, cafes and other amenities.

4. **Environmental sustainability.** Sustainable infrastructure management will also require a step-up in our capabilities to maximize the use of resources such as water, energy, green spaces and waste management. NUS' overall target is a 23% reduction in carbon emissions by 2020 on a Business As Usual (BAU) baseline. University-level oversight is exercised by a Sustainability Steering Committee, which monitors the implementation of sustainability programs, tracks a range of metrics, and includes stretch targets such as a recycling rate of 25%, Green Mark certification of 45 buildings, and an increase of green spaces in and on the roofs of buildings to 45,000 m^2.
5. **Greenway connectivity.** The Greenway is an eco-friendly, encircling connective loop for pedestrians and cyclists, designed to blend harmoniously within NUS' topographical layout. At designated points within each precinct, pedestrians and commuters can switch to more traditional forms of mass transport, including internal shuttle buses. The intended aim is to shift transportation within the campus to a more sustainable car-lite and bus-lite model, and encourage healthier modes of movement, such as walking and cycling.

CHARTING FUTURE DIRECTIONS

Over the past decade, NUS has embarked on an extensive program of Capital Projects across our campus, with some buildings from this phase slated for completion from 2017 to 2019.

When considering campus infrastructure development over a more distant timeframe, that is, over the next 20-30 years, decisions will be guided by several strategic considerations. These include postulations of how learning and research activities will evolve, as well as local conditions specific to the University.

- First, we think that IT, Big Data and a new generation of Smart Technologies will continue to impact and revolutionize teaching and learning. It will be difficult to predict with certainty which specific technologies will become ubiquitous or transformative, but it will be necessary for us to design study and learning spaces for continuous flexible adaption and re-configuration, while allowing for ease of technological upgrades and enablement.

- Second, the research spaces that we build must be capable of supporting the cutting-edge research of the future and the equipment and tools required for this. It will also be the norm to co-locate or integrate research spaces which span disciplines and include industry partners and associated spin-offs and start-ups. The translational linkage between research and enterprise will become more tightly knit.
- Third, even greater attention would need to be placed on reducing energy consumption and the carbon and environmental footprint of the university. New developments will need to be integrated as part of a holistic framework that is sensitive to the natural environment, and promotes ecologically friendly modes of mobility within the campus.
- Fourth, NUS will further expand the use of a range of new tools and technologies such as drone-based 3D mapping, Geographic Information System (GIS) spatial data analysis, as well as augmented reality (AR) devices to better map out and visualize new and possible campus development directions.

Campus planning and design are not a static exercise, but a creative tension that requires a careful balancing between future goals and present circumstances, so as to provide the best environment possible for the university community. The definition and application of key principles for the design and construction of buildings and precincts provide a useful framework for such work over the long-term.

REFERENCES

Cox, H. (2015). "A Model for Creating a Campus Sustainability Plan". *Planning for Higher Education*, V44 N1 (October-December), pp. 89-99.

Crawford, M. (2014). "A Century of Campus Planning: Past, Present, and Future." *Planning for Higher Education*, V42N3 (April-June).

Former University of Singapore (Bukit Timah Campus) (n.d.) Urban Redevelopment Authority, Singapore. Retrieved 19 May 2017, https://www.ura.gov.sg/uol/conservation/conservation-xml?id=BTC

Gorgati, V. & Savid-Buteler, P. (2016). "Why Campus Matters". *Planning for Higher Education*, V44 N3 (April-June), pp. 18-27.

Long, C. (2016). "There is a There There: Connected Learning Communities in a Digital Age". *Planning for Higher Education*, V44 N3 (April-June), pp. 61-85.

National University of Singapore. (n.d.) Retrieved 18 May 2017, from http://www.nus.edu.sg/uci/PPM/FirstMasterPlan.htm

O'Neil, M. (2013). "Limitless Learning: Creating Adaptable Environments to Support a Changing Campus." *Planning for Higher Education*, V41 N1 (October-December), pp. 11-27.

Rytkönen, E., Nenonen, S., Österlund, E. & Kojo, I. (2015). "Process dynamics of managing interdisciplinary, cross-organizational learning campus in change". *Facilities*, 33 (11), pp. 752-772.

Vel, J. & Higa, K. (2016). "Designing Innovative Campuses for Tomorrow's Students". *Planning for Higher Education*, V44 N4 (July-September), pp. 11-20.

CHAPTER 7

Global Research Collaboration: a Vital Resource in a Turbulent World

Meric S. Gertler

CONTEXT

Two powerful and contradictory forces are shaping the current geopolitical landscape. On the one hand, a movement to retreat from international engagement appears to be gaining momentum in some corners of the globe.

The Brexit campaign in the United Kingdom is a clear example. More than 17 million people, 52% of the population, voted to sever Britain's ties with the European Union, a region representing half a billion people and, at just over a fifth of global GDP, the world's third-largest economy. These ties had existed officially since 1993 and unofficially for the better part of half a century. Whatever one's views on Brexit, the vote has been read by many as expressing scepticism about international engagement, and an apparent enthusiasm for building barriers between countries rather than bridges. The resulting political, economic and social uncertainty in the UK has been well documented. But, despite this, political parties in France, Germany, the Netherlands, Italy, Austria, Sweden, Denmark and others have sounded similar themes.

Meanwhile, in the United States, President Donald Trump campaigned successfully on a vision of America's future that many regard as nativist, America-first, anti-immigration and isolationist. Nearly 63 million Americans voted for candidate Trump. Examples of nationalist policy were easy to find in the first months of his presidency: executive orders restricting immigration from certain predominantly Muslim countries, a budget proposal calling for increases in military spending and decreases in international aid, a call for proposals to build a "big, beautiful wall" along the US-Mexican border, a directive to review the H-1B foreign worker visa program, and so on.

One final example comes from the southern hemisphere. In March 2017, Australia's government replaced their 457 visa program for skilled temporary foreign workers with an "Australians first" policy. The new policy will reduce the term of temporary work visas from four to two years, introduce language and labour market testing, and eliminate or substantially reduce the opportunity for visa holders to pursue permanent residency and citizenship. More than 200 jobs will be removed from the list of occupations permitted to be filled by visa-holders, including historian, geophysicist, microbiologist and biochemist (Government of Australia, 2017). While commentators had argued that the 457 visa program needed revision and tightening, this initiative has been seen by many as an expression of troubling nationalist, anti-immigration sentiment (sarahinthesen8, 2017).

On the basis of these three significant cases, it certainly appears that major global forces are moving us away from mutual trust, cooperation and engagement on the international stage. Much has already been written about the economic, social and political causes of this retreat, and I will not add to that literature here. Instead, I wish to call attention to a growing and increasingly important counter-movement.

At precisely the time when these anti-international forces seem to be gathering steam, the international community is increasingly facing challenges that are global in nature, and whose solutions inevitably require international cooperation. Examples come easily to mind: health epidemics, international migration and refugee flows, cyber security, poverty and global inequality, threats to water and food security, and more. These challenges do not respect political borders, and may even be exacerbated by them. The existential threat posed by climate change is another striking case in point.

It is not just *implementing* solutions that requires cooperation; increasingly, *finding* solutions also requires cooperation. The best, and perhaps the only, answers to the most complex and pressing global challenges of our time will emerge from sharing data, ideas, perspectives, findings — and failures — between different research communities around the world. Indeed, particularly in these turbulent times, I would argue that international collaboration in research is a vital resource for universities and for prosperity, both domestic and global. Moreover, this phenomenon has the potential to counteract the mounting geopolitical backlash against international engagement noted above. What is my evidence? And, if I am right, what are the possible implications for policy-makers?

INTERNATIONAL COLLABORATION IS GROWING, GEOGRAPHICALLY CLUSTERED, AND VALUABLE

Let's begin with an intriguing observation. As Figure 1 shows, the growth in international co-publication activity since 1990 has far outstripped overall publication growth over the same period. Figure 1 compares the rate of growth in all research publications with the rate of growth in research publications involving one or more international co-authors. While the number of research publications has more than doubled since 1990, the number of research publications with one or more international co-authors has increased *more than tenfold*. International collaboration is clearly flourishing.

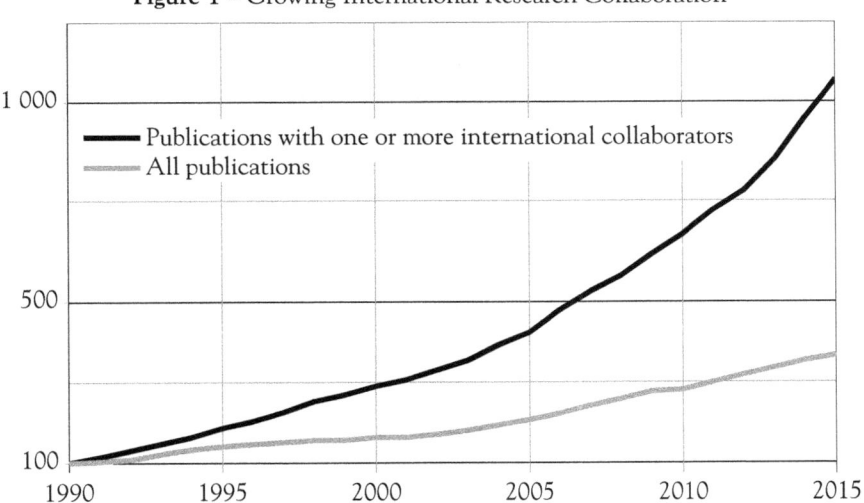

Figure 1 – Growing International Research Collaboration

Number of scholarly publications globally, 1990 to 2015, indexed to 1990 (1990 = 100).
Source: Web of Science® Thomson Reuters, Clarivate Analytics; University of Toronto.

Indeed, since 2010, scholars at the top 50 research-intensive universities in the world (measured by publication volume) have collaborated over a million times (an average of more than 400 collaborations a day) with international partners on peer-reviewed publications, creating a vast, shared knowledge network that crisscrosses the globe.

Figure 2 ranks urban regions by the number of times authors from universities and other research institutions in each respective region have collaborated with authors in other countries on co-authored, peer-reviewed publications. It is worth commenting on two points. First, the smaller than expected number, and relatively low rankings, of US urban regions shown in Figure 2 reflects the disproportionately large number of opportunities for US authors to engage in collaboration with scholars at other leading research institutions in the same country. While scholars at many US institutions are active international collaborators, the intensity of this activity may be offset to some extent by the scale of their opportunities for domestic collaboration. And second, European programs designed to encourage intra-European exchange and collaboration — including, for example, the European Commission's Marie Skłodowska-Curie actions, and the EU's Erasmus exchange program — may help explain the prominence of European countries in Figure 2. Collaborations among EU countries and collaborations among EU and non-EU countries are both growing; comparing the intra- and extra-EU collaboration rates would be an interesting question for future study.

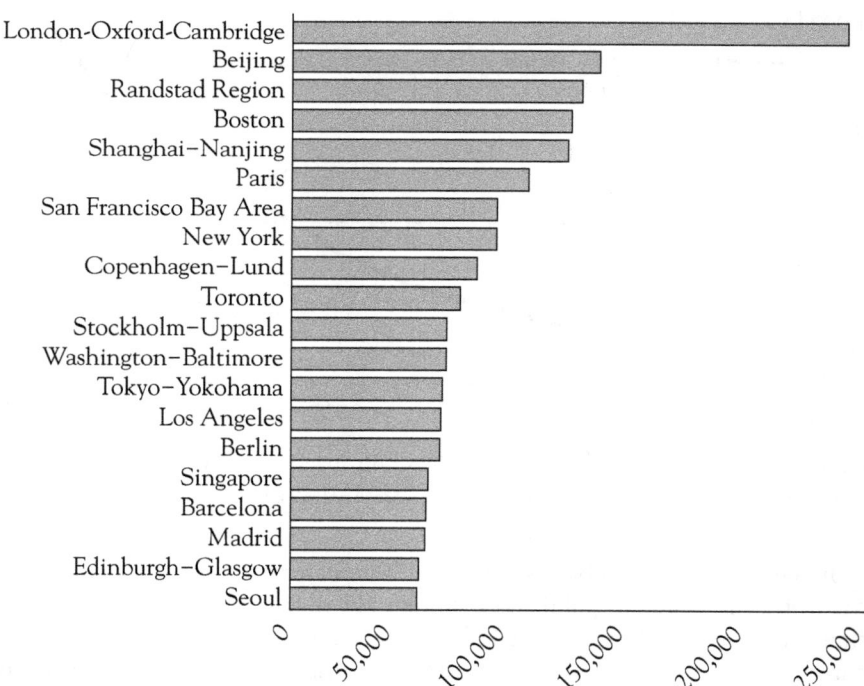

Figure 2 – Global Collaborations

Top 20 urban regions by total number of international co-authored publications, 2011-2016.
Source: Web of Science® Thomson Reuters, Clarivate Analytics; University of Toronto.

Figure 3 offers a geographical representation of the apex of this network. It shows the reach of international collaboration originating from the top 20 urban regions identified in Figure 2 between 2010 and 2015. Each line represents a partnership that produced 100 or more co-publications over the period. Here you can clearly see the role that major urban regions play in shaping — and dominating — global knowledge networks. We can think of these connections as the globe's arteries — creating and circulating ideas, opening up opportunities and fueling creativity and innovation.

Figure 3 – International Collaborations

Top 20 most active urban regions, 100 or more publications, 2010-2015.

This striking evidence raises an obvious question: what forces are driving this remarkable growth in international co-publication? One clue may be found in the recent literature on creativity, collaboration and innovation, which suggests that research conducted by teams that are more internally diverse is more likely to succeed in generating significant innovations (Nooteboom *et al.*, 2007; Spencer, 2011). Diversity can be measured in terms of a variety of dimensions, including occupation, discipline, nationality, culture and other social markers.

Studies in fields from economic geography (Nathan & Lee, 2013), management (Hunt *et al.*, 2015), psychology (Phillips *et al.*, 2008), and complex systems (Hong & Page, 2004), among others, have found that teams, firms, or regions collaborating under conditions of "resource heterogeneity" often perform better on creative, problem-solving, or innovative tasks than those collaborating under conditions of "resource homogeneity". Nooteboom *et al.*,

(2007, p. 1017) describes the phenomenon in the following way: "When people with different knowledge and perspectives interact, they stimulate and help each other to stretch their knowledge for the purpose of bridging and connecting diverse knowledge."

Hence, scholars may be more likely to seek international collaborators because they find such research collaborations especially productive. They may also believe the resulting publication will be more successful or innovative, or have a greater impact. These and other factors may help explain the increasing propensity to co-publish internationally.

Indeed, there is some hard evidence to support this conjecture. For example, at the University of Toronto, international collaboration accounted for just under half (46%) of all research publications between 2010 and 2015. But, in the same time span, internationally co-authored papers accounted for fully 82% of the University of Toronto's Highly Cited Publications (Clarivate Analytics TR, 2017). This pattern is repeated in every one of the top 20 collaborating regions highlighted in Figure 2, with international co-authors disproportionately represented among a region's most highly cited research. And this pattern is consistent with the findings established by others confirming that, all else equal, research publications featuring international collaborators do indeed tend to be more highly cited than those publications with exclusively domestic authors (Sin, 2011; Khor & Yu, 2016).

If one accepts citation frequency as a reasonable indicator of impact or influence, then it appears that international collaborations are in fact more likely to produce more impactful or influential publications. It stands to reason that exposure in different countries and research circles will increase a publication's impact as it naturally reaches a larger audience — perhaps through as simple a mechanism as being shared simultaneously in multiple localities by the various co-authors. This kind of profile is a valuable form of influence in itself. At the same time, the combination and cross-pollination of diverse methods, perspectives and frames of reference that are fostered by international collaboration create a particularly fertile environment for the production of new, influential — and highly cited — ideas, discoveries and innovations.

In this sense, research universities and the urban regions that host them are gateways to global knowledge networks, contributing and drawing benefits in a global process of joint knowledge production and exchange. Actively participating in this network is increasingly important for both the global impact and reputation of research universities and for the local and national prosperity of their host economies. Furthermore, global collaboration is, to a very large extent, a *positive-sum* interaction; it is an amplifying exchange. Collaborating with peers in other countries produces much more than local adaptations of discoveries made elsewhere: it often produces entirely new discoveries catalysed by the collaboration. Consequently, the size and quality of the global knowledge network are a powerful contributor to local and global prosperity.

I would suggest that there are interesting connections between this insight and the geopolitical dynamics discussed at the beginning of this chapter. A close look at a map of how the United Kingdom voted in the Brexit referendum offers a fascinating insight. Many commentators have pointed out that in most of the UK's major urban regions, a substantial majority voted to remain in the European Union. An examination of voting results by local authority district reveals a nuanced picture, but supports this general observation (Toly, 2017; Becker *et al.*, 2017).

What is less well appreciated is the striking observation that the strength of a region's "remain" vote was especially strongly correlated with the presence of a major research university. Indeed, there is evidence to suggest that the presence of a research-intensive university in a district was a better predictor of the strength of a district's "remain" vote than whether or not the district was part of an urban region.

One explanation for this correlation is that, as noted above, research universities connect their host regions to the world, and vice versa, in ways that bring many benefits to local residents. Hence, these are communities that recognize the value of international engagement because they are deeply embedded in it, from researchers and students to local cultural institutions, firms and industries.

This builds on the growing recognition that the relationship between universities and their host cities is fundamentally symbiotic (Gertler, 2016). It is a partnership that sparks innovation, economic dynamism, cultural vibrancy and urban resiliency. International collaboration is a vital part of this relationship. Complementary forms of knowledge, competence and experience acquired from colleagues in other centres of research and innovation through university collaborations, industry partnerships, faculty and student exchanges, or other forms of international engagement, enrich local communities, stimulate the local production of ideas and innovations, open new avenues of research and inspire creative solutions to unique or shared problems.

Viewed through this lens, international engagement, including collaboration in research, is an invaluable, continually renewable resource, advancing the global standing of research universities, pushing forward the frontiers of knowledge and driving domestic and global prosperity. Recalling the list of the world's leading urban regions by volume of international research collaboration (Figure 2), it is striking — and not at all surprising — that the world's top collaborating urban regions are also among the world's most dynamic metropolitan *economies*.

EVIDENCE FROM PATENT DENSITY AND VENTURE CAPITAL INVESTMENT

Evidence from the distribution and density of patenting activity, a commonly used (if limited) proxy for innovation, provides further support for the argument that global research collaboration constitutes an increasingly important resource. As with co-publications, international collaboration in patenting is exploding. Since 1980, the number of patent applications filed under the Patent Cooperation Treaty has boomed, rising in 2015 to roughly 75 times its level in 1980. Over the same period, patent applications listing co-inventors from different countries have risen a staggering 30000% — patents involving international collaboration are filed 300 times more often today than they were in 1980 (OECD, 2017).

Where are these co-inventors located? Figure 4 is a heatmap showing geographical variations in patent density around the world, based on US patent data (USPTO, 2107). It is telling that most of the same regions that lead the world in international collaboration on publications — those listed on Figure 2 — also lead the world in patent density. In other words, there is at least circumstantial evidence to suggest that international research collaboration produces favourable conditions for patent activity, perhaps by producing more patentable innovations.

Figure 4 – Patent Density

Global patents granted, USPTO. Heatmap by inventor location, 2015.

Evidence from the analysis of venture capital activity complements the picture. In a recent paper called "Rise of the Global Startup City", my colleagues in the Martin Prosperity Institute at the University of Toronto, Richard Florida and Karen King, studied the geography of recent venture capital investment data (Florida & King, 2016). Their list of the top 20 metropolitan regions by venture capital includes 10 of the top 20 leading metropolitan regions by international research collaboration, though with some variation in the order and with a couple of significant outliers. Notably, centres of international research collaboration feature prominently in each of the three regions that Florida and King profile — North America, Europe, and Asia. (Intriguingly, significant outliers include several urban regions in India: Mumbai, Delhi and Chennai.)

The overall pattern is clear. It appears that venture capital and other forms of mobile investment seek out these special nodal centres and the opportunities that are signaled by their world-leading research, their deep talent pools *and* their connections with other global centres of knowledge production and innovation through international research collaboration.

Connecting these various strands together, one can view them as comprising a larger cycle: from international collaboration in research to international co-invention and patenting to local venture capital investment. We can think of this as the path from knowledge creation to innovation to commercialization. In a challenging fiscal climate, stimulating this flow, as international research collaboration does, is of obvious value. The source of this stimulation, as I have argued throughout, lies in the fresh and unexpected ideas, perspectives and insights we glean from collaborating with our international peers. International collaboration often forces us to test our assumptions and shift our frames of reference. These are the conditions that spark creativity, discovery and innovation.

POLICY CONSIDERATIONS

These observations about international collaboration as a resource for cultivating prosperity — locally, nationally and internationally — suggest certain implications for both university leaders and national and sub-national policy-makers. Let me highlight three such considerations. The first concerns university priorities and the imperative to support international research collaboration actively. The second speaks to funding for advanced research — both international and domestic. The third brings the principles and spirit of international collaboration home, with important implications for immigration and higher education policy.

First, if the analysis presented here is correct, then supporting international collaboration between research centres should be a priority for research universities. Certainly, there are many mechanisms that can help achieve this goal, including supporting international collaboration with funding and administrative and other resources; exploring joint degrees and research projects; promoting student and faculty exchanges; and so on. These sorts of international engagements should not be limited to universities and other institutions of research and education, of course. They could also include private sector actors, civil society and public institutions more generally.

Second, the implications for public policy pertaining to research support are also important — and to some extent counterintuitive. There is no question that direct funding to support international collaboration should be an important objective for research policy. But, at the same time, *domestic* funding for advanced research is also absolutely vital in promoting international research collaboration. In this regard, it is important to recognize, as the evidence examined above clearly shows, that international partners in the development and exchange of knowledge and innovation are not randomly distributed around the globe. Instead, they are most frequently found at leading institutions located in major urban regions. Because "excellence seeks excellence", in the words of a 2013 editorial in *Nature*, (Adams, 2013), the pool of international collaborators is self-selecting and differentiated by discipline.

Forward-looking governments around the world are increasingly recognizing that, to take advantage of global knowledge networks and benefit from the resources found therein, it is necessary to *participate* actively in these networks. And excellence is required for participation. Consequently, many national and sub-national governments are concentrating their investments strategically in their top research universities, with the goal of building clusters of excellence. Such clusters differentially leverage regional strengths — for instance, strengths in specific university-based research fields, but also in related local industries, services, workforces, and so on.

The recently established Vector Institute in Toronto is an excellent example. Federal and Provincial governments, together with the University of Toronto and local industry partners, have invested some C$180M to build upon the Toronto region's research strength in artificial intelligence and machine learning. The goal is to help produce, attract and retain top talent — and further enhance Toronto's standing as a central node in the emerging global network of extraordinarily promising AI research and development.

Such initiatives take political courage, sustained investment and patience. These are often difficult challenges in democracies whose leaders must routinely face fickle, demanding, divided and impatient electorates. But spreading investments widely and thinly is directly at odds with the global knowledge landscape: it is spiky, not flat (Florida, 2005). To be most effective, to harness the resources of international collaboration, our local research investments must also be spiky.

Third, the same features that make international collaboration such a vital resource make *local* socio-economic, cultural and other kinds of diversity similarly vital resources. Attracting international students and scholars to our institutions, industries and communities fosters a kind of "international collaboration at home". To be sure, it opens opportunities for the more traditional sense of international collaboration, since these newcomers will bring their professional network contacts with them. But it also illustrates how outstanding scholarship, teaching, learning and innovation thrive only by examining a variety of ideas, discarding those that fail and improving those that work. As is the case with the more common understanding of international collaboration, by inviting the world to our cities, campuses and, especially, our classrooms, we encounter fresh, new ideas, perspectives and approaches that, in turn, inspire understanding and generate breakthroughs in knowledge and innovation. Thus, this kind of local international engagement takes its place in a larger virtuous circle of global collaboration.

As university leaders, we need to make the case for internationalization more forcefully — to our communities and political leaders as much as to our boards of trustees and governors. It can be hard to quantify the value of welcoming international students and scholars to our institutions and cities — though enumerating local startups founded by erstwhile international students or Nobel Prizes won at domestic institutions by international scholars should go a long way. It is sometimes hard to convince policy-makers to make the necessary investments to attract international talent when there are many other investments that seem more obviously beneficial to domestic audiences. But internationalization at home is every bit as valuable a resource as international collaboration with peers abroad, and the two trends are mutually reinforcing.

CONCLUSION

In today's world, in which geopolitical forces sometimes work to divide us, a renewed commitment to international collaboration and the understanding, learning, knowledge and innovation that result, can unite us. Indeed, the challenges we face as a global community will require this kind of collaboration, to implement answers as well as discover them. In this sense, international collaboration is a vital resource for advancing both the global standing of our universities and global prosperity itself. As the evidence demonstrates, universities, research institutions and major urban regions around the globe are at the forefront of this effort. Public policy should celebrate this and support it.

REFERENCES

Adams, J. (2013). "Collaborations: the fourth age of research", *Nature*, vol. 497, no. 7451, pp. 557-60.

Becker, S.O., Fetzer, T. & Novy, D. (2017). "Who voted for Brexit? A comprehensive district-level analysis", *CEP Discussion Paper No 1480*, London School of Economics.

Clarivate Analytics (2017). *Thomson Reuters Web of Science*, (data retrieved and analysed April 2017).

Florida, R. & King, K. (2016). "Rise of the global startup city", Martin Prosperity Institute, Rotman School of Management, University of Toronto.

Florida, R. (2005). "The world is spiky", *The Atlantic Monthly*, pp. 48-51.

Gertler, M.S. (2016). "Cities, research universities and the economic geography of innovation", in *University Priorities and Constraints*, Weber, L. E. & Duderstadt, J. J. (eds), Economica, Paris, pp. 235-48.

Government of Australia, Department of Immigration and Border Protection (2017). "List of removed occupations" https://www.border.gov.au/Trav/Work/Work/Skills-assessment-and-assessing-authorities/skilled-occupations-lists/removed-skilled-occupations. [March 2017]

Hong, L. & Page, S. (2004). "Groups of diverse problem solvers can outperform groups of high-ability problem solvers", *PNAS* vol. 101, no. 46, pp. 16385–16389.

Hunt, V., Layton, D., & Prince, S. (2015). "Diversity Matters", McKinsey & Company, http://www.mckinsey.com/business-functions/organization/our-insights/why-diversity-matters [March 2017]

Khor, K.A. & Yu, L.G. (2016). "Influence of international co-authorship on the research citation impact of young universities", *Scientometrics*, vol. 107, pp. 1095-1110. https://www.ncbi.nlm.nih.gov/pubmed/27239078

Nathan, M. & Lee, N. (2013). "Cultural diversity, innovation, and entrepreneurship: firm-level evidence from London", *Economic Geography*, vol. 89, no. 4, 367–394.

Nooteboom, B., Van Haverbeke, W., Duysters, G., Gilsing, V. & van den Oord, A. (2007). "Optimal cognitive distance and absorptive capacity", *Research Policy*, vol. 36, no. 7, 1016–1034.

OECD (2017). "Indicators of international co-operation", OECD Patent Statistics (database) <http://dx.doi.org/10.1787/data-00507-en> [March 2017]

Phillips, K.W., Liljenquist, K.A. & Neale, M.A. (2008). "Is the pain worth the gain? The advantages and liabilities of agreeing with socially distinct newcomers", *Personality and Social Psychology Bulletin*, vol. 35, no. 3, 336–350.

sarahinthesen8 (2017). Malcolm Turnbull's announcement to scrap 457 visas sounds more like a dog whistle than a genuine policy to grow jobs for young Australians. [Twitter post]. https://twitter.com/sarahinthesen8/status/854186387226087424. [March 2017]

Sin, S-C.J. (2011). "International coauthorship and citation impact: a bibliometric study of six LIS journals, 1980–2008", *Journal of the Association for Information Science and Technology*, vol. 62, pp. 1770-83.

Spencer, G.M. (2011). "Local diversity and the spatial concentration of creative economic activity in Canadian city-regions", in *Beyond Territory: Dynamic Geographies of Knowledge Creation and Innovation*. Bathelt, H., Feldman, M.P. & Kogler, D.F. eds, Routledge, New York, pp. 46-63.

Toly, N. (2017). "Brexit, global cities, and the future of world order", *Globalizations*, vol. 14, no. 1, 142-149.

United States Patent and Trademark Office (USPTO) (2017). http://www.uspto.gov [March 2017]

CHAPTER 8

Open Science: A Global Enterprise

Luc Henry and Martin Vetterli

INTRODUCTION

Over the past decade, "open" has become a mantra. "Open data", "open innovation", "open government" movements all call for a more fluid exchange of information between supply and demand. Similarly, initiatives aiming at making academic research more accessible have emerged in the early 2000s and claim their place under the umbrella of "open science". Due to a perceived reproducibility crisis and the explosion of digital technologies, the pace of the open science movement has recently accelerated. The adjustments it calls for have become a necessity to improve the access to and the diffusion of high-quality research results.

However, in order to establish a culture of robustness in academia, as well as find a new equilibrium between quantity and quality, the open science discourse should shift priority from mere access to careful curation. We believe that there is a need for the adoption of a new set of best practice in (digital) scholarship, and, as a consequence, the evaluation methods for both individual researchers and the results they publish should be revised. Considering the complexity of the task, we argue that individual countries, funding organizations or institutions alone cannot be responsible for the systemic change needed in order to make a swift transition to a sustainable digital scholarship.

WHAT IS OPEN SCIENCE?

"Open Science is at a stage where no-one is quite sure what it is, but they think it's a good idea." — Martyn Rittman, Publishing Services Manager MDPI

The diversity of initiatives that compose open science makes it difficult to agree on a unified definition. Although some have hijacked the term for commercial purposes, most of the open science practices — around open access and open research data for example — are aiming at making the output of (publicly funded) research freely accessible on the Internet, and reusable by anyone without restriction. Others want to transform the scientific endeavour and make it more fluid, more collaborative and participative, more fair and transparent in general.

A multitude of projects challenging the status quo of how knowledge is produced, disseminated and reused have adopted the terminology. These include non-traditional and dynamic publication formats, collaborative authoring tools, post publication peer-review, the widespread adoption of preprints (e.g. arXiv, bioRxiv, etc.) and other repositories, but also some forms of citizen science, the use of social media, etc. Taking this diversity into consideration, how can one separate the wheat from the chaff and decide which initiatives should be taken seriously and adopted by researchers and their host institutions?

The motivations of open science advocates are rooted as much in recent developments of the scientific method as they are in a set of values that have existed since the first scientific revolution in the 17th century. Instead of giving an exhaustive list of sound open science projects, some have tried to embrace the diversity and blurry definition. Benedikt Fecher and Sasha Friesike, at the Alexander von Humboldt Institute for Internet and Society in Berlin, have identified five schools of thought (see Table 1), each concerned with improving a different aspect of scholarship (Fecher & Friesike, 2013). Their categories help understand the value of the various approaches. After a critical assessment — beware of "openwashing", a term derived from "greenwashing", describing the act of portraying a product or company as open, although it is not — there is no doubt that research institutions will benefit from adopting the initiatives that have the clear objective of improving the quality and transparency of research practices and outputs.

Table 1: Open Science: Five Schools of Thought

Pragmatic school	Better, more efficient and collaborative research
Infrastructure school	Technological architecture supporting open science
Measurement school	Alternative impact evaluation methods
Democratic school	Unrestricted access to knowledge
Public school	Public participation to knowledge production

IF OPEN SCIENCE IS THE SOLUTION, WHAT IS THE PROBLEM?

A majority of open science initiatives have emerged from academia itself, usually under the impetus of researchers frustrated with a particular aspect of the scientific enterprise. Understanding the somehow unrelated — yet intertwined — concurrent situations that have led to the issues described below is important to evaluate the potential transformation that open science represents. Research evaluation, career promotion, access to the literature, funding allocation, are all being criticized, and whether open science initiatives represent answers to these critiques remains to be seen. This section summarizes the roots of the growing frustration in the scientific community that led to the emergence of the open science movement.

A Growing Commodification of Knowledge

The first — and most important — source of frustration is one of increasingly hindered access to information, and the consequence of private, for-profit companies taking an overly large responsibility for organizing the quality control and the distribution of scientific literature over the course of the 20th century. In a capitalist tradition, the near-monopolistic position of publishers allowed them to exploit a system in which researchers give away their intellectual property for free, while the dynamic molecules of the research process are fragmented into static and pay-walled atoms of knowledge, mostly documents in the PDF format.

Abusing their dominant position, several publishers have charged libraries ever-increasing fees to access new research, ultimately leading to the exclusion of institutions with limited resources. In the early 2000s, open access emerged as a promising solution to this problem. The movement proposed to reform the publishing industry and challenged funding agencies and research institutions to make all their outputs available online, free from all restrictions on access (e.g. access tolls) and free of many restrictions on use (e.g. licence restrictions). The three influential events that led to the establishment of the open access movement were the Budapest Open Access Initiative (Budapest Open Access Initiative, 2002) (see Box 1), the Bethesda Statement on Open Access Publishing (Suber *et al.*, 2003) and the Berlin Declaration (Berlin Declaration, 2003).

Although many expected it would kill two birds with one stone, open access is a disappointment to some. It is encouraging that, thanks to one open science project entitled Unpaywall, the share of legal open access (in opposition with illegal sharing platforms such as SciHub) is now believed to reach nearly half of the total volume of existing literature (Piwowar *et al.*, 2017). But for those who criticized the for-profit objectives of private commercial publishers, open access failed to break their monopolistic position. Indeed, the prerequisites for open access (accessible, reusable) are perfectly compatible with a for-profit approach. In a transition from one revenue model to the next — trading subscription fees, site licences or pay-per-view charges against article processing fees — the costs of publishing incurred on research institutions may even have increased (Cambridge Economic Policy Associates Ltd., 2017).

And because of the prestige one obtains when publishing in top-ranked closed journals, the moral imperative to make all research freely accessible was never completely met. An evaluation system based entirely on the reputation of publication venues and in which quantity prevails over content quality has another dramatic consequence: universities are in effect outsourcing their talent management to journals that use marketing strategies to compete for visibility. Because it failed to drift away from the notion of impact factors, the current implementation of open access does not completely solve the issues related to the loss of control over the allocation of scientific merit.

Box 1: *Excerpts from the Budapest Open Access Declaration*

> *An old tradition and a new technology have converged to make possible an unprecedented public good. The old tradition is the willingness of scientists and scholars to publish the fruits of their research in scholarly journals without payment, for the sake of inquiry and knowledge. The new technology is the internet. The public good they make possible is the world-wide electronic distribution of the peer-reviewed journal literature and completely free and unrestricted access to it by all scientists, scholars, teachers, students, and other curious minds.*
>
> *By "open access" to this literature, we mean its free availability on the public internet, permitting any users to read, download, copy, distribute, print, search, or link to the full texts of these articles, crawl them for indexing, pass them as data to software, or use them for any other lawful purpose, without financial, legal, or technical barriers other than those inseparable from gaining access to the internet itself. The only constraint on reproduction and distribution, and the only role for copyright in this domain, should be to give authors control over the integrity of their work and the right to be properly acknowledged and cited.*

The Reproducibility Crisis

The second crisis that academia is facing is a consequence of the decline in the reliability of the knowledge it produces. The reputation economy that drives scientific careers in academia has been using and abusing metrics that often reflect quantity more than quality. There is increasing evidence that using such proxy for productivity contributed in part to the lack of reproducibility for published scientific results (Ioannidis, 2014). Some disciplines are more affected than others, but, in general, both academic and corporate researchers now question the validity of what they can read in the literature.

Whether it is a consequence of fraud, honest mistakes or underpowered studies, the lack of reproducibility is likely rooted in the pressure to produce and publish (positive) results. With journals emphasizing the need for scientific originality in submissions, and a majority of science career moves requiring a long publication list in the most prestigious journals, making one's research stand out can come at the cost of cutting corners, or worse, fabricating results. This could explain why journals with higher impact factors have higher retraction rates. It could of course also be the consequence of an extensive scrutiny by more, and more careful, readers, who tend to notice mistakes more often (Fang, Casadevall & Morisson, 2011). In any case, the explosion of the retraction rates across all disciplines (Marcus & Oransky, 2015; Nature News, 2014) calls for a re-evaluation of peer-review process.

Altogether, this means that current research is less efficient than it could be. And the lower-than-expected quality of scientific facts per part of budget invested has led to frustrations. For example, a provocative estimate recently suggested that $28 billion a year is spent on irreproducible biomedical research in the US alone (Freedman, Cockburn & Simcoe, 2015). The reasons for the irreproducibility of scientific studies are diverse, but they are all rooted in an insufficient quality control and an incentive system that increasingly appears to be flawed. Fixing incentives, adopting standards, carefully documenting and sharing all methods and results; a list of solutions to the reproducibility problem is relatively easy to draft, but much more difficult to implement.

Rampant Digital Frustrations

Paradoxically, the advent of digital technologies has not always translated into an improvement of the scientific method. The very same academic community that invented email and the World Wide Web primarily to share scientific discoveries has been reluctant to explore the full potential of these technologies. In contrast with the fast digitalization of virtually every corner of society, the slow adoption by research communities has created tensions. Three aspects are particularly problematic.

First, while the technologies behind instrumentation have seen tremendous improvements, the format of scientific documentation — laboratory notebooks and scientific reports — is mostly unchanged since the 17th century. Pen and paper are still the norm in a majority of disciplines — although most observations are made with instruments that produce some form of digital medium — and the PDF has been a very poor and static digital substitute for printed documents. There is therefore an urgent need to fill the gap between the expectations and the reality of the current knowledge dissemination model. A generation of computer-literate researchers used to the web 2.0 is asking for a change in the way research results are communicated.

Second, with a peer-review system flooded with manuscripts, there are long delays from discovery to dissemination that are difficult to justify. A recent analysis of thousands of journals revealed the time between submission and acceptance and that between acceptance and publication (Woolston, 2015). For popular open access journals, the former was 75-175 days, and the latter 5-55 days. Although they have been used in some areas of physics and mathematics since the dawn of the Internet, pre-prints are now becoming increasingly popular in other disciplines, including the social sciences. One needs to welcome this with caution: pre-prints are not peer-reviewed articles and should not be considered as such. But, in light of the time it takes to formally publish a scientific discovery, pre-prints may be an opportunity to get results disseminated faster, prior to formal validation.

Last, with the emergence of information technologies, the scientific method is expending, however we fail to share the research output in formats beyond traditional publications. The two recent additions — computational and data-driven research (see Box 2) — have triggered an explosion in the number of computational methods and digital artefacts scientists use in their research projects. They can be new software, custom code, large data sets, photographs, sound and video recordings, etc. New platforms need to be developed in order to share them with the rest of the community and get credit for it. Although it could be at the expense of creativity, there is a need for some standardization in the way scientists deal with digital data in order to guarantee reusability and interoperability. Programming and statistics, life cycle management and database maintenance, all have become a crucial part of good scientific practice, yet very few scientists get trained accordingly.

Box 2: *The Four Branches of the Scientific Method*

> Branch 1: *Deductive (mathematics, formal logic)*
> Branch 2: *Empirical (controlled experiments, statistical analysis)*
> Branch 3: *Computational (simulations)*
> Branch 4: *Data driven (aka "Big Data")*

OPEN SCIENCE IN PRACTICE

Despite all the promises for a better, efficient, more inclusive scholarship, the adoption of open science principles at research institutions is still marginal. And EPFL is no exception. Apart from situations that call for legitimate exceptions — i.e. intellectual property, privacy and security — research should be an inherently open and global endeavour. However, we are in the presence of a series of paradoxes that introduce major obstacles to the widespread implementation of open science initiatives. Various factors play important roles in enabling or inhibiting their adoption.

To achieve a cultural change, EPFL is investigating actions that could lead to an increased awareness among researchers. We also need to guarantee the availability of infrastructure, training and career incentives. The following sections suggest how this can be done.

Building the right incentive frameworks

Several reports and studies that investigated the current state of data sharing have pointed out to the same issue: within the current incentive framework, what is in the best interest of the scientific community — not to mention that of the whole of society — is not necessarily in the best interest of individual scientists trying to build a career. Known as "the prisoner's dilemma", this paradox emerges in the reputation economy of science. Even if we disregard the fear of being scooped by other researchers, the practice of open science often represents a significant opportunity cost. The curation of increasingly complex and voluminous research data requires learning new skills and spending time not devoted to producing new data. It will not be encouraged unless it is recognized as a significant contribution to research. New forms of incentives will be necessary to promote this cultural change, while new infrastructures, tools and methods will contribute to an effortless transition (see below).

The San Francisco Declaration on Research Assessment (DORA, 2012) that was initiated by the American Society for Cell Biology represents one first step towards a change in evaluation methods. There are many further steps to take: promoting and rewarding reproducibility studies will improve the number of trusted results; enabling data citation and taking data sharing into consideration during evaluation will encourage the reuse and pooling of these valuable resources, with the potential of significantly improving the efficacy of science budgets.

Supporting bottom-up initiatives

Innovation often arises from frustrations and users are usually the best source of clever solutions to systemic problems. Open science initiatives are typically community-driven solutions but the majority of its most active supporters are not being recognized for their contributions. Institutions need to find ways to distribute resources to support the initiatives that are aligned with their values. This means that the research community has to investigate new revenue models for publishing services, new criteria for funding allocation, and new career paths for individuals making significant contributions to scientific best practice.

For example, one solution to the commodification of knowledge is the re-appropriation of the means of production. Until the 19th century, scientists controlled their journals entirely through learned societies. Many of these societies have now sold these publishing activities, outsourced them. When they are still independently publishing original research, they often fear open access publishing because it requires a new revenue model. Some have envisaged flipping journals, not just to meet the new open access paradigm, but also to put new governance models in place. However, the long hours put into editing, reviewing and formatting research articles written by other scientists is rarely viewed as a criterion for promotion. These tasks are crucial to the quality of academic research and should be rewarded as such.

Providing training and support

Putting open science into practice will require a continuous investment in training and support for our research communities. While librarians have been part of the research environment for a long time, there still is no equivalent for the management of digital scholarship. Training researchers how to properly generate, analyse and share their data is one crucial step towards reproducibility, but a career path for data scientists and statisticians, similar to that of librarians, has become crucial. The para-academic communities — data engineers who can write and maintain the code used to organize data, data analysts who can build models and visualizations, data stewards or information specialists — have become increasingly important to the research process and their work must be recognized.

EPFL and ETH Zürich have recently and jointly created the Swiss Data Science Center (SDSC) to make the barriers to best practice in data management and sharing as low as possible. With offices in both Lausanne and Zurich, its role will be to foster innovation in data science, catalyse multidisciplinary research and promote open science by providing tools to its users. The SDSC team will not only produce support to researchers, but also provide education at both institutions in the form of courses in data science at Master level.

Another initiative launched three years ago at EPFL is the deployment of electronic laboratory notebooks (ELN). The goal was to obtain a robust traceability of experiments and samples and to facilitate data management and further publication. Because each discipline has different requirements, there is no "one-size-fits-all" solution and researchers must have the freedom to choose the most appropriate tool. However, providing human resources to help them learn best practices has proven extremely efficient in facilitating the adoption of ELN across campus.

OPEN SCIENCE AS A GLOBAL ENTERPRISE

As a combination of both top-down and bottom-up initiatives, Open Science is a change in the way scholarship is produced, disseminated and evaluated. It represents a chance for the scientific community to increase the transparency and impact of research, as well as claim back ownership over quality control and talent management. A few years back, a report (The Royal Society, 2012) insisted on the fact that open enquiry is at the heart of the scientific enterprise. In 2017, it is time to reaffirm the global dimension of the scientific enterprise. We have to acknowledge that each of the challenges described earlier has a better chance to be tackled if institutions from around the world work together rather than in isolation.

Although one can only speculate about the reasons behind the absence of willingness to reward researchers who adopt open practices, it is likely to be due to the perceived high risk for a country or an institution to take this step and see its researchers being excluded from a competitive arena. Global and national institutions, whether they are research universities or funding agencies, need to take the following points seriously if they want to improve the quality of the research output and support general openness in science. In the coming years, EPFL will put in place initiatives that support the following actions:

- Value quality over quantity. In the spirit of the San Francisco Declaration on Research Assessment, we propose to use alternative assessment methods — i.e. other than impact factor and publication list — for evaluation, in order to promote the rights incentives and avoid outsourcing talent management to for-profit publishers.
- Increase, accessibility and visibility of all research outputs, beyond scientific articles. It has become crucial to explore novel knowledge dissemination routes and to enact sharing policies and standards that correspond to the requirements of different disciplines.
- Promote reproducibility and reuse of digital materials. Being open, in machine-readable formats and under appropriate licences is not sufficient. There must be incentives and rewards for those who create value and impact with scholarship provided openly by others.
- Support bottom-up initiatives — such as databases, journals, tools, etc. — that empower researchers by providing them with resources, training and infrastructures that enable them to share their research results.

The future of the scientific endeavour depends on it.

REFERENCES

Berlin Declaration (2003). [Online] Available from: https://openaccess.mpg.de/Berlin-Declaration [Accessed 9 August 2017].

Budapest Open Access Initiative (2002). [Online] Available from: http://www.budapestopenaccessinitiative.org [Accessed 9 August 2017].

Cambridge Economic Policy Associates Ltd. (2017). Financial Flows in Swiss Publishing. [Online] Available from: https://zenodo.org/record/240896 [Accessed 9 August 2017].

DORA (2012). The San Francisco Declaration on Research Assessment [Online] Available from: http://www.ascb.org/dora/ [Accessed 9 August 2017].

European Space Agency. (2008). ESA: Missions, Earth Observation: ENVISAT. [Online] Available from: http://envisat.esa.int/ [Accessed 3 July 2008].

Fang, F. C., Casadevall, A. & Morisson, R. P. (2011). "Retracted science and the retraction index". *Infect Immun.* 79, 3855-9.

Fecher, B. & Friesike, S. (2013). "Open Science: One Term, Five Schools of Thought." In Bartling, S. & Friesike, S. (Eds.), *Opening Science* (pp. 17-47). New York, NY: Springer.

Freedman, L. P., Cockburn, I. M. & Simcoe, T. S. (2015). "The Economics of Reproducibility in Preclinical Research." *PLOS Biology*, 13(6): e1002165.

Ioannidis J. P. A. (2014). "How to Make More Published Research True." *PLOS Medicine*, 11 (10): e1001747.

Marcus, A. & Oransky, I. (2015). "What's Behind Big Science Frauds?" *New York Times*, 22 May.

Nature News (2014). "Why high-profile journals have more retractions," *Nature Publishing Group*, 17 September [Online] Available from: http://www.nature.com/news/why-high-profile-journals-have-more-retractions-1.15951 [Accessed 9 August 2017].

Piwowar H. et al. (2017). "The State of OA: A large-scale analysis of the prevalence and impact of Open Access articles." *PeerJ Preprints* 5:e3119v1 (Online) Available from: https://doi.org/10.7287/peerj.preprints.3119v1 [Accessed 9 August 2017].

Suber, P. et al. (2003). *Bethesda Statement on Open Access Publishing.* (Online) Available from: http://www.earlham.edu/~peters/fos/bethesda.htm [Accessed 9 August 2017].

The Royal Society (2012). "Science as an Open Enterprise", *The Royal Society Policy Centre Report* [Online] Available from: https://royalsociety.org/topics-policy/projects/science-public-enterprise/report/ [Accessed 9 August 2017].

Woolston, C. (2015). "Long wait for publication plagues many journals", *Nature*, 523, 131.

CHAPTER 9

Impact of Disruptive Technologies on Employment and the Role of Universities

Atsushi Seike

INTRODUCTION

Various different concepts have been used to express disruptive technology. For example, it has been referred to as the Fourth Industrial Revolution (Schwab, 2017), and there have been government initiatives such as Industry 4.0 in Germany and Society 5.0, which the Japanese government recently proposed in order to keep up with the developments in Europe. As such, this new stage of technological development within society has been called by various names, and the interest given to the topic has varied slightly in scope, but the common focal point is the rapid pace in which technological innovation is transforming our society.

It is also apparent that the issues concerning employment are regarded as one of the most important aspects of the impact of disruptive technologies. This is not surprising at all because employment is considered a derived demand from production, and production basically depends on technology. On the other hand, employment is also decisively influenced by demography, which is its supply source. Especially in such countries as Japan, labour supply is significantly decreasing because of declining birth rates and population aging.

This paper aims to examine the impact of disruptive technologies on employment and possible measures to cope with it. It will also discuss the significance of disruptive technologies to cope with issues in a rapidly aging society such as Japan. And, based on these considerations, it will explore the role universities can play in responding to disruptive technologies.

HOW DISRUPTIVE TECHNOLOGIES AFFECT EMPLOYMENT

Disruptive technologies, such as AI and robotics, have the potential to make a huge impact on employment, both in terms of the amount of jobs and the quality and content of jobs. It is important to differentiate between these two aspects in terms of the measures that need to be taken.

Employment is a derived demand from production, so the amount of employment is determined by the amount of production. All other things being equal, companies increase the number of employees if production increases, and decrease the number of employees if production decreases, and if all else, including production amount, being equal, labour-saving technology will lead to a decrease in the amount of employment.

But if productivity improves because of technological progress, allowing for the prices of products to drop, the demand for the products will also become greater. If production increases due to increased demand of products, then employment, which is a derived demand from production, will also increase. Therefore, it is not clear whether disruptive technologies will lead to an increase or decrease in employment, as this depends on which factors described above dominate.

However, what modern industrial history tells us is that the long-term instead of the short-term consequences of technological advancement have always spurred economic growth and brought net employment growth. The Luddite movement in the 1810s is one such incident that occurred in early industrial Britain (Ashton & Hudson, 1997). A group of English textile workers and weavers protested against the use of machinery by destroying them, fearing that their jobs would be replaced by machines. However, despite their concern, the textile industry boomed during the Industrial Revolution — improved productivity resulted in lower prices and a significant increase in production capacity as well as the number of employees.

Better productivity meant higher wages, which expanded the purchasing power of workers, stimulated demand and led to more jobs. This kind of virtuous cycle has been observed repeatedly throughout history. For instance, Henry Ford, whose car company was responsible for advancing mass manufacturing technologies through the creation of the moving assembly line, increased his workers' wages twofold. Of course, this was partly a business decision to cope with the unionization of his workers, but he also stated that he doubled wages so that the workers could afford to buy the cars they made (Nevins & Hill, 1954). Japan's postwar economic growth was also characterized by a virtuous cycle — the gains from improved productivity were shared with the workers in the form of higher wages, which led to the expansion of the middle class, stimulating domestic demand and increasing employment.

These historical facts tell us that the key to creating a virtuous cycle of technological progress and employment is through increased demand of products driven by technological advancements, and translating this to higher wages for workers. In other words, the kind of impact technological innovation will have on employment is determined not by the technology itself, but whether the gains from increased productivity are shared among the workers.

The same thing can be said for disruptive technologies. The acceptance of the technologies by the people, especially workers, will depend on whether improved productivity can provide higher wages and increased employment.

However, the way technological progress will impact the quality and content of jobs is quite clear. Workers will no longer be required to do work that can be automated through AI and robots; they will be required to do what only humans can do. This outcome is unavoidable even if the amount of employment increases. The way we work has also changed from artisans taking on the entire process of manufacturing to the division of labour in which workers are responsible for only part of the manufacturing process. Therefore, factory work has become more about monitoring the process instead of physically doing the work.

Generally speaking, technological innovation has raised the quality and content of jobs and, as a result, the workforce structure has become more white-collar than blue-collar oriented. Over the long term, jobs have become more intellectual, as well as more comfortable, through technological innovation. As with history, there is no doubt that disruptive technologies will change the quality and content of jobs. But the fact that the impact of these technologies will spread widely to white-collar professions is markedly different to how the impact of technological innovation until now has been restricted mainly to the quality and content of blue-collar jobs.

WORK THAT ONLY HUMANS CAN DO

Disruptive technologies, and in particular AI, will create huge disruptions to white-collar professions. It is currently predicted that these technologies will replace white-collar jobs including the most highly skilled professions — and there is already evidence of this happening. Advances in information technology during the so-called Third Industrial Revolution replaced many tasks typically carried out in an office, such as filing or creating documents, but AI's influence will extend to more specialized high-paying jobs such as those in the legal, accounting and medical fields.

A well-known survey conducted by a team of researchers at the University of Oxford evaluated at-risk jobs against the probability of computerization within the coming decade or two among 702 occupations in the US in 2010 by distinguishing low-, middle- and high-risk groups. According to their analysis, 47% of the 702 occupations are in the high-risk category, and this will be the case especially for jobs in the "Office and Administrative Support", "Sales and Related" and "Service" fields. On the other hand, new technologies will not have a major effect on jobs in the "Education, Legal, Community Service, Arts and Media", "Healthcare Practitioners and Technical", "Management, Business, and Financial" and "Computer, Engineering and Science" fields (Frey & Osborne, 2013).

So what are jobs that only humans can do in a society with advanced AI? Before disruptive technologies gained so much attention, Robert Reich predicted in his book *The Future of Success* that two types of people will be in great demand in the new era: geeks and shrinks (Reich, 2000). Geeks are people who have the ability to create completely new things such as game-changing software, products, services and know-how, or come up with new ideas.

Reich explains that geeks find ultimate joy when their creations are recognized as being cool. This suggests that geeks are creators on the one hand, but are not so interested in the economic value of their creations. What motivates them is curiosity. They get pleasure out of inventing something new and are ecstatic when their creations are called "cool".

With geeks, you need shrinks. Shrinks are the type of people who can intuit what people want, especially those deepest yearnings and needs that even they themselves are not aware of. The relationship of a shrink to a geek is that shrinks have the insight into knowing which products or services created by geeks will sell, or what kind of products or services geeks should create in order for them to sell. Geeks are the creative people and shrinks are the imaginative people.

Geeks and shrinks do jobs that only humans can do, but this demands a certain talent that a lot of people do not have. In terms of high volume, other types of work that can only be performed by humans are those of a craftsperson in the broadest sense, and those that provide sophisticated services. Typically, a craftsperson would engage in make-to-order production such as building custom-made machines. This entails making a completely new piece of machinery, so quite often the client may not fully understand what kind of machinery they need. Jobs that provide sophisticated services are those that provide services that "hit the spot". These services cannot be manualized because they respond to the individual needs and desires of the client in different and sometimes unexpected situations. People in this profession must have the ability to produce added value by raising the level of services in medical care, long-term care, education and tourism, among other fields.

And another type of job that humans have to do is organizational jobs, most typically management jobs. Organizing a well-balanced team to achieve high level of performance, motivating people within the organization and adequately fostering people on the job are indispensable contributions that humans can make. Good organizational persons, geeks, shrinks, craftspersons and sophisticated service providers are capable of achieving high performance.

The work of a craftsperson is materializing the needs of the client into products. Sophisticated services that hit the spot are about perceiving the needs and desires of the customers or clients and providing services according to each specific situation. And organizational persons must have wide-ranging and deep insights. In all these cases, they must be resourceful, imaginative and empathetic, which is something that AI is not.

BIG HOPE IN DISRUPTIVE TECHNOLOGIES TO COPE WITH POPULATION AGING

Similar to the potential of disruptive technologies such as AI and robotics to significantly impact employment, we are already seeing evidence of drastic changes affecting the structure of labour supply, which basically determines employment. In this respect, in developed countries, particularly in Japan, the low birthrate and population aging are the most significant structural changes.

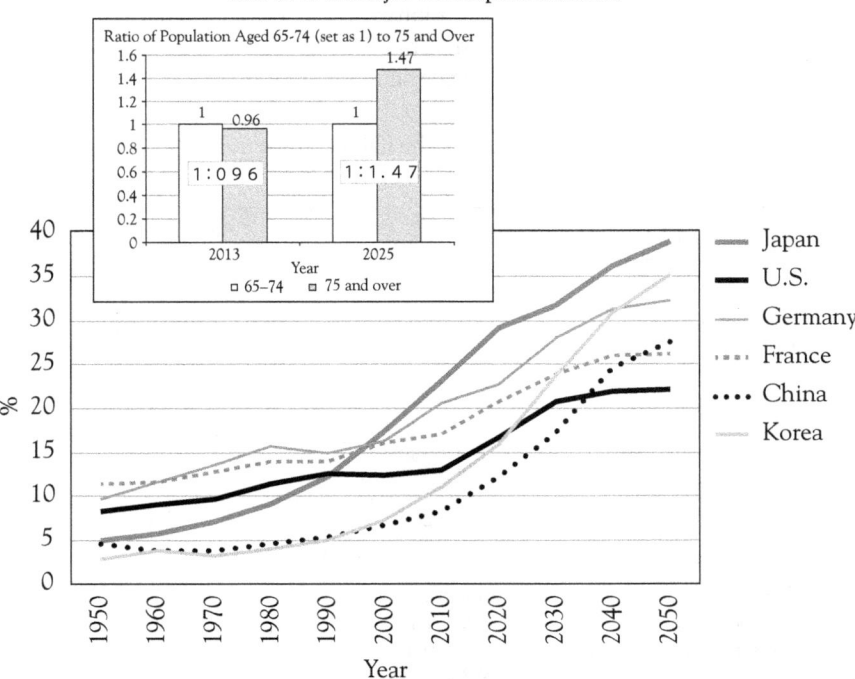

Figure 1 – Proportion of older population aged 65 and over in major developed countries

Source: Based on data from the World Population Prospects: The 2015 Revision, UN.

As seen in Figure 1, Japan's population aging is globally unprecedented in its level, speed and depth. The proportion of people aged 65 years old and over has now reached 27% of the total population of Japan, making it already the largest proportion in the world. The speed at which population aging is progressing in Japan is two to four times faster than that of European countries. For example, in France it took 114 years for the older population to increase from 7% to 14% of the total population, while in Japan it took only 24 years. Furthermore, as the baby boomers who were born between 1947 and 1949 reach the age of 75 by 2025, within the older population itself, the proportion of people aged 75 years and over is expected to increase rapidly. Now the ratio of people aged 65 to 74 and people aged 75 and over is 1 to 1, but it is projected to be 1 to 1.5 in 2025.

One significant impact of population aging is the shrinking of the labour force. Figure 2 shows how much Japan's labour force is predicted to shrink by comparing the actual figures in 2014 and the projection for 2030. If no measures are taken, the labour force is set to decrease from the present 66 million to 58 million in 2030. All other conditions being equal, a smaller labour force will lead to lower productivity, which means that economic growth will weaken in the supply side of the economy. Furthermore, lower wages will result in lower consumption, thus economic growth will weaken also in the demand side of the economy. If we consider that it is mainly the working population that pays tax and social security, this would naturally mean that a smaller labour force will challenge the sustainability of the social security system.

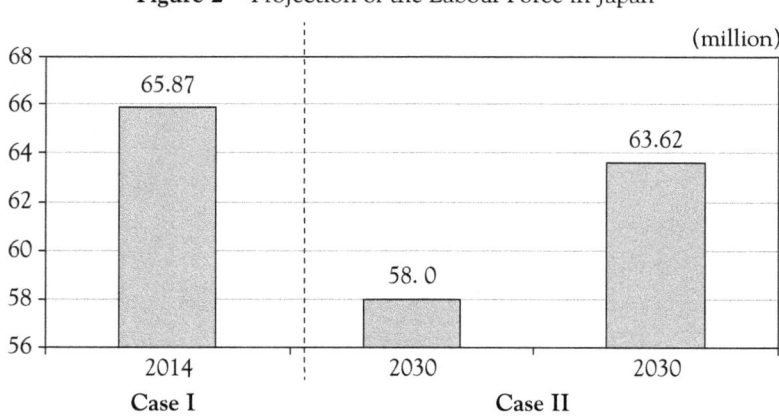

Figure 2 – Projection of the Labour Force in Japan

Case I: Labour force participation rates remain constant
Case II: Labour force participation rates of women and older people will increase
(The necessary increase of the labour force participation rate for Case II)

Males	60-64	77.6%	→	89.3%
	65-69	52.5%	→	67.9%
Females	30-34	71.0%	→	84.6%
	35-39	70.8%	→	83.8%

Source: The Study Group Report on Employment Policies (2015), Ministry of Health, Labour and Welfare.

However, population decline does not necessarily mean a reduction in the labour force. The size of the labour force is calculated by multiplying the population by the labour force participation rate, so if we are to increase the number of people who are willing to work, in other words the labour force participation rate, then we would be able to sustain the current numbers of the labour force, or at least minimize its reduction. Already, the labour force participation rate of prime-age male workers is close to 100%, so one of the ways that has the greatest potential to expand the size of the working population is the promotion of the labour force participation of women and older people (Seike, 2016b).

As can be seen in the lower rows of Figure 2, if the labour force participation rate for women in their 30s and men in their 60s can be increased by 10 to 15 percentage points, the size of the labour force could be maintained at a stable level of 64 million by 2030. And, needless to say, increasing the labour force participation rate of older people largely depends on to what extent they are healthy (Seike, 2001). In this respect, the major progress of disruptive technologies in the field of life sciences may play a major role in the prevention of lifestyle-related diseases and help maintain good health into old age and cognitive abilities among older people. This is highly expected to happen.

Also enhancing child care support is one of the most important conditions to raise the labour force participation rate of women, because without substantial improvement, they would have to leave their jobs to care for their children. In addition to improving childcare services, we also need to provide more opportunities for women to work from home, and improve conditions that allow women to look after their children while they work. In this aspect, major advances in information technology may help expand the possibilities of working from home.

Furthermore, we are now facing a more serious phenomenon in which middle-aged to older people and women are reluctantly leaving their jobs to care for their parents or spouse. Losing experienced workers at the prime of their working lives, as well as women who are wives or daughters of older people who need long-term care, from the work force is a huge loss of human resources. Even now, there are not enough care services available because of the shortage of care workers, and with the rapidly increasing number of older people needing long-term care, this problem will only become more acute.

Another pressing problem is the dramatic increase in the number of older people with cognitive decline. The number is expected to grow from 5 million to 7 million within the next decade (Ninomiya *et al.*, 2014). Older people with cognitive decline essentially need person-to-person care, so this may bring a sharp increase in the demand for care workers. Therefore, the shortage of care workers may worsen at a faster pace, which means that more people will have to quit their jobs to take care of older family members with cognitive decline.

Again in this respect, disruptive technologies, namely remarkable advances in the life sciences, may provide solutions for preventing older people from developing physical and cognitive decline; enable the deferment of its onset through advances in the medical sciences; or even accelerate the development of assistive technology or equipment that can support people suffering from physical and cognitive decline. The introduction of care-giving robots may replace care workers, eliminate the problem of shortage of care workers, and reduce the number of middle- to older-aged workers and women unwillingly leaving their jobs to care for their family members (Ushiba & Soekadar, 2016; Inamura et al., 2016).

Because of the literal interpretation, disruptive technologies are often thought to have a destructive impact on the economy and society, and this is particularly believed to be the case for employment. However, there are also high hopes, especially in a country such as Japan with a rapidly aging population, that new technologies will be a powerful tool for tackling problems related to population aging. In other words, disruptive technologies and aging may create a win-win relationship — we can be constructive with disruptive technologies. Japanese society should capitalize on this possibility and build a model for an aging society which can cope with problems caused by population aging through technological solutions for other countries that will soon face the same phenomena.

THE ROLE OF UNIVERSITIES

In any case, in order to ensure sustainable socioeconomic development amidst falling fertility rates and an aging population, it is essential to improve productivity. The advancement of technologies, such as IT, AI, IoT and robotics, is welcome news. These new technologies can replace some of the work that workers are now performing, while workers can specialize in work that can only be done by humans, producing added value that can only be created through human skills and ingenuity, and thus raising the value of labour productivity.

The important thing here is to ensure that the gains from raising value added productivity are distributed properly to the people who contributed to it. History has demonstrated that increased productivity through technological innovation has resulted in more demand for products, and therefore more employment, and raised the level of living standards. A virtuous cycle was created in which the fruits of improved productivity were shared among the workers in various forms, such as higher wages, and this in turn increased domestic demand. If the gains are not properly distributed, this could lead to the widening of disparities and shrinking of the economy.

The recent rise of populism, most notably in the UK, US and some European countries, is quite often attributed to the resentment people are feeling after losing their jobs through economic globalization and technological innovation or having their income reduced, or it is triggered from the fear that these things may occur. However, we cannot deny that globalization and technology advancements are real, and we should not stop these processes, because these advancements could either have detrimental consequences or they could bring enormous economic benefits. Instead, we need to focus on sharing the benefits with as many people as possible and push ahead with economic globalization and technological innovation.

Universities can play a major role in this aspect. This role can be divided into two areas.

Firstly, universities can contribute to the sound development of new technologies and innovation by carrying out cutting-edge research that directly promotes technological innovation in the fields of natural sciences, life sciences and technological sciences. At the same time, it is important to promote research in the social sciences and humanities in order to understand the conditions under which these technologies are accepted by society. Discussions of the ethical, legal, economic and even psychological aspects surrounding the emergence of new technologies have become increasingly more important (Kokuryo & Kaya, 2017).

Another role universities are expected to play is, of course, education. To make new technological innovation available to a wider public, there needs to be some kind of system of redistributing the benefits thereof. Broadly speaking, there are two ways this can be done.

The first is to redistribute the gains from increased productivity in the form of monetary redistribution. Recently the idea of Basic Income, proposed by several economists, has garnered attention, and the referendum on a universal basic income plan in Switzerland in 2016 is still fresh in many people's minds. However, income distribution is one of the most important incentives for working, and there is a possibility that a plan which guarantees a uniform income for all may have an adverse effect on work ethics. This may also impact labour productivity and even pose various kinds of moral hazards.

The second way is involving as many people as possible in improving productivity through technological innovation, so that they can directly have a share in the benefits. To achieve this, these people must be equipped with the work ability to adapt to new technologies. Universities can play a major role in helping them cultivate the necessary abilities that will allow them to develop the capacity to adapt to the technologies themselves, or through training received on the job. One way to achieve this is to strengthen lifelong education, which is a recurrent education program that allows students to catch up with the newest technology. Graduate schools and professional graduate schools, in particular, will play a huge role in this area.

On the other hand, another necessary ability is being able to adapt to changes associated with the emergence of new technologies and markets. A defining characteristic of disruptive technologies is the pace at which these changes will occur, so it is not always realistic to learn new skills at university each time there is technological change. Instead, it is generally more efficient to learn new work skills through on-the-job training.

Therefore, it is important for universities to help students develop the basic ability that allows them to adapt to changes and re-skill when new technologies emerge (Seike, 2016a). This is the ability to understand for themselves market and technology changes and respond appropriately based on this understanding. The ability to think for yourself is not about thinking aimlessly but systematically; it is the ability to identify a problem, form a theory that logically explains the problem, verify whether the theory is true or false, and, if proven true, take appropriate action. This is, needless to say, the learning methodology of taking an unsolved problem as a research topic, constructing a hypothesis to explain the problem and testing the hypothesis to reach a conclusion.

In other words, what university students must do to respond to disruptive technologies is to engage themselves properly in this learning process. They need to understand the meaning of learning through a liberal arts education, as well as by implementing the learning methodology of selecting a topic and researching it in depth. Among work that can only be performed by humans, honing the ability of thinking for yourself is particularly helpful for people who are engaged in work that requires the imagination. This can be effectively developed through the learning methodology described above.

CONCLUSION

New technologies will continue to make significant advances and the pace at which this is currently taking place is likely to get faster. It is important not to stop this process, but to adapt these technologies to improve the public welfare of society, which will allow more people to support technological innovation. To do so, we need to build a framework of distributing the benefits of new technologies to the people.

Firstly, a framework which prevents the negative side effects of disruptive technologies is needed, and moreover, which distributes the fruits of the technology to as many people as possible. Here, it is especially important that as many people as possible are involved in the realization and success of the technological innovation, and as explained above, universities have an important role to play in making this a reality.

On the contrary, if we consider that new technological innovations have great potential to help us tackle issues brought on by declining fertility rates and population aging, these new technologies are not destructive but rather are constructive. Since it is possible to forge a win-win relationship between aging and technological innovation, disruptive technologies can become constructive technologies in the long run. Allowing technologies to take their course in areas where they can replace humans, and humans to engage in work that only humans can do, is demonstrative of the kind of progress human society has made throughout history. Most people will engage in typically "human" work that involves creating new value, discerning its potential application, and responding flexibly to other people's needs.

With the appropriate response, the so-called disruptive technologies have a huge potential to help improve the wellbeing of humanity in the long run. Universities, too, can play a definitive role in assisting in the building of this win-win relationship between technological innovation and society.

REFERENCES

Ashton, T. S. & Hudson, Pat (1997). *The Industrial Revolution 1760-1830.* Oxford: Oxford University Press.

Frey, Carl Benedikt & Osborne, Michael A. (2013). *The Future of Employment: How Susceptible are Jobs to Computerisation?* Oxford Martin School, Department of Engineering Science, University of Oxford.

Inamura, Haruhiko, Tsuyoshi Hamano, Takehiko Michikawa, Fujimi Takeda-Imai, Takahiro Nakamura, Toru Takebayashi & Yuji Nishiwaki (2016). "Relationships of Community and Individual Level Social Capital with Activities of Daily Living and Death by Gender." *International Journal of Environmental Research and Public Health*, 13.

Kokuryo, Jiro & Kaya, Akiko (2017). "The Human-AI Ecosystem: A Nonhuman-Centric Approach." *Kindai Management Review*, Vol. 5.

Nevins, Alan & Hill, Frank Ernest (1954). *Ford: Expansion and Challenge 1915–1933.* New York: Charles Scribner's Sons.

Ninomiya, Toshiharu et al. (2014). "Nihon ni okeru ninchishō no kōreishajinkō no shōraisuikei ni kansuru kenkyū (Research on estimates of the future population of elderly people with dementia in Japan)," FY 2014 *Health and Labour Sciences Research Grants Report*, Ministry of Health, Labour and Welfare.

Reich, Robert (2000). *The Future of Success.* New York: Vintage Books.

Schwab, Klaus (2017). *The Fourth Industrial Revolution.* New York: Crown Business.

Seike, Atsushi (2001). "Beyond Lifetime Employment." *The Geneva Papers*, Vol. 26 No. 4.

Seike, Atsushi. (2016a). "The Role of Universities and Social Needs in Times of Great Change." In Luc E. Weber & James J. Duderstadt eds. *University Priorities and Constraints.* London, Paris and Geneva: Economica.

Seike, Atsushi (2016b). "Towards a Lifelong Active Society: Coping with Japan's Changing Population." *Asia and the Pacific Policy Studies*, Vol. 3, Issue 3.

Ushiba, J. & Soekadar, S.P. (2016). "Brain-Machine Interfaces for Rehabilitation of Poststroke: Hemiplegia." *Progress in Brain Research*, No. 228.

PART III

Leadership and Governance

CHAPTER 10

Leadership for Change: Some Simple Lessons from the University of Sydney

Michael Spence

In private many Vice-Chancellors are, like most academics, self-critical creatures, who can talk openly about their failures as much as they can their triumphs. But, for the public occasion, every Vice-Chancellor has a hero story in which they (though, for modesty's sake, it is usually their team) either brought an institution that was on its knees to academic and financial prosperity, or made a good institution great (again).

My hero story is broadly in the former genre, though I want to tell it for a very particular reason. Over the past seven or so years, we have brought real change to the University of Sydney and, in the process, been true to three leadership tools that I think are essential in such a process, particularly in conditions of uncertainty. I offer that story as a kind of case study in bringing change to an enormous institution more difficult to turn quickly than the *Titanic*.

In order to understand our story of change, it is important to understand something of the University to which I arrived from Oxford in 2008. The University of Sydney is enormous. It currently has 63,000 students and teaches everything from print-making to astrophysics. About 36% of our students are international students, of whom about half are from the People's Republic of China. The University is ranked within the Top 100 in all the major rankings, and in the Top 50 in the ones that we like to cite. We are said by the QS, for example, to be 4th in the world for the employability of our graduates.

The University of Sydney is Australia's oldest, and, at the time I arrived, was widely believed, at least within the institution itself and its alumni community, to be its richest and its best. In large part, we could believe that narrative because the institution kept very poor financial information (the statutory accounts of Australian universities were essentially cash accounts), and equally poor information about the quality of our research. In the government's first research assessment exercise, for example, approximately a third of our work was not returned because our data collection systems were poor and a sizeable group of our academics believed that it was none of the University's business whether they did, or did not, produce publications. Our sense of place in the research world came crashing down when, not surprisingly, we did not do as well as we thought we ought to have done in that first exercise. Our sense of our own wealth was even less supported by the facts; we had over A$300 million of backlog repairs and maintenance, and in my first year in office there was a month in which there was the real possibility that we might not have been able to meet the salary bill. The University was (on average) the highest-paying university in (on average) the highest-paying university system in the world, but had failed to invest in critical research and teaching infrastructure for several preceding decades. Six faculties of the University were generating most of its income; while ten were losing significant amounts of money with very little accountability.

A CORE PROBLEM

In essence the University had one core problem. It had forgotten what it meant to be a single university. It was instead a loose association of 16 faculties, warring states whose influence in university decision-making had more to do with internal politics than either the quality of their work or their contribution to the University's financial sustainability. This had many consequences, not least an inability to devise meaningful institutional strategy about research and education, and a byzantine, multi-layered system of university administration. This status quo was usually supported with two arguments, each of which contains a kernel of truth, but neither of which justified the lack of a coherent institutional strategy. The first was the argument that academic strategy ought to be devised at the level of the institution closest to the core disciplines. The second was that the most creative academic work happens in an environment in which "a thousand flowers bloom", and that institutional strategies usually empower university apparatchiks to "pick winners" who invariably turn out to be "losers".

The University is, I am pleased to say, now in a very different position. We have a coherent strategy focusing on the transformation of our undergraduate educational offerings to make them far more appropriate to the contemporary needs of our graduates; we have pioneered a new model for indigenous education and research; we have a strategy to strengthen both our disciplinary and interdisciplinary research that is yielding significant dividends; we have a strategy to improve the culture of the institution around our core values; have simplified the design of the organization by reducing the number of faculties from 16 to six; and have invested around $2 billion in the redevelopment of our main campus, and are only half-way through our planned program of investment in research and teaching infrastructure; we have raised over $750 million in our latest fundraising campaign when fundraising levels had been very low; and are in a much more financially sustainable position. All this has been possible because we have remembered what it means to be a single university.

FOUR ELEMENTS FOR CHANGE

Four key elements in leading change have been crucial. None of them is particularly innovative, but the Sydney experience demonstrates that the combination of these elements can be very powerful indeed.

The first is a deep commitment to collective leadership, supported by absolutely transparent research, teaching and financial performance information. Once the scale of the challenge at Sydney was clear, the first thing that we did was to commit to running the University through a fortnightly meeting of representatives of the faculties and to keeping that meeting accountable against reliable information. Many sought to undermine the process in one of two predictable ways: either by entering into a dispute about the data and the methodologies of its collection and analysis, or by developing conspiracy theories about why the whole exercise was really intended to persecute this or that faculty. But the antiseptic effect of information, and the difficulty of maintaining really spurious arguments or indulging in bad behaviour with the possibility of group censure, meant that the quality of decision-making and the accountability of individuals were significantly improved. It was important in this process that I myself lost some arguments in the group about things that I thought we should do; the group needed to be empowered to take responsibility. In addition to this central university meeting, faculties were organized into groups for the purpose of joint strategy development and common budgeting, a transition measure towards the later merger of faculties (mergers which would at the time have been politically impossible).

The second key element in leading change in a highly diverse and fragmented institution was to introduce an internal resources and costs allocation mechanism that set appropriate incentives. Like most such mechanisms, ours allocated to the faculties the income that they earned less levies for: university-wide services and strategic initiatives; the maintenance of infrastructure (a "space" charge); investment in infrastructure (a "capital" charge); the transfer of teaching income to support the costs of research in a system in which many of the direct, and most of the indirect, costs of research are met from student fee income (a "research transfer levy"); and, in a way open to constant revision, for meeting the particular costs of the ten faculties which at the beginning of the process were not breaking even financially. This last levy was obviously an important one in breaking open the activities of the faculties to university-wide conversation about choices that were being made at the local level that had university-wide implications. This was extremely challenging to the group of Deans, who had traditionally worked on the fiction that they had collective interests defined against the interests of the "University", or the "Centre" loosely understood, and who came to understand that the choices that they were making had consequences for their colleagues in other parts of the institution. The transition for them was from being advocates for their faculty in a complex political system, to being academic strategists, talent managers, fiscal stewards, fundraisers and external advocates. But the transition enabled the group to distinguish contexts in which the "losses" incurred by particular faculties were the product of external funding or other factors beyond the control of the faculty itself, from contexts in which they were the product of contestable choices being made by the faculty. In the latter contexts, the University could still take the decision to subsidise those choices, for example where an unusually expensive pedagogical method was preferred to a less expensive one because of a faculty's philosophy of education, but it was doing so knowingly and understanding what the trade-offs might be for other part of the institution.

The third key element in leading change was comprehensive and widespread consultation around the development of two consecutive five-year university strategies, that involved staff, students and external stakeholders in a variety of contexts and methods of input. Our 2010-2015 strategy involved almost 18 months of consultation with literally thousands of staff, students, alumni and external stakeholders as we educated the University community about the need for a coherent strategy, and then consulted on the shape that it should take. Inevitably our first strategy lacked the focus that a good strategy requires. In an extremely diverse institution, there was a desire by every part of the University to have their marker in the strategy, and therefore far too long a list of initiatives included within it. But it was important to accept that this was a first iteration in the exercise of attempting to become one university and in having the kind of conversations that we would need to have to become a more strategically effective organization. Importantly, the 2010-2015 strategy was positioned as the first part of a ten-year program; it is in the 2016-2020 strategy that pace of change is quickening.

One feature of a good strategy that often proves particularly elusive in a university context is its particularity. Many university strategies globally pronounce grand intentions about changing the world, and then set about investing resources in particular kinds of input into the academic process. They talk about investing in buildings, or in people, or in information systems and have various generic schemes for doing so. But a strategy ought to be focused on the core business of the university in teaching and research. And unless a university is one of the tiny handful that have almost limitless resources, excellence in teaching and research will inevitably involve concentrating strategic resources in particular disciplines or thematic areas of work. This requires real choices to be made: choices such as that between investing in existing excellence or building up new areas of work, investing in issues of great currency or trying to predict emergent topics of importance. The egalitarian ethos of a university and the fragility of academic egos mean that these choices between the commitment of resources to incommensurably good ends are at least initially very fraught. Moreover, while a university level strategy is core, individual faculty strategies that dovetail with it are at least equally important, and conversations about priorities become even more difficult at the local level unless those conversations are well supported. Academics need to be convinced that being a part of a university with a truly global reputation for excellence in particular fields has a halo effect for everyone.

Of course, alongside the difficulties of particularity, the agreement of key performance indicators for a university strategy often descends into a critique of the inadequacy of the available measures. In this context, we have found that the process of convincing a community that a vision of success does need to be articulated and that success ought, however crudely, to be able to be measured, is just as important in bringing a change to the focus of an institution, as the specific key performance indicators that are agreed.

The fourth crucial element in leading change was to ensure that the strategy built upon the authentic voice of the institution and was able to capture the imagination of the academic community. For Sydney, the key challenge was to become one university in our ability to respond to a challenging and changing environment. This had to be a matter not merely of our institutional, but also of our academic life. The University had been founded in 1850 with a commitment to equality and inclusion (there is a stirring speech in the New South Wales Legislative Council in which one of its founders advocates that the University be open to "every class" and to "Christian, Mohamedan, Jew or Heathen") and for the service of the people of New South Wales. A commitment to service inevitably involves asking, not just the questions that academics are asking one another, but also questions that the community are asking. Those questions, by their very nature, tend not to fall neatly within the purview of any one academic discipline and therefore require a multi-disciplinary response. By investing heavily in a range of multi-disciplinary initiatives from small scale seed funding schemes, all the way up to the Charles Perkins Centre, a $500 million investment in obesity, diabetes and cardio-vascular disease research, the strategy was able to draw on our tradition of community service and work against academic, as well as administrative, fragmentation in the institution.

MULTI-DISCIPLINARY RESEARCH

This investment in multi-disciplinary research has yielded extremely positive results. It has required us to develop new ways of facilitating multi-disciplinary research and therefore opened up conversations about the reducing barriers to interaction across the institution. This has been an academic conversation as we have drawn on complexity theory to think about how to create networks of academic cooperation, as well as an institutional one as we have thought about issues such as how our financial model can be used to incentivize participation in the multi-disciplinary activities. Our work in multi-disciplinary research and education has enabled us to recruit incredibly well in the core disciplines as scholars from around the world are attracted to some of our initiatives. It has attracted both philanthropic and industry support. One of the attractions to Microsoft in their significant corporate investment in research in quantum computing on our campus has been not only our existing expertise in that area, but the work of the Australian Institute of Nanoscale Science and Technology in drawing together disciplines such as engineering and physics in solving problems in quantum computing. Sometimes our commitment to multi-disciplinary research has simply allowed us to better develop existing work that was going on. For example, we have over 200 people who work across the disciplines on the issues facing China and a slightly larger number on issues facing Southeast Asia. By better coordinating their work in multi-disciplinary centres, we have been able to build on incredible existing strengths in these fields of area studies.

It was crucial in the development of strategy that the connection between our institutional life and our academic life was maintained. Becoming one university was not merely about "efficiency" or being more "agile" or being able better to respond to external pressures; it was also about recovering one of the academic purposes of the institution in multi-disciplinary research.

Leading change in a complex and large university such as my own has proved to be about empowering collective decision-making in conditions of information transparency; having a mechanism for the allocation of costs and resources that reflects University priorities; setting a strategy after a process of wide consultation that has a realistic number of achievable initiatives; and ensuring that the strategy of the institution captures the imagination of the academic community.

ACADEMIC LEADERSHIP

Of course, much of this is basic academic leadership. But it does require particular skills of a Vice-Chancellor and her team. Aside from the technical skills required to run a complex organization, there are three roles that I think a Vice-Chancellor has a particular duty to discharge during a process of significant institutional change.

The first is that she must be the chief advocate for change, and the most articulate in describing the good place towards which change is taking the institution. Much is made in the literature of the so-called "burning platform" as a justification for change. But, in my experience, academics, particularly at heritage institutions, never quite believe that the platform is on fire. Tales of constrained resources or declining standards of performance, or challenges from the digital revolution, are never as motivating for change as a story of how the university could be a better place in which to work and study, how it could contribute more, or how it could be more true to its founding ideals. Of course academic staff are trained to identify bogus claims at 1,000 metres, and so the story about change that the Vice-Chancellor offers must be simple, evidence-based and clear in its description of the process from the current to the future state. This is, of course, extremely challenging, because in practice much change delivers unanticipated benefits (and costs) and it is not always easy at the beginning to see every step in the way forward. But constant, consistent and honest messaging from the Vice-Chancellor and her team is crucial.

Second, and this is perhaps most difficult of all, the Vice-Chancellor needs to have a strong sense of the pace of change that an institution can bear. I mentioned that our two five-year strategies are part of what has been effectively a ten-year program of change. Throughout this period there has been a constant tension between the university's staff, who have found the pace of change almost dizzyingly quick, and the members of our governing body with a commercial background, who have found it painstakingly slow. Only the Vice-Chancellor and her team can mediate this issue of the pace of change. Going too slowly can result in a failure to achieve strategic objectives, but so too can endangering a program of change by pushing the institution far too quickly.

In 2011, in an attempt to meet a pressing financial challenge, we needed to undertake a redundancy program. We decided to achieve the required savings in a way that would increase the pace of cultural change that we were bringing to the institution and, in particular, the sense that our academic staff had an obligation to contribute to the University's research effort. We initiated a scheme that made around 100 academics redundant on the basis of a test of "contribution". If an academic had not produced the equivalent of a piece of research a year over the preceding three years, her name was submitted to a local panel of her peers to determine whether that was a fair assessment of her research output in the relevant period, and whether she was so essential to the teaching mission of the relevant unit that she ought not to be made redundant. If her name remained on the list as someone liable to be made compulsorily redundant, it went to a university-wide panel of her peers who determined whether the local panels had been fair and consistent in their treatment of individuals. In an institution in which a third of academic staff saw no obligation to report their research work to the University for submission to the research assessment exercise, and in which only around 25% of academic staff annually participated in a performance development conversation, this redundancy program let off a cultural explosion. There was no doubt that it increased the pace of cultural change in the organization; within a year 85% of academic staff were participating in a performance development conversation and there was a greatly increased sense of the need collectively to address issues in the research performance of the institution. But there were some ways in which the program pushed the culture of the institution to breaking point by bringing a change in expectations quite so quickly. It is a key role of the Vice-Chancellor to oversee the pace of change.

Finally, a Vice-Chancellor must not only be an advocate and apologist for change, she must not only oversee its pace, but she must also model the behaviours and attitudes of the institution that she hopes to see. A large part of our 2016-2020 strategy is work to bring change to the culture of the organization, so that we are not merely one university, but one university of a particular type. We have identified values of courage and creativity, respect and integrity, diversity and inclusion and openness and engagement as hallmarks of the institution that we want to be. Perhaps surprisingly, given the characteristically cynical caste of the academic mind, this part of the strategy is that which has garnered most staff discussion and which is bringing most strongly the sense of being a sense of a community with a common culture across close to 10,000 staff. I have been actively leading this conversation in the institution, because there is an imperative that if we are to think through what it means to embody those values, a demonstrable commitment to them must begin with the most senior leadership. In particular, staff must see university leaders take decisive action in contexts in which, for example, an institution's commitment to academic freedom, is called into question. It is these moments that build trust in leadership in a mission based organization.

THE HERO'S VULNERABILITY

In every good hero story, the hero must also be plagued by a vulnerability, a weakness that almost undoes the happy ending. My story of our work at Sydney is no different, and it relates to this third requirement of a Vice-Chancellor. In retrospect, I ought to have done more, and more quickly, to ensure both the calibre of my own team, and that it was working together effectively, modeling the type of unity and coherence that I was trying to build across the University. This was a challenge less easily met than it might seem because, arriving from overseas, and taking over a team in which there had been quite a bit of churn, I was keen not to replace too many of my deputies too quickly. Yet several of my team had a significant investment in the existing modus operandi, and there was deep spirit of competition amongst them. Moreover, I made some weak early appointments and could have invested more energy in creating a team out of my immediate reports, concerned as I was to get the Deans working together more closely. This meant that the core team did not very consistently model the ways of working together that I was trying to encourage across the University. I was fortunate to have some really fabulous individuals in the group, who deeply shared the vision that we were trying to implement, including my current Provost with whom I work extremely well. But it was only when the central team was strengthened that the project really began to gain momentum. In a context of change, it is crucial that the team at the centre is both highly capable and also working in lock step together.

Collective decision-making against transparent quality and financial information; a resources and costs allocation mechanism that sets the right incentives; a clear strategy the formulation of which involves extensive and genuine consultation and captures the imagination of the academic community; leadership that can communicate a vision, can moderate the pace of change, works effectively together and lives the values of the institution. This is not a complex recipe for change, but we have seen it to be a very powerful one even in an extremely fragmented and enormous institution with very different cultures across its different faculties and schools. I believe that it is going to become even more crucial as universities need to adapt more quickly to the increased pace of global competition and the challenges of technological change.

CHAPTER 11

The Public–to–Private Shift in Universities: Consequences for Leadership

Patrick Prendergast

CONTEXT

In whose interests do university leaders act? In the interests of specific groups: the students, the academics, or the alumni? Or do we act in the interests of industry, the state or the nation? Does the university exist to promote societal change or to maintain the status quo? Clear answers bring strong and consistent decision-making. Lack of clarity brings confusion and drift.

I gave the question much thought when I took office as a university president in 2011. I said at the time:

"Higher education is both a private and a public good since it gives the graduate potentially greater earning power and gives society a return by providing the research that drives economic growth and by educating the doctors, teachers, engineers, scientists, lawyers, artists, and entrepreneurs that society needs." (Prendergast, 2011)

I tried to strike a balance between private and public interests. I undertook to keep in mind that we must prepare students for rewarding careers in a fast-changing world, while also contributing to a dynamic economy and sustainable society.

In line with many authors, I saw the outputs of higher education in simple terms, with public goods on one side and private commodities on the other (Williams, 2016). But, in retrospect, this is probably the wrong way to see it; universities do not operate to produce one type of output only. They conduct a myriad of different inter-related activities that bring both private and public benefits. Indeed, it is efficient to do many of these activities simultaneously; most important of all, simultaneous teaching and research provide research-inspired education at the forefront of disciplines — performing in this way is the hallmark of research universities.

This paper is concerned with the changing ownership of the benefits — or outputs — of universities, and how university leaders should respond. As I will show, the shift in ownership is from public benefits to private benefits, and for brevity I term this the "public-to-private shift".

Daniels (2015), in a paper presented at the Glion Colloquium, discussed a different but related topic, the ownership of universities themselves: public ownership versus private ownership. He argued convincingly that the public/private balance in terms of outputs is similar in both, and is indeed converging. It is a question worth asking: are not-for-profit private universities, because they are not subject to political regulation, better able to produce outputs that enhance the public good?

If the public-to-private shift speeds up, what are the likely consequences? How might the public-to-private shift affect issues such as the composition of the student body; subjects taught in universities; and the prioritisation of research fields by academic faculty.

I begin by examining the example of Ireland before attempting to generalise to other situations.

PUBLIC-TO-PRIVATE SHIFT IN IRELAND

Education

In the middle of the 20th century, higher education in Ireland, as in most countries, was promoted as a public good. Joining the EEC in 1973 set Ireland along a path of integration with the global economy. Industrialization afforded new opportunities to a young population. In the period 1970–2000, Irish governments, no matter what their political philosophy, responded consistently by funding the growth of universities and widening participation to all socio-economic groups. (According to Clancy [2015], the proportion of the population participating in higher education rose from 5% in the mid-1960s to 66% in 2009.) The Irish university system changed from one of small universities, mainly educating teachers and professionals, to one of research universities competing successfully in European and other research programs. In addition, some 20 Institutes of Technology offering applied education were created, widely distributed around the country.

Throughout this period, Irish people were encouraged to take pride in the country's graduates and to see them as vital to economic development, and the basis of a prosperous society. Also in this period, students paid significant fees with a subvention of every student by a state grant to universities. In 1996, with the ostensible aim of further broadening access, Ireland went the way of other European countries by abolishing fees altogether, citing the rationale that "it would remove important psychological and financial barriers to participation at third-level". There were dissenters at the time, with one university president describing it as "a disastrous decision" (Sunday Business Post, 1997) but the initiative was followed by many years of economic growth during which Irish governments could afford to subsidise higher education. Looking back, this "total subsidization" disturbed the private/public balance that had established itself as acceptable in Irish society. Furthermore, as Denny (2014) has shown, the abolition of fees in Ireland had no appreciable effect on the socio-economic status of those accessing university education — it may even have exacerbated inequality of access by allowing middle-income families to use the money saved to buy private high school education (Denny & Flannery, 2017). Eventually, when the economic crash came in 2008, the public asked why it was paying all the costs, and higher education as a public good was brought into question. Swingeing cuts were made to public funding of universities. Fees were re-introduced, albeit at a limited level, and increased to €3,000 in 2015. And we may note that fees have been introduced around the world, with few exceptions (see Table 1).

When I took office in 2011, public funding per student had been reduced year-on-year for many years, and state investment in capital infrastructure in universities had all but dried up. In 2011, the student/staff ratio was increasing in all Irish universities and our positioning in the global rankings was slipping: in Trinity we went from a QS ranking of 43 in 2009 to 65 in 2011 — a slip of 22 places in just two years. There was no appetite in the political system to confront what was happening or to take preventive steps to halt decline — unsurprising, perhaps, given that the whole country was undergoing a financial crisis. As I saw it, state funding would continue to fall but, for electoral reasons, the government would be disinclined to allow universities to make up the shortfall by levying fees to cover costs. My decision to speak as I did in my inaugural address was because I felt the "private good" argument hadn't been heard enough in Ireland, and that it was an important counterbalance to the "public good" argument. It put the focus on who was benefiting most from higher education.

Although I was among those kickstarting the debate, I was still surprised when, six months later, the Minister for Education and Skills made a speech in which he referred to students as "consumers" who "could exercise their choice by moving to another supplier of the service"; his ministry "hadn't a clue", he said, whether universities were doing their job or not, and "the only people who can tell us that the contract between the lecturer and the institution, the department and the university, is being delivered on the ground, is the student body." (Sunday Independent, 2012)

I thought this was extraordinary market-economy language from a socialist minister in a state-regulated system, and also extraordinary was the implication that students were the only beneficiaries of higher education. And if students were indeed simply consumers, why was the state preventing universities from charging fees set by the market? Perhaps the minister's statement was signalling that the state should no longer shoulder the complete burden of the costs of higher education, and that increased private contributions were necessary.

In 2014 the Expert Group on Future Funding for Higher Education was set up. Its report to government confirmed what many of us in the universities had been saying for years: the current funding levels were unsustainable (Department of Education and Skills, 2016). As a result, in the ten months since the report was published, the private good and the economic argument is being made everywhere, and we're hearing a great deal less about the public or societal good of higher education and research. For instance, a recent editorial in *The Irish Times* had this revealing paragraph: "A recent OECD study measuring the benefits of a third level degree estimated that lifetime earnings for Irish graduates were boosted by about €320,000. It makes sense that those who benefit should pay back a relatively small proportion of their lifetime income in return" (*The Irish Times*, 2016). The editorial ignored, of course, the fact that higher earners pay higher rates of tax, so the matter is one of how to distribute exchequer revenue.

In 2017, we are still waiting for the government to decide whether to re-instate public funding or to allow universities to charge higher fees. In the meantime, Trinity, and other Irish universities, have sought to increase revenue from other sources — e.g. international and postgraduate student fees, philanthropy, industry collaboration and commercial activity.

Research

Up to the mid-1990s Ireland had only very small national research programs. In 1999, this changed with the establishment of the Programme for Research in Third-Level Institutions (PRTLI) which awarded €1.2 billion in five funding rounds. Next, in 2000, Science Foundation Ireland (SFI) was launched with a fund of €646 million. The argument for putting state funds into research was an economic one. The Technology Foresight Ireland report, which established SFI, noted that "a world class research capability in selected niches of these two enabling technologies [biotechnology and ICT] is an essential foundation for future growth" (Irish Council for Science, Technology and Innovation, 1999). Therefore the increased research funding was explicitly tied to economic growth. However, other than long-term goal setting, the political system did not influence the award of grants. Peer review of Principal Investigator grants was fully respected, and researchers had freedom to define research topics.

This was a revolution for Irish universities: funding was an order of magnitude higher, and grants were awarded based on scientific excellence as defined by international peers. Whereas previously universities were valued for education only, now a role for universities in directly stimulating innovation and, ultimately, economic growth was envisaged. The reports, focus papers and legal Acts which established the PRTLI and SFI didn't emphasize individual firms or private interests. The new direction was still being framed within a "public good" argument with the focus firmly on excellent science to ultimately benefit industry.

Since the economic recession that began in 2008, there has been a much greater emphasis on what industry needs to create jobs. The SFI Act of 2013 widened SFI's remit to include applied research so as "to enable the outcome of oriented basic research funded by SFI to be taken closer to market, which in turn increases the potential of research to yield commercial opportunities and jobs as well as other societal benefits" (Science Foundation Ireland, 2017). SFI has put the benefits of scientific research to industry foremost in its funding strategy. In this respect the "revolution" of the mid-1990s has moved from public benefits to private benefits.

Summary of Ireland's shift to the private

In post-war Ireland, higher education was funded as a public good. The percentage participation was low and research funding from the national exchequer was almost zero. Now, in 2017, the opposite is the case: participation is high and the arguments about education are almost all related to the private benefits of having a degree. Research is heavily funded, with the largest funding body making grants for "impact" rather than for arguments relating to the long-term benefits to society as a whole.

IMPLICATIONS OF THE SHIFT TO THE PRIVATE

When we try to envisage the consequences of this shift, we need to look at the implications for who we educate, what we teach them, what research we do, and how this translates to societal change.

Who will we teach?

The composition of the student body in universities is changing rapidly. Previously, students were drawn from a university's immediate hinterland. Nowadays, almost all universities — even small regional institutions — are attempting to recruit students globally. Young people living near Trinity College Dublin are going to Open Days in, for example, the Netherlands or the US, something that was unheard of before. It is stating the obvious that sourcing university education globally is only open to those who have the means to pay, or can access loans. If this phenomenon accelerates it will lead to a smaller number of elite universities accessed by those with private resources or, for universities with the resources to do needs-blind admission, those with the resources of cultural capital to compete for scholarships. This latter point is important because it is often said that needs-blind admission guarantees admission of students independent of financial means. However, the pre-admission spend on the prospective student (and indeed on their parents' education a generation earlier, as is seen in migrant families) is the major determinant of who enters universities. Such admission may be needs-blind, but it is not blind to family background and social position. In this respect the shift to the private could stifle social mobility. True elites have always been able to access excellent education globally.

What research will we do?

Motivation for conducting research in universities is very diverse. In an attempt to analyse this diversity, in Figure 1 I have plotted the public-private aspect on an X-axis and multi-disciplinarity on the Y-axis, allowing four quadrants of university research to be identified.

Up until very recently the gold standard in university research was basic, single-discipline research published in prestigious academic literature after peer-review. (see Figure 1, lower left quadrant).

However, there are at least two modes for shifting the public benefits of such basic research into the private domain: (a) by establishing intellectual property rights prior to publication — this may be mandated in the contract that funds the research or it may be the wish of the individual Principal Investigator to exploit the results commercially through licensing or spin-out ventures; or (b) by establishing a paywall around the research so that it is no longer a public good (see lower right quadrant). With (a) and (b) the results are privately owned and not released free to everyone.

For complex problems, multi-disciplinary partnerships are created, and industry takes a more hands-on approach to participating in the research (upper right quadrant). Again, the results are privately owned, and often not published at all.

In the fourth quadrant (upper left) is an emerging mode of research which uses multidisciplinary teams to address complex problems, or global challenges (Prendergast & Hennessy, 2016). Often this research is funded philanthropically, and produces results that are made publicly available in open-access repositories.

The trend created by the shift to the private is "to the right and upwards" in Fig. 1 — if this trend accelerates then the focus on creating impact and meeting the needs of industry will also accelerate. However, it is notable that

Chapter 11: The Public–to–Private Shift in Universities

recent interventions by non-governmental actors and by private philanthropists have advocated addressing global challenges. This has shifted a notable portion of global research activity into the fourth quadrant.

Figure 1 – Quadrants of university research

	Public Good	Private Good
Many Disciplines	**Global Research Challenges** Open data Publicly-available.	**Industry-defined Research** Outputs commercialised for products and services. Publication not a priority.
Interdisciplinarity		
One Discipline	**Basic Research** Outputs peer-reviewed and published under open-access.	**Basic Research** Outputs first IP protected and may be published after peer review.

Four related types of university research showing transitions between public and private benefits (X axis) and multi-disciplinarity (Y axis).

1. Traditional basic research is in the lower left quadrant, and the outputs of this research largely define a university's research ranking in terms of published papers and citations.
2. In the lower right quadrant, the outputs of the research are captured for private gain. This is a goal for many researchers as it can be the basis of profitable licensing agreements and/or the creation of spin-outs.
3. In the top left quadrant, complex industry-defined research problems are addressed by industry/academic teams often set up through university labs or research institutes.
4. In the top right quadrant results of multi-disciplinary studies are collected with the objective of making them freely available at the first opportunity, often in the first of large datasets that other researchers can also use. Often philanthropically-funded, this research is motivated towards solving a global challenge (e.g., malaria, ageing, climate change).

Most universities will be active in all four quadrants.

What will we teach?

The disciplines offered in universities have always reflected society's needs and interests, and have always been subject to change. In addition, in a university where the academic staff are active researchers or scholars the curriculum should keep up with the latest research results even before they appear in mainstream textbooks. Van der Zwaan (2017) presents a detailed discussion of how this happens, calling such universities "research universities". And what we teach is determined by pressures for change from outside academia: employers, industry and perhaps parents as they aim to maximize the employability of their offspring post-graduation (Prendergast 2015). Davies (2010) summed up such disciplinary transition briskly under three aspects:

"What we teach is
- part tradition,
- part response to emerging fields of knowledge, and
- part industrial practice to control entry to a profession."

If the shift to the private accelerates then how will each aspect be affected? Private interests will not give much attention to "tradition". As regards emerging fields of knowledge, these will be predominantly in areas where research is supported in the sciences and technology. Entry to professions will likely be less controlled.

Some acceleration of change in what universities teach is already evident: many new disciplines have appeared relatively recently — such as neuroscience, nanotechnology and bioengineering. Other disciplines are changing into something different: for example, modern languages are becoming more explicitly venues for cultural and political studies, and electrical engineering is spawning a host of new degree programs in "disciplines" such as Internet of Things (IoT) or media engineering.

DISCUSSION

Throughout this paper, the shift to the private means a shift to creating an environment where universities "make" private goods rather than public goods. Trinity College Dublin is a public university, as defined by legislation, and is answerable to the Minister for Education and Skills. I have set out to answer the question of how the mission of a public university such as Trinity will change with the shift to the private ownership of outputs.

In Trinity College Dublin we recently articulated our mission as follows:

"We provide a liberal environment where independence of thought is highly valued and where all are encouraged to achieve their full potential. We will:
   a) encompass an ever more diverse student community, providing a distinctive education based on academic excellence and a transformative student experience;
   b) undertake research at the frontiers of disciplines, spurring on the development of new interdisciplinary fields and making a catalysing impact on local innovation and on addressing global challenges; and
   c) fearlessly engage in actions that advance the cause of a pluralistic, just, and sustainable society."

This mission balances the private benefits with the public good, focusing on both the "student experience", a private good, and on "sustainable society", a public good. It makes the economic argument ("a catalysing impact on local innovation") but also the societal/civic argument ("a pluralistic, just and sustainable society" and "addressing global challenges" which is a reference to major global issues such as climate change, poverty and conflict). The focus on "independence of thought" and "academic excellence" is suggestive of a commitment to knowledge for its own sake, rather than for how it might benefit industry.

Staff in Trinity, as in most not-for-profit organizations, truly have a sense of working for the public good. But, given the changing public/private balance, the next Strategic Plan may need to be different to reflect changing circumstances.

- Will we need to emphasize more the return on investment for the individual student?
- Will we need to downplay the emphasis on "global challenges" and instead emphasize the needs of industry?
- Will we need to make more provision for economic growth, with comparatively less emphasis on pluralism and sustainability?

Such moves would not, I expect, be supported by the majority of the university community. But if the alternative is disconnect and hypocrisy — paying lip service to ideals which we can no longer translate into actions — I certainly wouldn't be happy with that situation. Fortunately, I don't think it has to come to this. But to avoid it, we need to better articulate the importance of the public good of higher education and research. Furthermore, we need to articulate that "the public good" is not synonymous with maximum economic growth. It is part of what we do, but it does not define it (see Walsh, 2012).

Table 1: Spectrum of funding arrangements in higher education. Department of Education and Skills (2016)

High State Grant Funding	High State Grant Funding	Moderate State Grant Funding	Low State Grant Funding	Low State Grant Funding
No student contribution	Moderate student contribution (€2,000)	Moderate to high student contribution (€6,000–$10,000) (€4,000–€7,000)	High student contribution (£9,000)/ (€12,000)	High student contribution ($9,000/€9,000– median)
	Income-contingent loan for tuition and living costs	Income-contingent loan for tuition only	Income-contingent loan for tuition and living costs	Subsidised and unsubsidised mortgage-type student loans
				High level philanthropy (with tax incentives for individuals)
Grants & loans for living expenses	Recent removal of universal grants Grants for low incomes	Grants for low incomes	Recent proposal to remove maintenance grant	Grants for low incomes
Norway	The Netherlands	Australia	England	US

In Ireland, as I suspect in other countries, creating a public debate about higher education is not a straightforward task. As Clancy (2015) has noted, one of the consequences of a state-funded system in Ireland is that the state aims to set the agenda of who, what and how universities should educate and research. He notes that, over the past decade in Ireland, "the state's dominant role as funder was progressively used to steer the entire higher education system towards the achievements of its goals [...] Universities have experienced a sharp decline in autonomy in the face of a more interventionist state which seeks to define more precisely what their role should be and how their outputs should be evaluated." This raises the question: who defines what "society's needs" are? Who defines the public good? In Ireland, the government represents the choice of the majority of the electorate, but it's recognized that one political grouping, focused on re-election, cannot be the sole decider of the public good. It is through a partnership between government and independent public institutions, such as universities, that the public good can be best decided. Historically, such independence and autonomy of action was given to the church, to parliament, to the judiciary and to the media, the so-called "fourth estate". Today, many would also recognize social actors, businesses and business representative groups, and artists/creatives, as key sectors who bring benefit to society when they act independently. The greater the degree of independence of a higher education institution the greater is its ability, together with government, to make public the benefits of higher education. Perhaps in this we have a paradox: the more private funding a university has, and the more autonomous it is, the greater the benefit it brings to the society of which it is part.

To some extent, therefore, the decline in state investment could enable greater autonomy for public universities, empowering them to operate more in the public good. According to Times Higher Education (2017), the former chancellor of the University of California at Berkeley, the highest ranking public university in the United States, recently said that "it would cause a huge political kerfuffle, but increasingly, in the US context, there needs to be a debate [about becoming a private university] that should be conducted in a serious way". Considering the matter for British universities, Chan (2017) writes: "The answer is not for British universities to secede from the public sector as in a privatization. The answer is to augment public sector financing with additional resources coming from the private sector. Some may call this the philanthropic sector, or the third sector. It is where private citizens act for the public good. What is required now is a public-private partnership."

CONCLUSION

At the start of this paper I posed the question: "In whose interests do university leaders act?" If we are clear about the value we bring, the public-to-private shift need not lead to us abandoning our mission or core principles; rather it may provide a leadership opportunity to define them anew. But can university presidents make any difference, given the decentralized organisational structures in universities? Freeland (2017) writes: "Presidents can and do lead by convincing key stakeholders whom they cannot directly control to support their goals. They do so by exercising persuasion, moral force and inspiration and by representing the inherent authority of the office. This is hard, but possible." In the face of the recent re-appearance of populism, "fake news", electoral manipulation and terrorist attacks, the question of articulating the public good in education and research has become more necessary than ever. It is essential that universities persuade all of the ultimate greater purpose that lies in the public good, whether achieved by public or private universities, or in a public/private partnership.

ACKNOWLEDGEMENT

I would like to thank Professor Brian Lucey of the Trinity Business School for some comments on a draft of this paper.

REFERENCES

Chan, G. (2017). *The Research University in Today's Society*. UCL Press, London.
Clancy, P. (2015). *Irish Higher Education, A Comparative Perspective*. Institute of Public Administration, Dublin.
Daniels, R. (2016). "Converging paths: public and private research universities in the 21st century", in *University Priorities and Constraints*, (L. E. Weber. & J. J. Duderstadt, Eds), Economica, London, Paris and Geneva, pp. 183–201.
Davies, G. (2010). *The Republic of Learning. Higher Education Transforms Australia*, p. 35.
Denny, K. (2014). "The effect of abolishing university tuition costs: Evidence from Ireland", *Labour Economics* Vol. 26, pp. 26-33.
Denny, K. & Flannery, D. (2017). "The economics of higher education participation", in *Economic Insights on Higher Education Policy in Ireland*, (J. Cullinan & D. Flannery, Eds.), p. 27.
Department of Education and Skills (2016). The Cassells Report. https://www.education.ie/en/Publications/Policy-Reports/Investing-in-National-Ambition-A-Strategy-for-Funding-Higher-Education.pdf page 28 [last accessed 28 September 2017]
Freeland, R. (2017). "Do university Presidents still matter?" https://theconversation.com/do-college-presidents-still-matter-81251 [last accessed 18 September 2017]
Irish Council for Science, "Technology and Innovation" (1999). *Technology Foresight Ireland. An ICSTI Overview*, Forfás, p. 9.
Irish Times (2016). "Dodging difficult decisions: Third-level funding." 9 May.
Lucey, B. M. (2017). More on funding universities. (https://brianmlucey.wordpress.com, [last accessed 18 September 2017]
Prendergast, P. J. (2015). "Forging a future: pressures on higher education", in *Perspectives on Manufacturing: Essays in Honour of John Monaghan*. (K. Kelly & G. O'Donnell, Eds), Trinity Centre for Bioengineering, Dublin, pp. 33–44.
Prendergast, P. J. (2011). Inaugural Address as Provost of Trinity College Dublin, 19 September.
Prendergast, P. J. & Hennessy, M. (2016). "Global research questions and institutional research strategies", in *University Priorities and Constraints*, (L. E. Weber & J. J. Duderstadt, Eds), Economica, pp. 143-154.
Science Foundation Ireland (2017). http://www.sfi.ie/about-us/about-sfi/history/ [last accessed 28 September 2017].
Sunday Business Post (1997). "UCC head hits out at 'disastrous' fees move." 15 June.
Sunday Independent (2012). " 'I haven't a clue if lecturers are doing their jobs', says minister." 5 February.

Times Higher Education (2017). "Berkeley needs 'serious debate' on public-private future — Dirks." September.

Van der Zwaan, B. (2017). *Higher Education in 2040. A Global Approach*, Amsterdam University Press.

Walsh, B. (2012). "Degrees of nonsense", in *Degrees of Nonsense. The Demise of the University in Ireland*. (B. Walsh, Ed.), Glasnevin Publishing, Dublin, pp. 169–196.

Williams, G. (2016). "Higher education: public good or private commodity?" *London Review of Education*, 14, pp. 131–141.

CHAPTER 12

University Governance: More Complex than it Appears

Tony Chan

"...*it was the best of times, it was the worst of times...*" Charles Dickens (1859)

INTRODUCTION

In recent years, there have been reports of controversies and events taking place across universities around the world, with issues from conflicts of interest and institutional autonomy to cases related to sexual harassment and racial discrimination. We have witnessed an increasing number of demonstrations across university campuses on issues such as the race debate, fossil-fuel divestment and academic freedom. While these might be isolated incidents, they offer food for thought for the higher-education sector, particularly in regard to university governance. On many occasions, there were discussions about university governance, with some challenging the robustness or legitimacy of the university governance structure or leadership team. This is unsurprising as university governance is key in determining the success and failure of any university. Thus, when incidents occur, concerns will often be directed at university governance. However, as universities, we are complex organizations with a myriad of stakeholders both internal and external, and these stakeholders have different and sometime conflicting expectations of the role of universities or how university leaders should respond to certain events.

This paper explores recent events which outline the complex relationships between universities and key stakeholder groups, and the implications they have for university governance. Particularly, Presidents and Vice Chancellors are often put under the spotlight. So the job of a university president can be the best of jobs and the worst of jobs.

UNIVERSITY AND SOCIETY

There are certain societal expectations bestowed upon universities and their leadership. Society expects university presidents to be "cleaner than clean" and hold themselves to the highest standards of ethics and integrity. Yet, there is no uniform policy on what the highest standards entail. Indeed, actions that are considered acceptable by its stakeholders in one institution or country might not apply at another. Also, public sentiment seldom remains constant, so behaviour or conduct that might have been standard practice can quickly escalate into public concerns. We will highlight examples of how these issues come into play, and the implications on university governance.

Societal expectations of University Presidents

The first example relates to the presence of university president on corporate boards. According to Inside Higher Education (Wexler, 2016), in the US, "nearly one-third of public college presidents serve on corporate boards". Yet, a decision by the University of Arizona's President to take a paid position on the board of DeVry University, a private, higher-education company, prompted criticism from students, faculty, lawmakers, alumni and community members. At that time, DeVry was facing allegations from the Federal Trade Commission, which claims that the company made false claims about its job placement rates and graduates' earnings. The President issued a statement defending her decision to stay on the board, citing that "I am using personal time for these activities and have fully complied with all Arizona Board of Regents (ABOR) policies. Just as faculty consult, university administrators serve on outside boards. This is true in Arizona, as well." (Barchfield, 2016). The event also drew criticism to the Arizona Board of Regents, which oversees the state's university system. The President was considered by its Board of Regents to have complied with ABOR policies, as a disclosure statement about the appointment was filed (Wexler, 2016). However, as articulated in one article, "the fact that a university president does not have to secure permission from the regents before taking a paid position at another university is a loophole that the regents need to close" (Arizona Daily Star, 2016). In a separate but related matter, the Chancellor of UC Davis signed on with DeVry on the same day as the President of the University of Arizona, but quit the board within days. According to Inside Higher Education (Wexler, 2016), the difference between their responses lies in the governance structure of their respective institutions. Under the UC system, presidents are required to go through approval processes to serve on external boards. Recently, the UC Regents introduced a new policy which limits top administrators to two outside paid jobs and adds another layer of approval to ensure such positions do not pose a conflict of interest or a "reputational risk" to the university system (Lambert & Stanton, 2016).

"Battleground" for Societal Concerns

As well as societal expectations of university leadership, a university campus can become a "battleground" where concerns and issues simmering in societies can surface. With faculty and students as members of society, they will have their own views and concerns, with some expecting their university to take a stance or introduce corresponding policies. In the US, race relations are a highly sensitive issue, which has been much debated across universities in recent years. For example, at the University of Missouri, students initially joined demonstrators over the police shooting of an unarmed black man in Ferguson, Missouri. According to the *Washington Post* (Izadi, 2015), in the light of the unrest in Ferguson, student groups lamented the university's lack of official response to racial tensions on campus. Following weeks of student protests and the threat of a football team boycott, the University's President resigned "amid complaints that he had done little to address racism and other incidents on campus" (Svrluga, 2015). The incident at the University of Missouri is not isolated, as universities campuses in the US increasingly become common venues for debates about race. At the University of Kansas, the administration called a town hall meeting to give students and faculty a chance "to be heard" before concerns about race on campus could grow (Hartocollis & Bidgood, 2015). Similarly, in Hong Kong, where we operate under "One Country, Two Systems", there are a lot of sensitivities and debates surrounding the relationship between the Hong Kong Government and the Mainland Government, and the interpretation of the Basic Law of the Hong Kong Special Administrative Region, which stipulates the basic governance framework for Hong Kong. University presidents in Hong Kong are often asked by their students, alumni and members of the community to express their views, and there have been student demonstrations across universities in Hong Kong.

While university campuses have historically been a place where societal concerns and new ideas are brought forward, what makes it more challenging for university leadership today is that universities are engaging with a much wider variety of stakeholders in an era of heightened transparency. Transparency means more than simply making information accessible – it inculcates a shared value that information should be available and disclosed in a timely manner. However, there are implications when information is disclosed prematurely as it can sometimes influence judgement in decision-making. The power of social media means that protests can quickly be mobilized, so what happens in one university can have the potential to escalate to another. So university leaderships are challenged not only to be accountable when information, either accurate or misleading, is widely distributed, but also expected to respond to events and activities in a manner which meets societal expectations that are far from homogeneous. Considering these circumstances, any university leadership will have to assess the risk that universities are willing to take to support innovation and safeguard academic freedom, and the implications if they become risk-adverse.

UNIVERSITY AND GOVERNMENT

The relationship between university and government is complex. With almost all universities receiving some form of government funding, public and private universities are expected to be publicly accountable, in terms of ensuring money is appropriately spent, and that learning and knowledge are being advanced. At the same time, universities need to safeguard institutional autonomy, as this supports academic freedom. As articulated in the Times Higher Education (Andrews, 2015), "Institutional autonomy is vital. It supports academic freedom and is its necessary corollary: without it, higher education cannot be self-governed, and if they are not, the danger is that external interference will ultimately limit academic freedom." This section will explore the relationship between university and government, and outline examples where the pivotal balance between public accountability and institutional autonomy can be tipped.

Demonstrating Public Accountability

First, we need to look at how universities are funded in different countries. In the US, state funding goes primarily to public institutions, while federal funding is generally awarded through student aid for students at public, private and for-profit colleges, and research grants. Indeed, US federal funding accounts for a significant portion of research funding across many public and private universities. So even private universities will need to demonstrate that government funding is appropriately spent. Recently, a tweet by the US President following a protest (which led the school to cancel the event) against the visit from a right-wing commentator to UC Berkeley, read "does not allow free speech and practices violence on innocent people with a different point of view. No Federal Funds" (Nasiripour, 2017). While the US President does not have the unilateral authority to execute this, as Congress would have to pass a law altering the rules governing the provision of federal funds to college and universities, this nonetheless set off discussions about the role of government funding and institutional autonomy.

In Hong Kong, the University Grant Committee (UGC) serves as a buffer between the Government and higher-education institutions. The UGC operates on the premise that its duty is to protect academic freedom and the institutional autonomy of the institutions, but, as publicly-funded organizations, universities must be responsible and accountable to the public. The UGC achieves this through its funding allocation, which comprises recurrent grants and capital grants. Recurrent grants are disbursed to universities on a triennial basis, to tie in with the academic planning cycle, in the form of a block grant to provide universities with flexibility in internal deployment. By receiving block grants, this represents "an important bulwark of institutional autonomy so that the universities maintain an arm's-length relationship with the Government over operational matters, including most academic affairs". (Newby, 2015, p. 24).

UK universities are expected to demonstrate that public money has been spent appropriately, with an officer of the university (usually the vice-chancellor) as the "accountable officer" for this expenditure. Each year, both the vice-chancellor and the chair of the governing body formally sign off the university's financial returns through an annual accounting procedure. Through this accountability framework, it gives assurance that public finance has been appropriately spent. Being publicly accountable encompasses also whether the money spent is delivering values in learning and knowledge through teaching and research. Unlike business entities, measuring the performance of universities is far from straightforward, as Albert Einstein says, "not everything that counts can be counted, and not everything that can be counted counts". There is also a danger in setting up inaccurate key performance indicators which only measure things that are measurable rather than measure the things that matter.

In Hong Kong, a recent review, commissioned by the Hong Kong Government Education Bureau and the UGC, and conducted by Sir Howard Newby, examined the governance of UGC-funded institutions. Fundamentally, the report pointed that good governance helps "to guarantee the autonomy of universities by sustaining and nourishing public confidence" in universities (Newby, 2015, p. 3). The Report outlined six recommendations to further strengthen university governance. First, each institution should identify board/council candidates against a skill template individually. Once selected, the board/council members should receive training and professional development, to ensure that they are familiar with the internal workings of the university, the policy context in which the university operates and the global pressures universities are increasingly subject to. Second, the establishment of a written accountability framework in which the vice chancellor or president and the council chairmen report annually to the government. Third, for each university to draw up a set of key performance indicators which allows its board/council to assess the progress towards the priorities agreed in the strategic plan. Fourth, for each board/council to draw up a risk register which will be reviewed annually. Fifth, for each board/council to publish a scheme of delegation, which set out the sub-structure of its committees. The final recommendation suggested a review of university governance, ideally every five years. If the six recommendations are implemented, it would mean that university boards/councils and the university administration will work more closely together to further enhance accountability to safeguard the autonomy of universities.

In the same report, Newby (2015) cited the development of codes of conduct in the UK, which seeks to establish the principles of university governance, has helped to ensure that university autonomy is nurtured and sustained based on clear lines of accountability. In Singapore, the accountability framework for university is not only widely accepted but continues to sustain the trust of key stakeholders, especially the government, in the good governance and excellent senior management of the university sector.

Government Influence

Government policies can have direct or indirect implications on higher-education institutions. For example, a new bill in Missouri seeks to end tenure for all new faculty hires starting in 2018 and requires more student access to information about the job market for majors (Flaherty, 2017). Faculty expressed concerns as tenure helps to protect academic freedom and encourage cutting-edge research, and helps faculty engage in shared governance, which is important to the long-term success of any institution. There are concerns that universities in that state will become less competitive in hiring top faculty candidates.

Government policies which are not education-specific can pose challenges to higher education. Yale and Stanford are among 17 elite universities which launched a legal challenge to President Trump's ban on refugees and citizens of Muslim-majority nations entering the US. Harvard's President voiced apprehension that a climate hostile to immigrants might detract from Harvard's ability to attract international faculty (Parker, 2017). With Brexit, UK universities expressed their disappointment and concerns. As outlined in the Universities UK statement on the triggering of Article 50 (Universities UK, 2017), "with more than 125,000 students from other EU countries studying at UK universities and 17% of academic staff from EU countries, and UK as the major beneficiary of the EU's Horizon 2020 research, the future relationship with the EU has clear implications for universities in the UK."

Third, many governments around the world appoint council members or have officials serve on their board/council. This is the case in Hong Kong where the Chief Executive of the Hong Kong Special Administrative Region is the Chancellor (head of university) to all UGC-funded institutions. In Singapore, the Ministry of Education's Permanent Secretaries are members of the Board of Trustees for Nanyang Technology University and the National University of Singapore. In Denmark, in March 2017, the Danish Minister of Higher Education and Science put forward a new legislative proposal on the governance of higher-education institutions, giving government the final choice on the appointment of heads of university boards (Myklebust, 2017). This demonstrates that there really is no universally accepted form of university governance, and this is an evolving process.

These events highlight how intertwined government affairs and universities are at times. Changing governments and government policies can push universities into unknown territory which requires strong university leadership to navigate. For governments to trust that the higher-education sector can be self-governing, universities are required to provide supporting evidence to demonstrate that their actions and activities are accountable. The stakes are high if universities fail to achieve this, as institutional autonomy can be taken away easily if trust is broken.

UNIVERSITY ADMINISTRATION AND BOARD/COUNCIL

To understand the relationship between university administration and board/council, we must examine their distinct roles and responsibilities. Like a corporate board, the university board/council, which usually consists of non-executive and un-compensated members, provides financial and strategic oversight and risk management, and not direct management, which is the role of the university administration. In many university systems, there is some form of shared governance with the senior administration, as well as faculty, staff and students, which helps to safeguard academic freedom.

Clear Roles and Responsibilities?

However, recent events suggest that the roles and responsibilities between the university administration and board/council might not be so clearly defined in practice, as local and international politics can affect university governance. For example, at the University of Illinois, a faculty recruit had his job offer rescinded after his social media posts about Israeli military action in Gaza (Cohen, 2014a, 2014b). The Chancellor maintained the board had never voted to approve his hiring, and argued that his comments on Twitter raised questions about his ability to interact with students and to embrace campus values of civility (Jaschik, 2015). The University of Illinois Board backed the Chancellor's decision and voted not to hire him. Questions were raised over whether the University violated the recruit's right to free speech and academic freedom. A report by a national group of professors says the University of Illinois "violated the principles of academic freedom when it withdrew an offer of a tenured faculty appointment" and the university administration and the board of trustees violated the faculty's "due process rights as a faculty member, acted outside the widely acceptable standard of academic governance and created an uncertain climate for academic freedom on campus" (O'Connell, 2015).

One-Size-Fits-All?

Given the important role that the board/council plays, there are great variations. In the US, the size of boards and method of appointment vary significantly with nine at the University of Colorado and 55 at the University of Chicago. In England, the Further and Higher Education Act 1992 requires post-1992 universities to be governed by a board of no fewer than 12 and not more than 24 members. Oxford University and Cambridge University are excluded from this legislation, with Oxford Congregation having more than 4,500 members, comprising academic staff, heads and members of governing bodies of colleges, senior research and administrative staff. In Hong Kong, the size of a council at the Chinese University of Hong Kong (CUHK) is nearly twice the size of the Hong Kong University of Science and Technology (HKUST) and the University of Hong Kong (HKU). The composition of boards/councils also differs slightly. There are slightly more student representatives and two members (who are not students or staff) elected by the Court at HKU. At CUHK, the deans of each faculty and graduate school are members of their Council, while at HKUST no more than two deans are appointed as council members, and they are by rotation among the deans of faculties, schools and the dean of undergraduate education.

While there is no optimum number of board/council members, it is the proportionality and composition that are key, as the right mix will foster constructive and challenging working relationships between the university board/council and university administration, which is conducive to good governance. As mentioned earlier, it is desirable to have a set of board/council members with the right collective "skill sets". As leaders in higher education face greater challenges than ever before in a highly competitive market, the ability of leaders to respond to change is critical. Research by the Leadership Foundation for Higher Education sampled views from more than 60 governors in UK universities, and found 89% of governors felt that change in their institution is managed well, compared with less than 45% of staff. When asked about challenges facing leaders in higher education, only 9% of governors identified increasing diversity as a means to improve leadership, compared with 51% of higher education staff who thought that their institution's governing body did not take diversity and equality into account in appointments (Legrand, 2016). While the sample size of the survey cannot claim to be wholly representative, the research highlights the need to "develop more effective ways to support governors in staying in touch with issues and ensure that they are making the best possible impact".

The relationship between the board/council and senior administrators is crucial. Both parties need to fully understand each other's responsibilities and roles. Effective communication also remains vastly important. Finally, checks and balances in the governance structure will also help to ensure that personalities and politics do not cloud decisions or impact the university's operation and mission.

UNIVERSITY AND STUDENTS, FACULTY AND ALUMNI

Students, faculty and alumni are a university's most important stakeholders. Universities are underpinned by the success of their students, faculty and alumni, and any decisions or actions that a university makes will have the most direct impacts on them. It is therefore unsurprising that students, faculty and alumni are often vocal about their views and concerns, and there are expectations for university leaderships to consult them on key decisions. Indeed, in many universities, there are seats on board/council reserved for their representatives. Universities are also expected to reflect the views of their students, faculty and alumni which can be challenging as their views are far from homogeneous.

Managing Stakeholder Expectations

In recent years, the issue of academic freedom has been debated across campuses around the world. Universities face the challenge of ensuring academic freedom while at the same time meeting their duty to provide an inclusive learning environment. At Middlebury College, in Vermont in the U.S., students chanted and shouted at a controversial writer, preventing him from giving a public lecture at the college. The speaker was eventually moved to another location on campus where a discussion with a faculty was livestreamed back to the original lecture site. College officials explained the decision to allow the event to take place as being about free speech, but an open letter signed by Middlebury alumni says that "This is not an issue of freedom of speech. We think it is necessary to allow a diverse range of perspectives to be voiced at Middlebury…However, in this case we find the principle does not apply, due to not only the nature, but also the quality, of Dr Murray's scholarship. He paints arguments for the biological and intellectual superiority of white men with a thin veneer of quantitative rhetoric and academic authority." (Jaschik, 2017). As universities, we are indeed challenged to protect values which we think define our institution, but can at times contradict the views of some students, faculty and alumni.

There are also ongoing debates over how institutions should balance their historic roots with the need to appeal to a modern and diverse range of students. In November 2015, a protest led by a student group demanded that Princeton disassociate itself from former US president Woodrow Wilson due to his "racist legacy" (Lawler, 2015). Similarly, Yale changed the name of its Calhoun College, which honors a 19th century alumnus and former US Vice President who is now viewed as an active proponent of slavery when many condemned it (Washington Post, 2017). Similar debates took place in Oxford, with students arguing that the statue of British mining magnate and African colonizer Cecil Rhodes, who is now seen as racist, should be taken down as this is considered incompatible with the "inclusive culture" at the university (BBC News, 2016).

Managing Stakeholder Relationships

As well as meeting expectations of our students, faculty and alumni, our relationships with these stakeholder groups can be scrutinized. For example, as university leaders, we need to investigate and take actions to handle faculty, students and staff misconduct, as any universities and employers are required to. The sexual harassment case of a faculty at UC Berkeley was under much scrutiny in the media and among the UC Berkeley community. After the resignation of one of their deans, who was alleged to have committed sexual harassment, UC Berkeley issued a statement which read "the initial decision not to remove the dean from his position is the subject of legitimate criticism. We can and must do better as a campus administration. We must move in the direction of stronger sanctions, and in doing this we want and need the broad input of the campus community. We will act quickly to generate action that will produce lasting change in our culture and practices." (Berkeley News, 2016).

As well as handling faculty, student and staff misconduct, there are occasions when our practice or treatment of stakeholders falls short of expectations, and there are indeed consequences. Recently, the University of Iowa agreed to pay US$6.5 million to settle discrimination lawsuits by former employees, as jurors found that school official discriminated against an employee based on her gender and sexual orientation (Foley, 2017). The case in point is that our response to incidents like this puts our leadership skills to the test as we are challenged to act appropriately and in a timely manner, and the robustness of the governance structure will undoubtedly be tested.

The examples highlight incidents and events university leadership must manage effectively. University leaders are increasingly expected to express their views and take a stance on issues that students, faculty and alumni consider important. Secondly, there are expectations that those views should represent students, faculty and alumni, even though their views might not be homogeneous. It remains vastly important that students, faculty and alumni have channels through which they can voice their concerns and ideas, and for universities to consult them on key issues, but, at the same time, we are required to safeguard our values, namely, academic freedom, and ensure that our actions, along with our faculty and students, comply with laws and regulations that underpin the higher-education sector and society.

CONCLUSION

The job of a university president can be the best of jobs and also the worst of jobs. The president plays a pivotal role in balancing stakeholder interests, while ensuring that these align with the university's long-term development.

The events outlined highlight the complex relationships between universities and key stakeholder groups, and their implications for university governance. With universities engaging with a wider range of stakeholders, there are different and sometimes conflicting expectations in the role of universities in society or how university leadership should respond to certain events. Along with our stakeholders, universities today are required to navigate at a time of uncertainties and into unknown territories, including political events at the national level, as well as major economical and societal changes.

University governance is increasingly tested as we operate in a more complex and competitive environment. Yet, there are often different interpretations of what constitutes good governance, and these differences do not necessarily mean that one is more superior, as there is no foolproof governance system, but those that can successfully minimize the likelihood of human vagaries and extreme acts or decisions by implementing checks and balances in the system. Also, there can sometimes be confusion in what constitutes governance and management, as well as governance and accountability. At what point does governance become interference into academic freedom and how much is too much accountability so that it hinders innovation?

There is a need to balance accountability and institutional autonomy so that universities are accountable for their actions, while safeguarding academic freedom. The key will always be to achieve the right balance between different variables, namely accountability and institutional autonomy; however politics, personalities and societal expectations will have the potential to push the balance to one side or the other. Indeed, even a more mature governance system can be impacted by its leadership or external political environment such as Brexit and the Trump Administration.

REFERENCES

Andrews, M. (2015). "University autonomy: not the only principle we should defend", *Times Higher Education*, 23 July 2015. Available at: https://www.timeshighereducation.com/opinion/university-autonomy-not-the-only-principle-we-should-defend

Arizona Daily Star (2016). "UA President Hart must choose: Devry, or the UA", 9 April 2016. Available at: http://tucson.com/news/opinion/editorial/ua-president-hart-must-choose-devry-or-the-ua/article_e31b9b2e-49b1-5035-934e-a4c87a722c95.html

Barchfield, V. (2016). "Arizona Lawmakers Call for UA President Hart's Resignation", Arizona Public Media Broadcast, 6 April 2016. Available at: https://www.azpm.org/s/38228-arizona-lawmakers-call-for-ua-presidents-resignation-following-appointment-to-board-of-for-profit-college-company/

BBC News (2016). "Cecil Rhodes statue to be kept by Oxford University College," 29 January 2016. Available at: http://www.bbc.com/news/uk-england-oxfordshire-35435805

Berkeley News (2016). "Berkeley Law's Choudhry resigns as dean", 10 March 2016. Available at: http://news.berkeley.edu/2016/03/10/a-statement-on-the-berkeley-law-dean/

Berkeley News (2017a). Free speech? Hate speech? Or Both?, 31 January 2017. Available at: http://news.berkeley.edu/2017/01/31/free-speech-hate-speech-yiannopoulos/

Berkeley News (2017b). "Milo Yiannopoulos event canceled after violence erupts", 1 February 2017. Available at: http://news.berkeley.edu/2017/02/01/yiannopoulos-event-canceled/

Cohen, J. S. (2014a). "U. of I. pulls professor's job offer after tweets criticizing Israel", *Chicago Tribune*, 14 August 2014. Available at: http://www.chicagotribune.com/news/nationworld/chi-illinois-professor-israel-20140813-story.html

Cohen, J. S. (2014b). "U. of I. trustees vote 8 – 1 to reject Salaita", *Chicago Tribune*, 11 September 2014. Available at: http://www.chicagotribune.com/news/ct-salaitia-board-decision-20140911-story.html

Dickens, C. (1859). *A tale of two cities*, Philadelphia, Pa: Courage Books, 1992, (original publication, 1859).

Flaherty, C. (2017). "Killing tenure", *Inside Higher Education*, 13 January 2017. Available at: https://www.insidehighered.com/news/2017/01/13/legislation-two-states-seeks-eliminate-tenure-public-higher-education

Foley, R. J. (2017). "Iowa to pay $6.5M to settle landmark sports bias lawsuit", *Associated Press Business Insider*, 19 May 2017. Available at: http://www.businessinsider.com/ap-iowa-to-pay-65m-to-settle-landmark-sports-bias-lawsuits-2017-5

Hartocollis, A. & Bidgood, J. (2015). "Racial Discrimination Protests Ignite at Colleges Across the U.S", *New York Times*, 11 Nov 2015. Available at: https://www.nytimes.com/2015/11/12/us/racial-discrimination-protests-ignite-at-colleges-across-the-us.html?_r=0

Izadi, E. (2015). "The incidents that led to the University of Missouri president's resignation", *Washington Post*, 9 November 2015. Available at: https://www.washingtonpost.com/news/grade-point/wp/2015/11/09/the-incidents-that-led-to-the-university-of-missouri-presidents-resignation/?utm_term=.70307b82a2dd

Scott, J. (2015). "Illinois Chancellor Quits", *Inside Higher Education*, 7 August 2015. Available at: https://www.insidehighered.com/news/2015/08/07/chancellor-u-illinois-urbana-champaign-resigns

Scott, J. (2017), "Shouting Down a Lecture", *Inside Higher Education*, 3 March 2017. Available at: https://www.insidehighered.com/news/2017/03/03/middlebury-students-shout-down-lecture-charles-murray

Lambert, D. & Stanton, S. (2016). "UC Regents approve new limits on moonlighting by administrators", *Sacramento Bee*, 21 July 2016. Available at: http://www.sacbee.com/news/local/education/article91109637.html

Lawler, D. (2015). "Princeton University students protest Woodrow Wilson's "racist legacy"," *Telegraph*, 19 November 2015. Available at: http://www.telegraph.co.uk/news/worldnews/northamerica/usa/12006430/Princeton-University-students-protest-Woodrow-Wilsons-racist-legacy.html

Legrand, J. (2016). "Universities must make better use of their governors," *Times Higher Education*, 10 February 2016. Available at: https://www.timeshighereducation.com/blog/universities-must-make-better-use-their-governors

Myklebust, J. P. (2017). "Government strengthens grip on universities again", *University World News*, 1 March 2017. Available at: http://www.universityworldnews.com/article.php?story=20170301231102859

Shahien, N., (2017). "No, Trump can't cut UC Berkeley's federal funding by himself", *Bloomberg*, 3 February 2017. Available at: https://www.bloomberg.com/news/articles/2017-02-02/no-trump-can-t-cut-u-c-berkeley-s-federal-funding-by-himself

Newby, Sir H. (2015). *Governance in UGC-funded Higher Education Institutions in Hong Kong – Report of the University Grants Committee*, University Grants Committee.

O'Connell, P. M. (2015). "Group blasts University of Illinois for yanking Steven Salaita job offer", *Chicago Tribune*, 28 April 2015. Available at: http://www.chicagotribune.com/news/local/breaking/ct-steven-salaita-university-of-illinois-aaup-report-met-20150427-story.html

Parker, C. R. (2017). "Sharpening critiques of Trump's Policies, Faust Talks Federal Policy at Bloomberg Event", *Harvard Crimson*, 28 February 2017. Available at: http://www.thecrimson.com/article/2017/2/28/faust-bloomberg-roundtable/

Svrluga, S. (2015). "University of Missouri president, chancellor resign amid racial tensions", *Chicago Tribune*, 10 November 2015. Available at: http://www.chicagotribune.com/sports/college/ct-missouri-protest-football-players-faculty-20151109-story.html

Universities UK (2017). Universities UK statement on the triggering of Article 50, 29 March 2017. Available at: http://www.universitiesuk.ac.uk/news/Pages/Universities-UK-statement-on-the-triggering-of-Article-50.aspx http://www.chicagotribune.com/news/local/breaking/ct-university-of-chicago-safe-spaces-letter-met-20160825-story.html

Washington Post (2017). "Yale's smart choice in renaming Calhoun College", 19 February 2017. Available at: https://www.washingtonpost.com/opinions/yales-smart-choice-in-renaming-calhoun-college/2017/02/19/fd391418-f235-11e6-b9c9-e83fce42fb61_story.html?utm_term=.de8bd36d7a41

Wexler, E.(2016). "Dual loyalties", *Inside Higher Education*, 13 April 2016. Available at: https://www.insidehighered.com/news/2016/04/13/presidents-public-universities-criticized-joining-boards-profit-university

CHAPTER 13

The Geneva-Tsinghua Initiative as a Test bench of the Future of Universities

Yves Flückiger and Pablo Achard

UNIVERSITIES IN THE TURMOIL OF DEEP CHANGES

To secure Europe's future economic prosperity and competitiveness against an extremely challenging internal and external environment, many actions have to be taken. Above all, continued substantial investments in research and innovation capabilities are fundamental to the knowledge economy that Europe needs to drive private sector investment, human capital formation, employment and sustainable growth. The rapidly changing global economic and political landscape, the exponential development of computing power and technological capacities, and the multiple challenges that confront all our societies in the years to come make these long-term investments more crucial than ever before.

Our future prosperity and well-being depend on world-class research and innovation. Even a small increase in R&D has the potential to translate into per capita growth and have a significant and long-term effect on employment. The rate of return for publicly funded R&D usually exceeds 30% (Glover et al., n.d.) and there are significant benefits to cross-countries programs that complement significant national investments in excellent research and innovation. In particular, EU funding enables the best researchers in Europe to work with each other, resulting in higher quality of research as evidenced for example by their citation impact. So investing in excellent research and innovation should be a top priority for all who want smart, sustainable and inclusive growth.

In this context, universities all over the world are experiencing deep transformations that have been described in many books and articles (Achard, 2016; Flückiger & Achard, 2016; Barnett, 2012; Crow & Dabars, 2015; Van der Zwaan, 2017). Let us summarize some of these global trends.

The first one is a massification of the demand for higher education (HE). This trend is pushed by converging factors: demography, an economic boom of some regions of the world that triggers an explosion of the "middle class" and increasing needs of the knowledge economy. If this massification is slowing down in western countries, it is clearly visible at a global scale where Asia and Africa have an increasing share of student population. By 2020, China and India will train 40% of world's newly graduates.

Working hand-in-hand with massification is a diversification of student cohorts. For a long time a sanctuary of privileged, young, white males, universities are becoming more similar to society at large: gender, racial, demographical and socio-economical diversity is blooming. Not only "non-traditional" students are expanding, but "non-traditional" HE pathways are also increasing. More and more, people are returning to university at various stages of their professional careers to acquire new skills, certificates or knowledge. This Life Long Learning trend is a long-term one, gaining traction due to the acceleration of socio-technological innovations.

A more worrying consequence of massification is the decrease in state investment in universities, at least on a per student basis if not on an absolute one. This disinvestment has different consequences depending on national policies. US universities have seen a rising cost of student fees over several decades and much above inflation. In Europe, universities are increasingly seeking money from third parties: private companies, alumni, charity funds, etc. Both governmental and third party partners demand a more transparent and higher "return on investment". This drives HE institutions to emphasize and pay closer attention to their economical and social impact.

Diversification of the student population together with the increasing cost of HE makes a strong argument for increased attention to the needs and potential obstacles encountered by each and every student. Two routes are followed to reduce attrition as much as possible: the diversification of teaching methods, and the use of big data to tailor personal support. Online learning, blended learning, flipped classrooms, crossover learning, mastery learning, hands-on learning, learning-by-doing and a variety of other innovative learning methods are being experimented, tested and discussed in most academic institutions. Most of these aren't new, but their pros and cons are better known and professors and instructors have a larger toolbox than ever. In parallel, the amount of data collected on student activities, particularly during online activities, is exponentially increasing, following Moore's law. New analytical tools are therefore developed to improve admissions, prevent drop-off or create personal course contents (Lane, 2014; Wilson & Nichols, 2015.)

Forecasting is a difficult craft in an era where disruptive technological changes are arriving at a fast pace. By definition, breakthroughs and discoveries are almost impossible to predict. But we can imagine what the future will look like if the current trends amplify. We can even do more than that and try to experiment some of these ideas in pilot programs. That's what the University of Geneva and Tsinghua University are currently doing together in the field of the SDGs.

THE GENEVA-TSINGHUA INITIATIVE

In 2015 the UN General Assembly formally accepted a new set of 17 measurable Sustainable Development Goals (SDGs), ranging from ending world poverty to achieving gender equality and empowering women by 2030. These are to succeed the Millennium Development Goals, a set of eight measurable goals which were signed in September 2000.

Education for sustainable development (ESD) is explicitly recognized in the SDGs as part of Target 4.7 of the SDG on education, together with Global Citizenship Education. At the same time, it is important to emphasize ESD's crucial importance for all the other 16 SDGs. With its overall aim to develop cross-cutting sustainability competencies in learners, ESD is an essential contribution to all efforts to achieve the SDGs, enabling individuals to contribute to sustainable development by promoting societal, economic and political change as well as by transforming their own behaviour.

The Geneva-Tsinghua Initiative for Sustainable Development Goals (GTI) is a comprehensive portfolio of teaching, exchange and innovation programs aimed at contributing concretely to the achievement of United Nations' Sustainable Development Goals (SDGs, also known as "Global Goals"). It includes a Summer school ("ODD summer"), a Master's degree program in "Innovation, human development and sustainability", a Certificate (continuous education) program, a scholar's exchange program, an accelerator, online courses, hackathons and conferences.

Mobility is at the heart of this initiative and students spend time in at least two places: Geneva, the city with the most international organizations in the world, where they can learn about the practical reality of the SDGs from field experts who are on the front line of tackling the SDGs (UNEP, UNDP, WHO, ITU, UNITAR…), and Beijing and Shenzhen, China's leading clusters for software and hardware innovation, where they can learn what it takes to bring their ideas and prototypes to market in the world's largest economy and how they can contribute in one way or another to the implementation of SDGs.

The GTI's pedagogical approach is characterized by a focus on hands-on learning inspired by real-world problems. Group challenges are the backbone of this methodology, where students from different disciplinary and cultural backgrounds are invited to work together.

The GTI, in its first years, is made possible thanks to generous support of charities and alumni in each institution.

HOW GTI SERVES AS A TEST BENCH OF FUTURE EVOLUTIONS

GTI allows our two institutions to make a real test of new educational and translational models. We don't test different hypotheses separately but all of them together as they form a consistent system.

First of all, this portfolio is conceived globally for a continuum of audiences: summer students, Master students, life-long learners, scholars, online students, citizens interested in some events. The difference between these audiences is blurring, and bridges and modularity must be created from the very beginning between the different programs. It forces us to rethink students' pathways. A summer student can become a Master student, a life-long learner can participate in an accelerator activity, an online student can participate in a hackathon, etc. Moreover, these different audiences must find places, projects and opportunities to interact, share questions and ideas, give specific insights to each other's projects.

This diversity is also constructed from the start by mixing disciplinary backgrounds and by immersing students in two cultures (International Geneva, Entrepreneurial China). The goal is to teach them to think and act outside of their comfort zones, as well as to be prepared for "real life" situations where interactions with people from different backgrounds, cultures, ages, are the everyday business of most companies or institutions. In other words, to prepare students for the transition from the academic world to a global economy transformed by digital technology and the challenges of sustainable development.

This "real world" approach is also the opportunity to consolidate teaching by solving concrete problems. This is an opportunity to foster learning-by-doing, but also social impact and innovation. Indeed, in order to accelerate innovation and maximize its positive social impact, stakeholders from different disciplines need a platform to exchange and discuss their ideas and experiences. The GTI provides in this respect a crucial platform for knowledge exchange, enabling students and researchers to present their findings and practitioners to outline their needs and insights, while relating their experiences from the field. In the GTI, students are coming up with innovative solutions to some of the world's most pressing problems. By working collaboratively at the grassroots level, students are moving ideas forward to address a wide array of SDGs challenges.

Last, the GTI crystallizes the convergence between international organizations, the academic world and the business sector. This is true in the construction of the programs as well as in the financing of the whole endeavour where partnerships with non-governmental entities were keys factors of our ability to start so broadly. The coherence of the initiative was crucial for that matter.

REFERENCES

Achard, P. (2016). *Les MOOCs — Cours en ligne et transformations des universités*, Presses Universitaires de Montréal.

Barnett, R. (ed) (2012). *The Future University — Ideas and Possibilities*, Routledge.

Crow, M. & Dabars, W. (2015). *Designing the New American University*. Johns Hopkins University Press.

Flückiger, Y. & Achard, P. (2016). "From MOOCs to MOORs: a movement towards Humboldt 2.0." in Weber, L. E. & Duderstadt, J. J. (eds) *University Priorities and Constraints*. Economica, Paris.

Glover, M. et al. (n.d.) Estimating the returns to UK publicly funded cancer-related research in terms of the net value of improved health outcomes. *BMC Med.*

Lane, J. E. (ed) (2014). *Building a smarter university — Big data, Innovation, and Analytics*. State University of New York Press.

Van der Zwaan, B. (2017). *Higher education in 2040 — A global approach*. Amsterdam University Press.

Wilson, K. & Nichols, Z. (2015). *The Knewton Platform — A General-Purpose Adaptive Learning Infrastructure*. A Newton White Paper. www.knewton.com

CHAPTER 14

Leadership and Governance — How to 'Manage' Change in Universities?

Nicholas B. Dirks

"The two greatest gifts to the University of California have been the institutional autonomy given to its Board of Regents in the Constitution of 1878 and the unprecedented grant of authority the board assigned to the Academic Senate in 1920."
Clark Kerr, September 1997

BERKELEY CASE STUDY PART I: PAST ACCOMPLISHMENTS

The University of California was established in 1868. Within 50 years, it became one of the best universities in the US, whether public or private. Indeed, by the middle of the 20th century, it had more top ranked departments, schools, programs and colleges than any other university, including Harvard. Before the University could emerge as a serious contender among American universities, however, it had to weather a major political crisis, in which the fundamental purposes, and governance, of the university became the grist for sustained political turmoil and struggle.

Henry Durant, the inaugural President, aimed to create a "comprehensive" university. This vision was reinforced in 1872 when Yale's Daniel Coit Gilman took up the Presidency with a vow to develop a modern university in California, based on Yale's liberal curriculum, but wide in its scope and offerings, and adapted to the state's "public and private schools, to its peculiar geographical position, to the requirements of its new society and its undeveloped resources" (Gilman, 1872).

Very soon after Gilman took the helm of UC, however, the director of the university's college of agriculture, Ezra Carr, mobilized the agricultural interests in California and pressed the state legislature to condemn the university for neglecting the study of farming and the mechanical arts. In the political struggle that followed, Gilman became profoundly disillusioned as he realized that every one of his initiatives could be questioned if not undone by external forces with little understanding of either academic affairs or scientific inquiry. He lamented that, "however well we may build up the University of California, its foundations are unstable, because it is dependent on legislative control and popular clamour". He left in 1875, after only three years in California, to become the first president of Johns Hopkins University.

Gilman's quick departure constituted a warning to many legislators of the need for greater clarity about university governance. It was doubtless part of the reason why, when the new California constitution was finally passed in May 1879, the university was named a "public trust" — that is, formally "subject only to such legislative control as may be necessary to insure compliance with the terms of its endowment and the proper investment of and security of its funds". So, although the university lost a fine leader in Gilman, it acquired the necessary foundation for what was to become a great educational institution: autonomy from political interference and independent governance.

Gilman's anxieties gave way to a subsequent history of extraordinary success, but they never disappeared entirely. The loyalty oath controversy of the post-World War II years made it clear that political interference could take different forms, and the politically charged governor's race of 1966, during which Ronald Reagan ran on his pledge to clean up the mess at Berkeley, demonstrated how easy it was to mobilize public opinion against the University at a time of growing student unrest in the 1960s.

In recent years, however, the objective of curtailing the university's constitutional autonomy has surfaced again on several occasions in the state legislature, fed in large part by a pervasive sense on the part of politicians and the public that the university's commitment to academic excellence is not sufficiently tethered to the direct concerns of taxpayers in the state of California. Although political autonomy is widely seen as critical for excellence, the university is regularly under attack, whether around the increasing selectivity of its admissions process, its growing number of "out of state" students, a succession of largely media-driven "scandals" or simply the general misunderstanding of how a great research institution must function if it is to remain excellent and compete with peer private universities. All of these issues are used to argue for increasingly less autonomy. Paradoxically, at the same time criticism mounts, the campuses of the University of California are ranked higher and higher both for their academic excellence and for their demonstrated commitment to educating large numbers of students from low socio-economic backgrounds.

These crises, whether across the university system or at Berkeley, have been driven largely, if not entirely, by economic issues. After multiple cycles of cuts, especially since the early 1990s, the percentage of state appropriation making up university budgets steadily declined, though not yet at the same rate that affected most other public universities at the time. The great recession of 2008, however, hit the university system in California particularly hard. Berkeley lost more than half its state funding between 2008 and 2010, and, even after the recovery of the state economy, today receives only 11% of its budget from the state appropriation (down from 33% in 2004), only a little more than half what it received before the recession. While the immediate shortfall was made up by dramatic increases in tuition and students from out of state, the lack of public support for both led first to a six-year tuition freeze and then to a cap on out-of-state students.

The long-term structural financial strains have in turn created a governance crisis for the university, now more dependent than ever on its own entrepreneurial capacity and its campus specific initiatives rather than on claims for greater state funding. The governance crisis consists of issues related both to the administration of the "system" from above and governance of each campus from below. At a time when the preponderance of funding came from the state, the old governance system worked well. Now, however, each campus needs more attention from a governing board than the Board of Regents as a single board for ten campuses can provide, and more autonomy for its operations given both the differences of each campus and need for greater local administrative authority and control in order to cope with the new — and highly differentiated — financial environment.

At the same time, the remarkable and historically critical system of faculty governance, which emerged out of a faculty revolt against the autocratic "rule" of Benjamin Ide Wheeler in 1919, has struggled to accommodate itself to the enormity of the financial and institutional challenges ahead. The role of the Academic Senate has been critical to the development of Berkeley's academic excellence, playing a significant role not just in curricular and faculty affairs, but in setting academic priorities across the institution. And yet the changed budgetary realities of the university have been causing disruption to traditional ways of managing not just budgets but issues of faculty participation in financial governance as well.

BERKELEY CASE STUDY PART II: PRESENT CHALLENGES

I accepted an offer to become the 10th Chancellor of UC Berkeley on 7 November 2012, the day after Proposition 30 passed in California. The proposition was to increase taxes for education and, from afar at least, suggested very good news for the University of California, still reeling from budget cuts after the great recession of 2008. Unfortunately, it turned out that the passage of this proposition did not increase the state allocation to higher education, but rather only ensured that another precipitous round of cuts would not take place. And yet, the financial outlook seemed promising, and the state of California was finally showing pronounced economic growth and vitality after the great recession.

When I came to Berkeley some months later, however, I realized that there would be serious headwinds. First, the Governor, Jerry Brown, was adamantly opposed to any further tuition increases (he was fond of saying that when he went to Berkeley the tuition had only been $70 a semester, as if it should go back to those days without the ample state funding that made a virtually tuition free education possible), and that he wished to find a way to bend the cost curve of higher education. He was convinced that salaries were too high, teaching workloads too low, research too irrelevant, bureaucratic processes too byzantine and administrators too numerous, while betraying little understanding of or interest in the institutional realities of major public research universities.

Second, as I studied the budget, I learned that Berkeley was almost out of additional debt capacity and had begun to show alarming financial trends. Institutional contributions to the retirement program had skyrocketed from zero to 12% (now at 14%). A new formula for the allocation of state funding meant that Berkeley was left with a smaller share of the total pie than it had received earlier. New building (including renovating the football stadium, as well as several other projects that relied heavily on debt) had been necessary given the age and seismic vulnerability of the campus, but had been done without any state funding. Tuition increases and increased out of state enrolment had made recovery possible, but in a precarious way.

Six months after I had arrived in Berkeley, my Vice Chancellor of Administration and Finance, John Wilton, published a two-part paper entitled, "Time is not on our Side" (Wilton, 2013), arguing that without greater control over tuition and enrolment, UC Berkeley would face an increasingly difficult financial future. Wilton had already co-written, along with former Chancellor Robert Birgeneau and Executive Vice Chancellor and Provost George Breslauer, a paper arguing for greater political autonomy for Berkeley (and, by implication, for all the UC campuses), now making a similar argument by different means, showing that without control over the principal revenue levers, Berkeley's finances would founder, portending growing problems for the entire sector of public higher education.

Thirty per cent of Berkeley's revenues were provided by tuition (almost three times as much as state support), and we were in the third year of a tuition freeze that the Governor had endorsed as part of his own re-election platform for 2014. It was therefore deeply encouraging that in November 2014, on the day after Jerry Brown was re-elected for his last term as Governor, President Janet Napolitano announced that UC would propose 5% tuition increases for each of the next five years (Los Angeles Times, 2014). This move alone would have overcome close to two thirds of the structural deficit Berkeley would be facing. While it still would have been necessary to cut the budget and focus on raising new forms of revenue, the task would have been manageable. The only problem with this proposal, which was approved later in November by the Regents, was that the governor opposed it, and instead entered into direct negotiations with the University of California over financing.

On 20 January 2015, in the wake of a heated exchange in the November Regents' meeting, Napolitano had little choice but to accept Brown's invitation to form the "Committee of Two" to hammer out a "compromise". Negotiations took place behind closed doors over the next four months. On 14 May 2015, Napolitano and Brown announced their "Budget Framework Agreement" (SFGATE, 2015).

This agreement entailed a two-year extension of the tuition freeze, bringing the period of flat tuition to six years. In exchange, Brown promised to increase appropriations from the state by 5% for two years, and 4% thereafter. This sounded generous, but not only was it precisely what the state had been proposing in the fall (now with conditions), it was on a base that was still (for Berkeley) little more than half of what the state allocation had been back in 2008. Napolitano was able to persuade Brown to invest some of the state's "rainy day funds" into the UC retirement program, important given the underfunded level of the pension fund. And yet, especially for Berkeley and other heavily tuition dependent campuses, the increases in state funding were insufficient to cover rising expenses.

It was now clear that Berkeley would have to take dramatic action to curb expenditures and maximize revenues. Throughout the summer and early fall, I met with the Cabinet and the leadership of the Academic Senate to draw up scenarios of potential strategic initiatives that could help shift the financial direction of the campus without compromising our twin commitment to excellence and access. These ranged from administrative streamlining to reduction in the size and scope of the athletics budget, from the possible consolidation of administrative services for some smaller departments and professional schools to the development of new revenue-generating professional (and other) Master's degree. Given the number of initiatives and the complexity of the decision-making processes, in November 2015 the administration created a bespoke governance structure, supported by a small staff in an Office of Strategic Initiatives (OSI).

OSI represented an effort to set up an inclusive analytic and decision-making process — not to make any immediate decisions. The proposal to begin a strategic planning exercise was initially welcomed enthusiastically and broadly by faculty who attended workshops and special meetings, and we were encouraged by senate leadership to think aggressively and outside the box about academic as well as administrative restructuring. The fact that this conversation was taking place in relationship to a major budget deficit, however, produced a growing sense of nervousness across the campus. Besides, OSI looked to many on campus to be far too similar to the office that had been created for Campus Shared Services in the previous administration (which had not yet lowered costs or provided better service, as promised). The administration nevertheless attempted to design a community-wide process that would look well into the future, and seek to determine which areas were the keys to the long-term excellence of the university. With encouragement from the leadership of the academic senate, this was an opportunity to reconsider, and restructure, some of the key components of university life to adapt to a new and changing future.

As much as this process was to put everything on the table, it was to focus principally on finding new sources of revenue: developing new professional (and other) Master's programs, and soliciting more private support, both through philanthropy and through partnerships of different kinds. Since these deliberations were commenced in the context of a shrinking budget, however, they were seen as entailing significant cuts in programs that had entrenched constituencies. The administration thus confronted the reality that it was easy and attractive to create new areas of focus, but much more difficult to discontinue areas that might have (at least in relative terms) outlived their initial relevance and excitement.

On 10 February 2016, we formally announced the scale of the deficit and the general plan to confront it, warning that it could and doubtless would require "serious pain", including the reduction of hundreds of administrative positions (Berkeleyside, 2016)

As Clark Kerr once wrote, however, "the status quo is the only solution that cannot be vetoed". Discussions in departments and around the lunch tables of the faculty club rumbled with declarations of concern about any changes that might made to academic programs before the last drop of blood had been squeezed from the administrative stone. The institution of shared governance was in short order overtaken by a generalized set of antibodies designed to fend off major change. And some faculty began to mobilize not just against the idea of any kind of academic restructuring, but against other initiatives that had been launched to use new and promising measures to enhance university revenues and funding opportunities (including in the global arena), even as the administration and faculty struggled to cope with urgent issues ranging from sexual harassment among Berkeley faculty and administrators to the strength and training program of the football team.

Much of the roiling disaffection was expressed through faculty groups that were already generally and broadly sceptical about the role of any administration in managing change. The Berkeley Faculty Association, an informal group with no structural relationship to the Academic Senate, hosts faculty "list-servs" that raised alarms, while being chaired by two faculty leaders who professed to believe that government funding was the only acceptable revenue stream, that fundraising was categorically at odds with the fundamental purposes of the university, and that the administration should be run by faculty committees. At this stage, Senate leaders began to be petitioned to hold ad hoc meetings to ventilate faculty concern. In the spring of 2016, one such meeting eventuated in the passage of a resolution that, "all proposals for mergers or closures of academic programs, departments, schools, and colleges shall be removed from current plans by the UC Berkeley administration to reduce UC Berkeley's structural deficit."

While I subsequently disbanded the Office of Strategic Services, I felt that we had to continue with a strategic exercise to guide budget decisions. Given growing resistance even to this, and a small though coordinated campaign — using a direct line to the local media — to discredit my administration, I decided to step down as chancellor at the end of the subsequent academic year. Explaining this whirlwind of events to the student newspaper, "former UC Berkeley chancellor and current physics professor Robert Birgeneau, who himself faced backlash during his tenure, said in an email that the chancellor's multiple responsibilities — compounded by outside pressure from the UC Board of Regents, the UC president, professors, union leaders and politicians, among others — make the job 'impossible…There are too many forces operating on the Chancellor coming from too many directions', he said in the email. 'Further, the Berkeley Chancellor does not have control over enough of the basic variables like student tuition, faculty and staff salaries, the make up of the undergraduate student body'." (Dailycal, 2016). And a commentator from the Harvard Business School, taking the situation at Berkeley as a case study, asked whether indeed UC Berkeley had become "ungovernable" (Kirby & Eby, 2016).

During my last year as Chancellor, when I worried less about faculty resistance, we succeeded in cutting over 500 administrative positions, reducing the deficit from $150m to $110m and setting a course to reduce it by the end of the subsequent year to $56m, in large part through new plans for revenue generation. By the end of the year, the faculty — and for that matter the campus at large — genuinely began, for the most part anyway, to recognize and accept the need to address the structural conditions of the deficit, no longer content to wait for the state of California or the Office of the President to bail us out.

However, when I finally left office, my successor still confronted the need to make many more painful cuts, while working with as many academic units as possible to reorient themselves to programs and activities that could create new revenues.

The Berkeley administration has to do all this, however, even as it is structurally positioned between two struggling governance regimes. On the one side, while shared governance with the faculty through the Academic Senate has been a critical ingredient in Berkeley's excellence in academic matters, it has to take greater responsibility for addressing new budgetary and institutional realities, as well as capturing the concerns and participation of significant groups of faculty in parallel informal organizations who believe the senate is overly bureaucratized and under representative. On the other, while the system office has been appropriately preoccupied with the task of securing political support for the university both in the state legislature and across the public at large, it has not only been fully absorbed by that political challenge, it is simply not in a position to manage or support significant change in the face of current challenges on a campus-by-campus basis.

LESSONS FOR THE FUTURE OF HIGHER EDUCATION

In their recent book entitled *Locus of Authority: The Evolution of Faculty Roles in the Governance of Higher Education*, William Bowen and Eugene Tobin (2015) argue that modes of faculty governance are indeed ripe for rethinking across institutions of higher education, public and private. They suggest that "shared governance" should direct itself to new modes of shared responsibility, stressing collaboration rather than, as they document in a number of cases, their own separate authority. Given the scope and nature of issues confronting universities in the 21st century, faculty need to be partners with, rather than antagonists to, university administrations. While the authors stress the importance of "trust", they give examples that show how easily that trust can be eroded when an organization has a culture of mutual suspicion about the motives and priorities of other groups.

Using my experience at Berkeley as a case study, I believe there should be increased consideration at many universities of possible reforms of governance both from "above" and from "below", with genuine collective scrutiny of the role of administrative leadership at times of massive challenge and change. It is clear that functional organizational cultures are dependent on robust and appropriate forms of governance. Ineffective governance structures and sceptical cultural predispositions around the work of administrations produce significant liabilities for academic institutions as a whole, not just the administrations themselves. While academic leaders are often criticized for being reactive rather than proactive, and for not being genuinely visionary voices both for their institutions and for higher education at large, it is not always obvious how that could be any different under current governance regimes.

To be sure, administrations must do everything possible to be inclusive and transparent, while sponsoring widespread participation and active engagement. Shared governance traditionally entails a necessary recognition of the extent to which faculty are the core constituency of the university. However, changing financial models, as well as innovative institutional strategies, invariably open up the spectre of different groups, units, departments, colleges and schools competing over resources in ways that do not serve the collective interests of the university as a whole. Accordingly, at a time of major financial challenges, questions of governance come quickly to the fore.

In part, the institutional conservatism of universities protects against passing fads and undue political pressure. When online MOOCS (massive open online courses) were introduced to great fanfare in 2011, some university leaders proclaimed that a tsunami was going to hit the university as we knew it. This turned out not to be the case, both because of the continuing draw for students of residential college life, and because online courses operated better as supplements than as substitutes for more traditional teaching methods (not to mention the thorny issues around credentialing and accreditation). And when political leaders have called disciplines into question for their apparent irrelevance (as Florida Governor Rick Scott did with anthropology a few years ago), institutions resist simply (and necessarily) by virtue of their powerful commitment to traditional disciplines and bodies of knowledge.

And yet, we know that all universities in the early 21st century (a period not unlike the decades after World War II in this regard) are at a time of critical transformation. This is especially so for public universities in the US, almost all of which are struggling to adjust to the ongoing realities of public de-funding. Within universities, both public and private, academic structures must continue to adapt to a world that is changing at ever greater velocity. Technology will increasingly change how we educate students — on campus and off. And the changing world around us will require a re-evaluation of the traditional structures of knowledge creation and reproduction across the academy. Not only do traditional disciplines often set arbitrary boundaries around their fields of study (with separate journals, separate criteria for evaluation and modes of professional reference that tend to insulate each discipline from the other), most important discoveries and insights, in the sciences and the social sciences as well as the humanities, come from scholars and researchers interacting across disciplines. In addition, changes in technology — ranging from machine learning and artificial intelligence to automation and the internet of things — have already begun to eclipse older forms of "knowledge work", while globalization has accelerated at a pace that requires global literacy for most highly skilled employment in the future. Clark Kerr's prescient vision of the 1960s university as a site for training future workers in the knowledge industry seems increasingly outmoded. The university is now a site that must both create the new knowledge-scape of the future and produce ideas and frameworks to help us navigate a world in which everything — from the kind of work we do to the relationships of work and leisure, the local and the global, the climate and the planet, and the human and the non-human — will be changing quickly.

We cannot know what the university of the future should or will look like, but we do know that we should orient ourselves as much towards the future as towards the past. To do this in ways that will best position universities to lead in the years ahead, however, requires broad acceptance of the need to consider fundamental change, not just the incremental and minor changes that have often been the default parameters set by most university communities for too long. This must also entail the willingness to engage in serious collective efforts to rethink issues not just of leadership, but of governance, and the inherent responsibilities of all members of the community to play constructive roles in this process. Change is coming, and universities will be part of this change whether we like it or not. The point here, however, is that if universities are to fulfil our public mission — to change the world to make it a better place — they must be prepared to change themselves as well.

REFERENCES

Berkeleyside (2016). www.berkeleyside.com/2016/02/10/chancellor-dirks-warns-of-uc-berkeleys-unsustainable-structural-deficit

Bowen, W. & Tobin, E. (2015). *Locus of Authority: The Evolution of Faculty Roles in the Governance of Higher Education*, Princeton University Press.

Dailycal (2016). http://www.dailycal.org/2016/08/17/uc-berkeley-faculty-speculate-on-factors-behind-dirks-resignation/

Gilman (1872). Inaugural Address of UC President Daniel Coit Gilman.

Los Angeles Times (2014). http://www.latimes.com/local/education/la-me-ln-uc-tuition-20141105-story.html

Kirby, W. C. & Eby, J. W. (2016). "Public Mission, Private Funding: The University of California, Berkeley," *Harvard Business School case N9-317-023*, 24 August. https://canvas.harvard.edu/files/3194991/download?download_frd=1&verifier=D6k3SVOVvi7NBJzSACQY5DbnU0D5B4F49pkyoguC

SFGATE (2015). http://www.sfgate.com/education/article/Napolitano-Jerry-Brown-strike-deal-on-UC-tuition-6263588.php

Wilton, J. (2013). "Time is not on our Side". http://vcaf.berkeley.edu/sites/default/files/Time%20is%20not%20on%20our%20side%201%2011.29.13.pdf

CHAPTER 15

Managing Change in Change-Resistant Universities

Rebecca M. Blank

INTRODUCTION

Higher education is in a time of substantial change. For a variety of reasons, universities tend to be institutions that change slowly. Motivating university faculty and staff to adopt new ways of operating is a challenging but important part of any leader's job in higher education.

In this paper, I focus particularly on the flagship high-reputation, large research institutions, many of which have been in existence for well over 100 years. I refer to these as "older" or "traditional" universities throughout this paper. These are schools that have a primary business model of offering residential education on their campus to large numbers of undergraduates and graduate students. I am particularly concerned with public universities, in part because these are the places that educate and train the most students, at the undergraduate, professional and PhD level.

THE CHANGES FACING HIGHER EDUCATION

The higher education market is facing a number of changes that are disrupting and challenging older research universities. For instance, new technologies have vastly expanded the ability to deliver educational services to people at almost any place and any time; this is a potential challenge to those whose model of education is focused on residential campuses. These technologies have also changed the tools available to teachers in more traditional classrooms, allowing them to engage students in more active learning.

Meanwhile, competition among higher education institutions is also increasing. A growing number of high-quality schools in nations around the world are courting international students. American and British universities that have dominated the world market for higher education can no longer assume that they will attract the best and brightest from other countries. The growth in higher-income families with substantial resources to invest in their children has meant a growing group of potential students who are shopping nationally and (increasingly) globally for the best educational experience. That means schools have to compete harder to bring in top students.

At the same time, the demands of millennial students are often different than those of previous generations. Having grown up with a constant flow of information — much of it packaged as entertainment — they expect teachers to teach more interactively and with more visual content. They seek out information from multiple sources, and are often unfamiliar with traditional ideas about which sources have more credibility.

In many countries, including the United States, a decade of slower growth and higher unemployment has made young adults more instrumental in what they expect college to provide. They are more concerned with internships, career opportunities and the value of education to their future job choices.

As the world of teaching and students is shifting, the world of research and scientific knowledge accumulation continues to move at an extremely fast pace. In some fields, scientists are sharing results in real time, thereby speeding up the knowledge transmission and collaboration between previously siloed research efforts. In other fields, recent scientific advances (such as genome sequencing abilities or the technological ability to handle very big datasets) have opened up entirely new fields.

These changes create both opportunities and stresses within long-established research universities. Changes in the external environment require nimbleness on the part of an institution. To take advantage of the new opportunities that change provides, and to avoid losing competitive position in the midst of a changing environment, universities are reassessing their business models. This can be very difficult in older and more traditional university settings.

UNIVERSITY RESISTANCE TO CHANGE

One of the strengths of universities has been their long-term stability. Universities are among the oldest institutions in many communities, with far more continuity than most private-sector firms. This stability is a source of strength and has led to internal cultures within these institutions that last over decades (or even centuries) and are important aspects of the institutions' identity and reputation. But this stability also creates barriers to change.

Chapter 15: Managing Change in Change-Resistant Universities

Something I have long mused about is how institutions that are filled with highly creative and innovative individuals — people selected for their intellectual curiosity and fearless pursuit of new ideas — can be so resistant to change. Let me speculate on at least three reasons.

First, being creative is hard work. Anybody who has spent time in a job that requires creativity, seeking to solve difficult problems, knows how challenging this type of intellectual work can be. Research professors are constantly facing pressure to generate new research ideas and new ways of looking at the world. This requires many faculty members to "live in their heads" much more than people in other jobs. And the best way to do this effectively is to live in an external environment that is entirely predictable. The less one has to worry about a new office, a new course to teach, a new staff member to deal with or a new set of demands from the administration, the more time one has to actually work on and think about the big questions in one's research. This means that many professors are resistant to changes in their environment. Such changes take mental time and energy away from their work. Hence the ironic result that I have observed as a university leader: many of my most creative and innovative faculty are extremely resistant to institutional change.

Second, the long-term stability and the cultural identity that many universities exhibit can lead individuals in those institutions to mistake tradition for organizational excellence. More than once, when proposing an operational change, I have heard a response from faculty or staff that essentially says: "We've always done it this way. And, because our institution is so highly regarded, this must be the right way to do it." Faculty often are fiercely proud of the reputations of their institution. This leads them to assume that excellence depends upon the current business and organization model, and to worry that any change might lower that reputation. In contrast, many university leaders will tell you that their universities manage to achieve excellence despite their quite dysfunctional organizational structures.

Third, these institutions are typically very decentralized, which means that faculty and staff are often quite tribal in their loyalty to their department or their school or college. Big research and teaching universities have evolved over time, adding new disciplines or new colleges as new fields of knowledge emerge. Different departments and colleges are intellectually diverse, with very different markets for students and research results. As a result, most universities have allowed strong local governance and decision-making. Hence, the faculty and staff within disciplinarily-defined sub-units of the university often have a separate sense of identity from the overall institution, sometimes with their own unique organizational structure. Efforts to impose changes that affect the entire institution (common HR systems, integrated IT systems or involvement with on-line teaching) are often vociferously resisted as "okay for everybody else, but not for my unit".

DIFFICULTIES IN IMPLEMENTING CHANGE IN PUBLIC UNIVERSITIES

The difficulty of motivating and implementing operational changes is even more acute in public universities. Public universities suffer from additional institutional barriers that can make nimbleness and creative, forward-thinking leadership difficult to achieve.

First, public universities have multiple stakeholders outside the university that can influence or directly control university actions. State universities are typically regulated by legislatures, which often impose bureaucratic rules that govern hiring and pay, procurement and facilities changes, or financial processes and systems. Publicly elected officials often impose pricing rules on tuition or rules about which students have priority for admission. All of these restrictions reduce the ability of university leadership to change the operational model without substantial consultation or (in some cases) actual legislative changes.

Second, all of this consultation happens in the midst of constant public attention and commentary. Public institutions often are required to operate with great transparency. This includes strong faculty governance that requires extensive on-campus discussion before any decision is reached, as well as off-campus attention from the public media and elected officials. This gives those opposed to change more opportunity to organize and block proposed new programs or organizational restructuring.

Third, public universities typically are run by publicly-appointed boards. At times, these boards may include individuals with limited knowledge of the higher-education environment, or individuals who may have personal or political agendas that do not always mesh with the agendas of university leadership. In the United States there have been a number of public conflicts between university boards and university leadership in recent years, often leading to the departure of the university's president or chancellor. Some of these occurred because the board wanted changes that the president did not support; others occurred because the board opposed changes the president proposed.

Fourth, the large size and diversity of these universities adds to the complexity of their governance. For instance, the University of Wisconsin-Madison includes the health science schools (medicine, nursing and pharmacy); the college of agriculture and the schools that emerged from it over time (agriculture and life sciences, veterinary medicine and human ecology); the professional schools (engineering, law, business and education); as well as an extensive college of liberal arts. These schools were established by the state, and the university is committed to maintaining them, even though there are wide differences in the financial viability of these different schools. The resulting diversity in business models, operational culture and intellectual approaches makes implementing changes across the university cumbersome and slow, and means that special agreements for any proposed change often have to occur in at least some units.

Finally, in more recent years the challenges to public universities have become even greater due to changes in the larger economic and political environments in which they operate. Recession, followed by slower economic growth, has meant substantial cuts in public funding for these institutions in many cases. The rise of more populist politics has been associated with greater suspicion of public institutions, particularly elite public institutions such as universities. The rise of deep partisan divides in US politics has led both parties to use universities as political pawns in their arguments. This ranges from those on the left who campaign for "free college", without typically having a plan to provide the funds necessary to support their proposals, to those on the right, who attack particular types of scientific inquiry.

Dealing with these political, budgetary and decision-making problems takes a great deal of time and attention on the part of leaders in public institutions. These problems are often highlighted on the front page of the local newspaper. They demand immediate responses and take energy, time and capacity away from efforts to respond to the changing higher-education landscape. It can be difficult to find the dollars or create the institutional desire to invest in changes in how education is delivered or to deliver education to new groups of students. Yet, the changes confronting higher education demand a response from any institution that wants to retain its excellence and competitiveness.

MAKING CHANGE HAPPEN

There are many ways in which the changing external environment might force higher-education institutions to change. For some, this will mean attracting more students in a world where demographic shifts and greater competition may be reducing traditional applications. This could mean diversifying away from these institutions' historical business model of residential education by offering more on-line education or collaborating with institutions that provide and market distance learning. It could mean establishing satellite campuses to reach more students and to build reputation in other parts of the country or the globe.

In many cases, these educational changes will require organizational changes. This could mean eliminating or combining smaller departments or schools that are no longer financially viable or that are having difficulty attracting and placing students. It could mean greater centralization of IT resources to assure central control over IT security. Or it could mean streamlining or centralizing services to assure greater cost controls or more uniform quality.

For some, the major reason for change may be to create new revenue sources to offset declining public funding. This can mean increasing admissions or changing tuition models. It may mean training deans and department heads to be more effective fund-raisers. It may mean offering expanded degree opportunities through professional masters, certificate or licensing courses, either on campus or online.

How do older universities, with all of their change-resistant institutional structures and individuals, react more nimbly to their evolving external environment to take advantage of the opportunities or meet the challenges that these changes create? There are no simple answers to this, but at least three things are necessary to engage more traditional higher-education institutions in ways that will motivate change.

Communication

Communication is key, both internal and external. Internally, university leaders need to make the case for change, communicating the ways in which the environment is changing and the risks of continuing to do business as usual. Identifying a few respected faculty from across the institution to help make this argument is important, so that champions for change are present in the schools, colleges and departments that will be affected. The budgetary problems that have hit public universities in the past decade provide a particularly salient opportunity to make this case for change. As state dollars become more restricted, the need to find new ways to rethink business models and generate revenue has become apparent to more and more stakeholders.

Communication with outside stakeholders is equally important. Political leaders and alumni need to hear the same messages about the need for change. It may be important to show evidence of the success that other universities have had with these strategies. In some cases, institutional constraints imposed by the Board or by the legislature may need to be modified.

In all cases, the argument for change has to be placed in the midst of a larger strategic vision for the university. Stakeholders have to know that university leaders understand the reputation and value of the university and that proposed changes are designed to strengthen the institution through greater access to more students, greater reputation and increased revenues, all of which can be invested not only in new programs but also in strengthening and supporting the traditional research and education mission of these schools.

Implement Strategically

Strategically choosing where changes are first implemented is highly important. There will be plenty of sceptics and resistance to any new program or reorganization, so it is important to demonstrate that a proposed change can be successfully implemented and will deliver benefits (more revenue, more students, greater visibility, etc) as promised. Starting small may be more effective than trying to implement large changes across the whole university. This means identifying departments or schools where there are strong champions for change and/or opportunities to take advantage of change more quickly. Once some places in the universities have implemented changes, this gives leaders the ammunition they need to approach other more resistant parts of the institution and push them to adopt similar changes as well.

Create Incentives

It is important to set up the right incentives for change. Changes involve costs. Faculty and staff have to learn new ways of doing business; more students require a larger infrastructure to serve them, etc. Anticipating those costs and making them palatable is important.

For example, if a change will require more teaching resources, fund and hire additional instructors up front, so a department knows they will have the resources to serve more students. If a change requires staff to operate in a different way, provide some sort of bonus to those who acquire the training early. If a new program is being launched in order to bring more resources into the university, make some up-front commitments about where those resources will be spent, to assure faculty and staff that they will benefit from the new dollars and to make sure that faculty and staff are invested in the success of the new program.

The financial incentives faced by deans and department chairs need to reinforce the messages from leadership about new ways of doing business. This often means sharing any new revenue directly with the unit that produces it. And those units that implement changes early and well need to be recognized and applauded.

An Example

Let me give one example from the University of Wisconsin-Madison (UW). Several years ago, we were looking for ways to deal with state budget cuts. One way to increase our student enrolments and our tuition dollars was to improve and expand our summer semester offerings. While UW had a carefully planned curriculum during fall and spring semesters, very few courses were taught in the summer and there was no strategy about which courses would be offered. Whoever wanted to teach was allowed to, if the department had funds to pay them. As a result there were lots of small, specialized classes taught in the summer, with no overall coherence to the curricular offerings.

Our Dean of Continuing Studies took on the leadership responsibility to make changes. He worked with the other deans and with faculty leadership to oversee a process that identified courses that we needed to teach in the summer, such as high-demand classes that students needed to fulfil distribution requirements. He established rules about how summer semester classes should be selected. He proposed a funding model that would return a substantial share of any new summer semester revenue to the schools and colleges. He worked with a marketing group to put together a campaign to market the value of taking summer semester courses to our students, as well as to students outside UW who might want to be in Madison for the summer. He also worked to identify courses that could be offered on-line in the summer, asked for and received funding to develop these courses and identified faculty who would create and lead these on-line offerings. This has further expanded the reach of the summer program beyond those students living in Madison for the summer.

While the impetus to make this change was generated by a need to increase tuition revenue, the value of an expanded summer semester went far beyond this and it was important for faculty and staff to understand that the expanded summer semester could improve our educational reputation and performance. It offers an opportunity for students to complete distribution requirements or to take classes in the summer so that they can be away from campus on study abroad or internship programs in another semester. It is cheaper to take a summer class in order to complete a degree on time than it is to stay for a full additional semester. As a result, we hoped this effort would increase our four-year graduation rate and reduce student debt. The summer semester also allows us to pull in summer-only students, expanding our educational outreach and connections. As we moved forward, I and other campus leaders talked with every on-campus group that we met with about the need and the value of expanding summer semester.

In part because of the promise of new revenues, the deans became strong partners in this effort and pushed their departments to participate. In the first summer, we offered 71 new courses, increased undergraduate summer student enrolments by 15% and summer revenues by 21%. Our established target is to increase revenues by at least 10% per year for five years. As we head into the second expanded summer term, we are well on target to meet this year's goal. Departments that were more reluctant to expand their offerings in the first summer are now active supporters of this effort, as they see the success (and new revenues) attained by departments that offered summer classes with strong enrolments.

Our successful launch of expanded summer terms was due to many things, including the financial incentives that brought the deans into partnership, the communication from top leaders about the educational value of this effort, and excellent planning and leadership by one of our best deans. As the program has shown success, it has generated more interest and involvement.

CONCLUSION

Higher education is in a time of enormous change. While older, high-reputation universities may be less affected by these changes or feel their impacts more slowly than other institutions, virtually all universities are now engaged in efforts to adapt and change as the market, the finances and the technologies of higher education evolve. Particularly for large and complex universities, with a strong sense of their past and their reputation, these changes can be difficult and face both internal and external resistance. Providing the vision and the management skill to move such changes forward is a key part of the job for leaders in these organizations.

When I was hired, the Chief of the UW Police Force told me the following story. About 10 years ago, several of her senior leaders had come up with an excellent idea about how to reorganize their operations to serve campus more effectively. She discussed this with some of her colleagues at a meeting of Big 10 schools and all of them were highly complementary about the creativity and promise of this suggestion. The changes proposed had enough campus implications that both the staff and faculty governance groups felt they needed to study and debate the proposal. The initial reaction by these groups was negative, so the issue got reworked multiple times. It was finally seven years later when these changes were implemented. By that time, UW was the last school in the Big 10 to makes this change. In short, we went from being the creative leader to the slow follower. That isn't a story any university leader can afford to repeat on their campus.

PART IV

∙∙∙∙∙∙∙∙∙

The Future of the University
in a Polarizing World

CHAPTER 16

The Future of the University — Preparing for Change: Building a Nimble and Responsive University

Thiam Soon Tan

KEY DEVELOPMENTS FORCING CHANGES

In the next decade or so, many societies will have to manage the impact of an accelerated pace of technology changes which are often disruptive structurally to the workplace. The impact of these challenges will continue to evolve and will be different in different countries depending on the readiness to address them. We are already witnessing impact at varying levels of severity in different places, for example, in the form of an increasing pool of frustrated workers unable to participate effectively in an increasingly technologically complex economy.

For those of us in education, especially at the university level, we have a mission to deliver an education that will prepare well the next generation to meet these challenges. Some of the more discernible issues especially in the more developed economies include:

1. Fewer "ordinary" jobs left — jobs that are routine and predictable will continue to be replaced by technology or designed out of the systems. While new jobs will be created, they will need a higher level of skills, both hard and soft; or the so-called hi-tech or hi-touch skills and often, a blending of both. This continuing shift will also mean more frequent churning of the job market. How do we help virtually

everyone acquire the requisite skills and receive an education that can help them to navigate that future will be a challenge?
2. Reluctance of companies to invest in the development of new talent pool, relying instead on market forces to provide the increasing sophisticated workforce needed (Cappelli, 2011). While universities traditionally view their role as providing an education, there is an increasing pressure to help the expanding cohort of students get their first jobs. Even for those universities which are aware of the needs to provide an education that also helps the graduates get their first job through some degree of specialization, there is the added pressure and worry about these very skills getting obsolete due to technological changes. But the truth is that increasingly, no matter how much you teach now, it is going to be a case of never enough!

IMPACT ON THE EDUCATION SECTOR IN SINGAPORE

Singapore is one of the most open economies in the world, and thus is subject to the full brunt of the forces of globalization and technological disruptions. Adding to the challenge is the fact that it is also one of the smallest in terms of population or area. While smallness is beneficial in some ways, it poses severe challenges to generate enough capacity, capability and buzz to deal with all the impending changes and challenges, foreseen and unforeseen, so that the economy can continue to be vibrant.

Singapore has moved from third world to first world in about half a century. Its economic development during this period can roughly be divided into 5 distinct stages of about a decade each (Agency for Science, Technology and Research, 2011), namely the labour-intensive 1960s, the skills-intensive 1970s, the capital intensive 1980s, the technology intensive 1990s and the current knowledge/innovation-intensive new millennium. The education system has also evolved during this period to keep pace with the economic development.

The development of the polytechnic sector

Up until 1990, Singapore had only two polytechnics, Singapore Polytechnic and Ngee Ann Polytechnic. A notable difference of Singapore's polytechnics from most polytechnics elsewhere is that studying in a polytechnic is an alternate pathway to a 2-year pre-university education in junior colleges. The polytechnics train the students to be work-ready on graduation, but with adequate foundation for further education if they choose to do so. To be able to do this competently, the polytechnic education is over 3 years, a year longer than the pre-university education.

In 1990, after their secondary education (10 years), only 22% of each cohort attended the polytechnics, while about 26% would go to junior colleges and 11% went to vocational schools. This means roughly 60% of a cohort would receive more than 10 years of education (MInistry of Education, 2016a). To keep pace with the technology intensive period of the 1990s, the polytechnic pathway was ramped up rapidly. Temasek Polytechnic was set up in 1990, followed by Nanyang Polytechnic in 1992 and finally Republic Polytechnics in 2002 to increase the pool of people who would receive more than 10 years of education with an emphasis on skills that were needed by industry. By 2015, the picture had shifted dramatically with the 5 polytechnics accounting for about 47% of each cohort, while 28% would go to junior colleges, hardly changed from the 26% in 1990 (Ministry of Education, 2016b). Combined with the Institute of Technical Education (ITE), which took in about 24% for vocational training, the professional/vocational route accounted for close to two-thirds of the cohort (some double counting as a number of students from the ITE would continue their education in the Polytechnics). This emphasis on the professional/vocational education as the main pathway over the last quarter of a century is a shift towards the German/Swiss system, though, in Singapore's case, the professional/vocational education is school-based with structured internship, and not apprenticeship based.

This shift to get more young people to attend polytechnics and ITE played a key role in providing the necessary skilled manpower during the technology intensive period of the 1990s and early 2000s when Singapore became a global power house in electronic, chemical, offshore and marine manufacturing. More importantly, even up to this day, it has ensured low youth unemployment as polytechnic graduates are well sought after with high employment rates and good starting salaries. In the latest 2016 employment survey for polytechnic graduates, the overall employment rate is 90.6% six months after graduation with a gross median salary of SGD$2,200 (Graduate Employment Survey, 2017). This shift towards a polytechnic education was the realization since the early 1990s that senior high school leavers, without any further education or skill training, would find it increasingly difficult to land good jobs in a modern technologically oriented economy.

The University Sector

In the public university sector, the growth has been equally spectacular, albeit a little later than the development of the polytechnic sector. In 1980, there was only one university, the National University of Singapore (NUS) and only 5% of each cohort was able to enter NUS. In 1982, Nanyang Technological Institute was set up and became Nanyang Technological University (NTU) in 1991. By 1990, 15% of each cohort entered the two institutions.

But as the economy shifted towards being knowledge/innovation intensive since the new millennium, more university graduates were needed and this led to a significant growth in the university sector with Singapore Management University formed in 2000 and the cohort participation rate increased to 21%. In 2006, all the public universities were corporatized and became known as autonomous universities (AUs), to signal that they would operate "autonomously" with significant independence on academic matters subject to annual performance review by the Ministry of Education and also an external review once every five years (Ministry of Education, 2005). In 2011, Singapore University of Technology and Design became the fourth autonomous university, and Singapore Institute of Technology (SIT) became the fifth in March 2014. The latest addition is UniSIM, the only private university in Singapore. It is now the sixth autonomous university and has been renamed as Singapore University of Social Sciences (SUSS). The cohort participation in the autonomous universities continues to increase, with 26% in 2010 and 32% in 2015. The current plan is to expand the cohort participation rate to 40% by 2020, with the growth mainly catered to by the two latest autonomous universities, SIT and SUSS. Together with a history of a significant number of students going overseas to receive their university education as well as attending degree programs offered by overseas universities through private education institutes in Singapore, the number of graduates from each cohort who will receive a university education is likely to exceed 50%.

BUILDING A NIMBLER AND MORE RESPONSIVE UNIVERSITY – SINGAPORE INSTITUTE OF TECHNOLOGY

In the early 2000s, some of the polytechnics began to forge twinning programs with overseas universities to offer their degrees through the polytechnics for their own students only. But, towards the end of the 2000s, there was an increasing realization for the polytechnics not only to stay true to their original mission to train students to be work ready with skills that were sought after by industry, but in fact to strengthen this. So a decision was made in 2009 to set up the Singapore Institute of Technology (SIT) to take over that role to provide twinning programs for polytechnic students but managed at the national level instead of by the individual polytechnic. In this role, SIT had a number of unique characteristics:

- It was NOT a university in its own right, but partnered with various reputable overseas universities to develop twinning programs in Singapore. The students were admitted by SIT and their education subsidized by the government just as if they were attending the other autonomous universities.

- The students were almost all from the polytechnics students where there was pent up demand.
- SIT operated with a distributed campus, with a presence in each of the polytechnics (altogether 5 nationally).

This model allowed SIT to ramp up almost immediately. Though it was set up in September 2009, a year later it was able to take in the first 500 students through 5 partner universities offering 10 programs. The growth continued to be rapid with about 1,000 students in 17 programs from 7 universities in 2011, and about 1,500 students in 27 programs from 11 universities in 2012.

In August 2012, a high-level government committee, known as the Committee on University Education Pathways Beyond 2015 (Ministry of Education, 2012) recommended that Singapore should increase its cohort participation rate in university education to 40% by 2020 from the 30% target that was set for 2015, and SIT together with UniSIM (now SUSS) would cater to this growth. A very significant proportion of the increased participation would come from the polytechnic students. To do this well, the Committee also recommended that SIT develop a differentiated pathway from the other autonomous universities in Singapore and build a pedagogy that would place a greater emphasis on applied learning. This is to align with the earlier decision to get the polytechnics to refocus on training students with deep skills needed by industry. To drive this transformation, the Committee felt it was necessary for SIT to evolve from its original role of "aggregating" overseas university degrees to become an autonomous university in its own right. A new management was put in by early 2013 and, by March 2014, SIT was gazetted as the fifth autonomous university in Singapore and, in September of that year, offered 3 programs under its own name, the first that were not done through one of the overseas partners.

SIT's Strategies

In charting its future, SIT took the cue from the recommendations of the Committee on University Education Pathways Beyond 2015. The Committee envisaged that SIT would offer a new applied degree pathway and formed a close nexus with industry to produce graduates equipped with a strong foundation and a keen understanding of its real-life applications. Thus the management, together with its Board of Trustees, crafted a vision for SIT in 2013 to be "a leader in innovative university education by integrating learning, industry and community" to align with the Committee's recommendations. Further, given its partnership with overseas universities then, the trustees also challenged SIT to develop a nurturing learning environment "that is uniquely enriched by world-class partners".

If SIT wants to focus on applied learning and form a close nexus with industry, and if industry has to adapt to the many disruptive changes, a key strategic imperative is that SIT itself must be nimble and responsive, so that it is able to help its students and its industry partners to meet those challenges. For a university, this is not an easy task. Throughout 2013 and part of 2014, a series of debates and discussion led to a number of key strategies, some of them not commonly found in universities. The key strategies were

- Forge a symbiotic relation with industry as the central strategy for a university of applied learning
- Build an extended eco-system with overseas university through strategic partnerships
- Develop a flatter structure that promotes greater collaboration among academic themselves and with professional colleagues
- To develop a SIT-Industry continuum where its graduates can return, time and again, for upskilling and reskilling — adopting the motto of Once a SITizen, Always a SITizen!

SIT has been executing this set of strategies in the past 3 years and thus the success of this model is yet to be proven. More importantly, these strategies are continually being refined when problems arise during implementation. In spite of its young age, SIT has continued to grow, rapidly taking in 2,560 new students in 2016 out of a pool of 13,000 applicants, a vast majority from the polytechnics (over 90%). By the size of its intake, it is already the third biggest university in Singapore after the National University of Singapore and Nanyang Technological University, even though it is the youngest university (SUSS is the sixth autonomous university, but its predecessor has been a university since 2007). The current plan is for SIT to increase its intake to about 3,500 by 2020. Works to build a brand new centralized campus have just begun.

By redefining the admission criteria, SIT admits students on the basis of a demonstrated interest and passion for specialized program areas, for example, by having completed specialized diploma courses in the Polytechnics or through a portfolio of work and achievements. This results in a lower leakage rate, which is already apparent from our early Graduate Employment Survey results.

Forge a symbiotic relation with industry

In developing a university of applied learning, SIT spent much effort to examine the success of the universities of applied sciences in Switzerland, Germany and Austria. But it was clear that the approach by SIT would have to be different due to significant differences in the cultural context. A key difference that makes the job of setting up a university of applied learning in Singapore much more challenging is the fact that, historically, all the three countries mentioned above have a culture of strong apprenticeship with significant ownership by industry. An example of such an approach is Dual Hochschule Baden-Württemberg (DHBW), a university of applied sciences in the German state of Baden-Wuttenberg which has about 34,000 students and where its admission policy requires students to sign a training contract with a workplace training provider, most often an accredited company, before they can read a program at DHBW. In Switzerland, most students who enter the universities of applied sciences would have typically at least 3 years of apprenticeship.

In contrast, the ownership of apprenticeships by companies is not strong in Singapore. Many companies take in interns but the standard of supervision is highly variable and often without structured learning objectives. So, SIT decides to build a platform called the Integrated Work Study Programme (IWSP) that will be compulsory for all students reading either SIT's own degrees or SIT-overseas partner joint degrees. This platform helps students to integrate learning and acquisition of knowledge in real work situations and SIT has devoted significant efforts to convince employers that IWSP is more than internship. To strengthen the learning outcome of the students, especially those that are attached to smaller companies without strong supervisory capability, SIT also makes an institutional commitment to provide support to the students to ensure learning outcomes are met.

A few things work in favour of SIT in developing this applied learning platform. The most important one is the fact that the polytechnics students are trained to be work-ready after their graduation. Each year, a large number of polytechnic students do enter the job market instead of going to university. Thus most companies are comfortable in employing these graduates as borne out by annual surveys of the graduation outcome of polytechnic students, which has been consistently high and also with increasing wages.

Second, in the last four years, there has been a big push in Singapore to get more students to spend more time with industry. A national committee known as ASPIRE was set up in 2013 (Ministry of Education, 2014) and this was then subsumed into a bigger effort known as SkillsFuture which was launched in 2015 (Government of Singapore, 2015). The motivation for this push was more complicated. Under ASPIRE, the key push was to get polytechnic students to have enhanced structured internships in industry while they were studying and to encourage more to enter the job market instead of heading straight for university without any idea of the needs of the workplace or their own. Together with this was an effort to push companies to recognize and pay for skills mastery instead of relying on academic qualifications as a proxy, especially in jobs and professions where skills mastery counts. If this push is successful, it will slow down the trend where more and more young people yearns for "any" university degree immediately after graduation from the polytechnics.

Another motivation, and one that has become more relevant recently, is an effort to get workers used to the idea of lifelong learning for upskilling and reskilling to cope with increasing disruptions at the work place. Thus getting more to work first and then return to university at a later date will help these students have a clearer idea what they want to pursue and seed the idea of returning to school after working for a while. A big part of this push is to encourage greater ownership of this effort by companies with incentive for companies to work with institutes of higher learnings (both universities and polytechnics) to offer work-study programs (Today Online, 2017). In these programs, the student can choose to alternate trimesters between university and the workplace, or alternatively spend 3-4 days at the workplace and 1-2 days at the university, much like the dual programs in Switzerland or the DHBW model in Germany. This push has helped to make SIT's IWSP more attractive.

For SIT, its effort to make the IWSP a central feature of its curriculum has two key objectives. The first, and the one that is aligned with the objectives of ASPIRE and later SkillsFuture is for students to be more work ready and also help to improve the students' employability. A second motivation is really that when the students are on IWSP, the professors and professional officers will follow them and link up with the industry supervisor. This follow-up is much more intense than that in most universities offering internships as this is a structured part of the curriculum. This allows the professors and professional officers to form a closer relation with the companies and develop applied research projects with them. Further, through IWSP, SIT will receive a valuable continuous feedback mechanism from industry for its curriculum and a conduit to understand industry needs and develop collaborations. In that sense, IWSP is more a platform with an ideal is for industry to regard SIT as a true partner and for SIT to be a university that is "integrating learning, industry and community".

Building an extended eco-system with overseas universities through strategic partnerships

A second challenge is Singapore's smallness — one of the most globalized countries in the world but with a very small population of 5.6 million of which the resident population is about 3.9 million (Department of Statistics Singapore, 2016). Building capability to launch new programs to cope with the changing needs of industry will always be a challenge. The severity of this challenge increases with the pace of disruptions.

SIT started in 2009 by working with overseas universities. So when it became a fully-fledged university in March 2014, SIT had learnt how to work with a network of universities in a mutually beneficial way. A key strategic decision, made after it became an autonomous university in 2014, was to continue working closely with a network of selected overseas university partners to enable SIT to respond very quickly to new or morphing industry needs, and to mount new programs swiftly in response even when such expertise is not available in Singapore. Through this approach, SIT is able to build an extended eco-system. To be sustainable over the long run and consistent with the fact that SIT is now a public university in its own right, it was also decided that the nature of that collaboration would evolve from degrees offered directly by the oversea universities to one in which the degrees would be joint degrees. This approach of building a network of partner universities to create an extended eco-system is an innovation.

Building and managing such a network and to blend in the different culture brought by each university into a coherent one within SIT is a non-trivial challenge. If this effort succeeds even partially, it will provide a distinctive educational experience to prepare students for a globally-competitive economy and a unique feature among world universities. Over the last 2 years since the implementation of this strategy, three of the existing partners and one new partner have come on board to offer joint degrees to SIT students in Singapore. Discussion is now under way with the other partners about this evolution. This approach has already shown its versatility with SIT being able to launch new programs rapidly and ramp up intake number aggressively even though it is still a very young and small university.

In some way, this innovative approach is another form of the new "sharing economy" whereby different entities learn to share each other's limited resources to ensure scarce resources are optimally utilized. Such an approach is probably more pertinent to small universities in small countries that still have to cope with the full force of technological disruptions and globalization. Another powerful possibility, and one that is just in progress, is an effort to integrate the faculty from the various partner universities that through SIT, can work with each other and with SIT in applied research projects.

Not A Traditional Academic Structure

From its beginning in 2009, SIT has recognized that it cannot organize its academic structure in the form of Faculties/Schools and Departments like traditional universities. SIT has to be nimble, cost effective, multi-disciplinary in applied learning platforms, and highly responsive to industry and community needs. Besides leveraging on overseas university partners to build an extended eco-system, another key strategy is to build an academic structure that promotes inter-disciplinary collaborations and allows faculty to teach across numerous industry clustered or related discipline programs. A corps of professional officers complements the work of the academics.

As SIT aims to be a university of applied learning, it is necessary to build a pool of professionals who know industry and can help mentor students on projects within SIT as well as when they are out on IWSP. To use only academics for this purpose may not be the ideal solution. The strategy developed is to recruit working professionals, calling them Professional Officers, to complement the academics in mentoring students on the more applied side of their learning. To make the role unique and challenging enough to attract the right people, these professional officers will cover four roles as a group:

- To manage laboratories in shared facilities;
- To mentor students working on projects, especially, those that are more applied;
- To mentor students while they are out on IWSP, and to help them if they encounter problems at the workplace in which even their supervisors may not be able to help and
- To work on projects from industry wherever possible.

The development of a corps of professional officers has been challenging thus far, due mainly to difficulties in finding enough relevant professionals from industry and for those who joined, teaching them how to mentor students. But this is a strategic development and will continue to receive high level attention.

CONCLUSION

The confluence of technological disruptions and globalization is causing dislocations in society, in particular the disappearance of ordinary jobs. University has an important role to play to help more people acquire skills and an education that help prepare them for a continually changing future. To do so, the pedagogical approach and the way the university is organized must be able to response to those changes directly. This paper describes the early stage development of a new autonomous university in Singapore, the Singapore Institute of Technology. The strategies shared are meant to ensure the development of a nimbler and more responsive university. Singapore Institute of Technology is only just over 3 years old as an autonomous university and thus this development is still very much a work-in-progress. Thus far, we have started the journey and made some progress, but the hardest and perhaps the best part is yet to come.

REFERENCES

Agency for Science, Technology and Research (2011). *Science, Technology & Enterprise Plan 2015*. http://www.a-star.edu.sg/portals/0/media/otherpubs/step2015_1jun.pdf

Cappelli, P. (2011). "Why companies aren't getting the employees they need", *The Wall Street Journal*, 24 October.

Department of Statistics Singapore (2016). *Residential Population Profile*. http://www.singstat.gov.sg/statistics/latest-data#17

Government of Singapore (2015). *Budget 2015*, http://www.singaporebudget.gov.sg/budget_2015/pc.aspx

Graduate Employment Survey (2016). http://www.polyges.sg/downloads/GES2016PR.pdf

Ministry of Education (2005). *Autonomous Universities – Towards Peaks of Excellence*. https://www.moe.gov.sg/media/press/2005/UAGF%20Preliminary%20Report.pdf

Ministry of Education (2012). *Report of the Committee on University Education Pathways Beyond 2015(CUEP)*. Singapore. https://www.moe.gov.sg/media/press/files/2012/08/cuep-report-greater-diversity-more-opportunities.pdf

Ministry of Education (2014). *Applied Studies in Polytechnics and ITE Review (ASPIRE)*. Singapore. https://www.parliament.gov.sg/lib/sites/default/files/paperpresented/pdf/2014/Misc.%203%20of%202014_0.pdf

Ministry of Education (2016a). *Education Statistics Digest 2016*. https://www.moe.gov.sg/docs/default-source/document/publications/education-statistics-digest/esd-2016.pdf

Ministry of Education (2016b). *Cohort Participation Rate*. Specific Information Requested, Research and Management Information Division.

The Straits Times (2016). 13 Oct. http://straitstimes.com/singapore/unisim-set-to-be-sixth-autonomous-university

The Straits Times (2017). 17 March. http://straitstimes.com/singapore/education/sim-university-to-be-renamed-singapore-university-of-social-sciences

Today Online (2017). *UniSIM and SIT to offer work-study degree programmes*, 25 Feb. https://www.gov.sg/news/content/today-online---unisim-and-sit-to-offer-work-study-degree-programmes

CHAPTER 17

National Strategy for Higher Education and Research: Challenges and Pitfalls from a French Perspective

Alain Beretz

INTRODUCTION: STRATEGIES, A NECESSARY EVIL?

For hundreds of years, science has had a privileged position. But it no longer sits on this pedestal. There is this increasing confusion and distrust of scientific advice among citizens. As a result, the role of science in policy-making has become extremely complex.

Governmental strategies for higher education and research can have various motivations, from a sincere trust that investment in science will be beneficial to the society, to the project that science can help to gain or to maintain leadership in a specific field, usually technical or industrial. Bert van der Zwaan (2017) has reminded us that universities are now under scrutiny, and are "under the spell of production and quality". Indeed, no strategy goes without specific deliverables and milestones. And, sometimes, just as when a finger points to the moon, the fool watches the finger, these milestones and deliverables become the centre of all passions, and one forgets the values and basic objectives that the strategy is supposed to target to.

The prospectus of our meeting asked how we can: "perceive the future challenges faced by our institutions" and "provide the leadership to prepare them to undergo the necessary changes". The purpose of this paper is to explore the possibilities and the limits of an answer to these basic questions in the form of a national strategy. Of course, I do not intend to demonstrate what is a good or a bad strategy, but merely to point out some lessons from shared experiences about these strategies, their advantages and their pitfalls. I will merely attempt to analyse some of the mechanisms for their elaboration, and try to draw some very basic lessons for both the policy-maker and the actors of these policies, especially the universities. And, of course, writing this paper as a new member of the Parisian technocracy, I have to be careful that I don't suffer from the "Stockholm syndrome", which would lead the former university president to defend administrative attitudes which he has criticized in the past.

GOVERNMENT STRATEGIES FOR SCIENCE AND UNIVERSITIES: EXAMPLES

French national strategy for research

A French "National strategy for research" was issued in 2015 (French Ministry for Higher education and research, 2015). It was written after a long process of consultation of institutional stakeholders. It proposes a coordinated strategic vision of French priorities for research. Let us stress two words in this definition: "coordinated" and "French".

Coordinated: this is not a straightforward issue, as the situation in France is very diverse, with many stakeholders working more or less independently. In a parliamentary report on this strategy, it was said, in an ironic tone, that France could only be the absolute world leader for research, "because we have 14 ministers of research" (Le Déaut & Sido, 2017). Coordination is therefore a major goal of such a national strategy.

French priorities: of course, the French government is pushing its own strategy, but this questions the role of a national strategy in a totally globalized field. Even though the strategy's punchline is "France Europe 2020", it is sometimes hard to combine national and global issues. To attempt to bridge this gap, it aligns with the European policies for science and innovation and the Horizon 2020 program, thus focusing on three axes: 1. Excellent science, 2. Industrial leadership, 3. Societal challenges. The intention to make research strategies cross-readable and compatible is, in theory, a very positive goal, considering the international nature of modern research. In a recent report of the European Commission that he coordinated, Pascal Lamy stressed in his introduction that their recommendations would be effective only if applied not only at the level of the European institutions, "but also by other stakeholders, national governments, companies, universities, research institutes, non-governmental organisations and all others engaged in research and innovation within the EU and beyond" (European Commission 2017b).

The strategy has led to select a restricted number of scientific priorities in order to respond to the grand economical and societal challenges confronting the country, prioritize these priorities and avoid a global coverage of the whole scientific field. It aims at federating all the stakeholders around this global national strategy and to initiate a prospective view, with all stakeholders (the various administrations, academic and industrial scientists, companies).

Another issue is that this was a research-only strategy; in parallel, a national strategy for higher education was also issued, and rather independently! As both did not seem to be coordinated enough, a white book was published in 2016, which has attempted to synthesize these strategies into a global approach (Monthubert, 2017). The fact that after the last elections, a fully-fledged minister was appointed, responsible for all aspects of the "knowledge triangle", can only reinforce the idea that we need a global strategy involving simultaneously all aspects of the academic world, i.e. education, research and innovation.

The Dutch National Research Agenda

The Dutch National Research Agenda was conceived in a very different way, its elaboration process started with a unique bottom-up procedure. The general public was invited in early 2015 to submit questions about science. This resulted in 11700 questions submitted by the general public, academic institutions, the business community and civil society organisations. Five academic juries were appointed to meet and assess the questions. This was followed by three conferences in June 2015 whose purpose was to bring order to the questions, and to further aggregate the questions where possible, based on these three perspectives.

This process ultimately led to 140 overarching scientific questions and 16 example routes. The questions reveal the complexity of the issues challenging Dutch society today, and provide a glimpse into the areas where Dutch scientific research plans to focus on in the coming years (Dutch National Research Agenda, 2016).

The Japanese Society 5.0 plan

Japan has been writing five-year planning strategies for 20 years. The latest one is called Society 5.0 (Council for Science, Technology and Innovation Cabinet Office (2015)). It is not the purpose of this paper to present it in detail, but only to point to some of its specific characteristics. The plan contains unusually sharp warnings that Japan is dropping in competitiveness.

What is interesting is that the plan does not list research and development priorities on a detailed level, but rather the ambition of the government to identify important broad research areas as well as its aspiration for system innovation. One of the key principles is to "enhance preparedness for an unforeseeable future". This issue is addressed with improved political coordination between and within departments and research councils, as well as a clearer focus on the basic components of the R&D system (people and excellence), together with more open innovation.

Thus the title "Society 5.0" points to a new type of strategic attitude, more globally oriented, which is summarized by the word "preparedness". It is also important that it stresses shared values such as sustainability, inclusiveness, efficiency, and power of intellect. Concepts like open science, networked science and citizen science indicate a more inclusive approach to managing the country's R&D system. But the plan also proposes specific goals for the coming five years and points to priorities in several key technology areas (for example Internet of things and Artificial intelligence), as well as numerical goals (for example, increase of the proportion of female researchers, increase in the proportion of faculty members less than 40 years old, or increase in the number of licence agreements on university patents). Innovation and knowledge transfer to the economy are a major goal, addressed through concrete actions such as public procurement, or aggressive intellectual property management.

The European research strategy and quest for "impact"

Research Councils UK (RCUK) defines research impact as "the demonstrable contribution that excellent research makes to society and the economy. This can involve academic impact, economic and societal impact". (Economic and social research council, n.d.).

A good policy should ensure that it pursues the three types of impacts in a balanced manner. But, let's face it, the tendency is nowadays to place, officially or not, the economic impact in the front row.

The interim evaluation of horizon 2020 points out very clearly that: "Research and innovation programs are notoriously difficult to evaluate. The causal relation between research and innovation investment on the one hand and impact on the other hand is often indirect, and difficult to identify, measure, demonstrate and attribute" (European Commission, 2017). Nevertheless, the actual vocabulary of the European Commission when addressing the elaboration of the future framework program (FP9) is to emphasize the importance of research impact, or mission-driven research. The so-called "Lamy report" is the answer of a high- level working group to the question of maximizing the impact of future European Union research and innovation programs. There is a continuing debate on this subject, including on one of the recommendations of the working group to adopt a mission-oriented, impact-focused approach to address global challenges (European Commission, 2017b).

The nature of the impact proxies chosen plays a major role. Very often, governments now attribute national ambitions to a position in the rankings, while we know that rankings, when used as the main indicator of impact of national policies, can have deleterious effects (Hazelkorn, 2007). Hazelkorn insists that the priority should not be on rankings but on "a skilled labour force, equity, regional growth, better citizens, future Einsteins and global competitiveness", and it is these priorities that should be translated into policy." (Hazelkorn, 2013)

The individualist approach

Most often a strategy is designed around some specific and global goals, should it be a technology (artificial intelligence, Hindi & Janin 2017), a disease (war against cancer, Ledford & Tollefson, 2016) or a societal goal (radicalization, Fuchs, 2016). But another type of strategy is to target people, not subjects. One could, of course, say that this is a very selfish attitude, and that it does not allow to target global issues. The two following examples show that this is not the case.

A first example comes from the Weizmann Institute of Science, which was ranked sixth worldwide in the Nature Index 2017 Innovation ranking. This index is a measure of how effectively basic research translates into commercial applications (Nature Index 2017 Innovation, 2017). One could therefore assume that this is the result of a strong "market-pull" strategy, where research is targeted top-down to satisfy industrial needs. But this is not the case, the strategy of the Institute being "people-driven, not subject-driven". According to Weizmann's President Daniel Zajfman: "Research at the Institute is driven by the curiosity of our scientists, and (..) the Institute doesn't work on the basis of a well-defined marketing, outcome-oriented or translational strategy." He adds that the philosophy of the Weizmann Institute has always been to attract the best and the brightest scientists, and provide them with the necessary infrastructure to perform their cutting-edge, curiosity-driven research. "The best strategy is, in fact, to bet on excellent people, and not on a specific target." (Weizmann Institute, 2017).

Another strategy targeted on supporting talented individuals, whatever their field of research, is the European Research Council. The ERC funds investigator-driven, bottom-up research. This approach allows researchers to identify new opportunities and directions in any field of research, rather than being led by priorities set by politicians. Excellence is the only condition, and this strategy has a great impact: ERC grantees have won many prestigious prizes, including 6 Nobel Prizes, 4 Fields Medals, 5 Wolf Prizes and more. A bibliometric analysis shows that research funded by the ERC has a scientific impact far above average (European Research Council, 2016).

GENERAL PRINCIPLES AND PITFALLS

What priorities?

Indeed, no country can do without national priorities or strategic choices. Without some top-down incentives, major societal challenges such as energy transition, cybersecurity or antibioresistance would probably not be addressed in a proper way. However there is a constitutive ambiguity in fixing priorities, in the sense that it could mean excluding from the national efforts any subject which is not deeply rooted in theses priorities. Also, care should be taken to avoid "patchwork strategies" looking more like emergency measures to cope with a few rapidly-growing demands, but without an underlying ambition and no global sustainability (for a general discussion see Henningsen et al., (2013)).

Who fuels the strategy?

A strategy should translate a policy. An example often cited is the "War on cancer" that was initiated by Richard Nixon in 1971, massively funding research on cancer and making it a national priority (Brennan et al., 2010). Similarly, Barack Obama launched the "cancer moonshot" in 2016, with the goal to double the rate of progress against cancer, achieving in five years what otherwise would have taken ten (Ledford & Tollefson, 2016). Another interesting example is the recent initiative by President Emmanuel Macron to "Make our planet great again" (Butler, 2017). Of course, these major political impulses do not guarantee that the scientific outcomes will meet expectations, but they provide a major push that cannot come from the scientific community alone, and also act as a kind of "branding tool" for a country or a region.

Who elaborates the strategy?

The few examples mentioned in this paper show that the paths leading to a strategy could be highly variable. A strategy can stem from compiling many institutional contributions (which was the main method for the French national research strategy), be the result of an initial project designed a small group (the method leading to the Japanese Society 5.0 plan), or come from wide consultation of the public (for the Dutch National Research Agenda). It is far beyond the purpose of this paper to evaluate or rank these various pathways, it is my impression that they might matter less than the final result and the use which is made thereof.

A strategy needs a budget

There is a big difference between a strategy that is set up to funnel an additional, voluntary budget, and another which would be there to concentrate limited funds only on some targeted areas of research.

A parliamentary committee has recommended that, for implementation of the French strategy described above, a five-year budgetary effort of 1.2 to 1.5 billion €/year over 5 years was necessary (Le Déaut & Sido, 2017). Unfortunately, the present budget will not reach this figure, but this type of assessment is of the greatest importance, and stresses a neglected effect of these strategies, which is to provide sound arguments to lobby for the place of higher education and research in political and budgetary decisions. Global strategies can provide decision-makers and taxpayers alike with simple arguments to convince them that investing in higher education and research are global priorities they should support. In this sense, a good budget needs a supporting strategy.

A strategy should be evaluated

One of the ways to escape the abrupt debate about the validity and importance of a national strategy is to evaluate it. Milestones and outcomes should be designed in order to report on the efficiency of this strategy, but this not a straightforward issue.

To be significant, the evaluation of a national strategy should address as much as possible the following points: efficacy (have the targets been reached?), efficiency (relationship between the resources used and the changes generated), relevance (adequacy of the strategy to the problems), impact (effects of the strategy), relevance (between the means and the problem). These are the items that will be monitored for the evaluation of the Horizon 2020 program.

Some strategies include from the start robust evaluation schemes, but, at least in the French system, very often this is a weak spot. It is important to stress that the quality of indicators should not be discussed in the post-evaluation process, but included from the start in the design of the strategy. Nevertheless the link between governance or strategy and performance is very hard to make, and attributing good or bad performance to the various strategies and mechanisms summarized here is still highly unreliable.

CONCLUSION: AUTONOMY AND NATIONAL STRATEGY, THE IMPOSSIBLE SYNTHESIS?

This paper did not propose to deliver a scholarly analysis of governmental strategies for higher education and research, but only to summarize a few remarks derived from my own experience of the two sides of the mirror, university and government. There is scholarly literature on the subject, which I did not intend to review; but it remains partial, and research on that field should certainly be encouraged. For example, Ferlie *et al.* have connected the study of higher education policies and strategies with wider concepts drawn from political science, organization theory and an emergent body of work in public management. They have suggested that "many of the organizational and managerial reforms apparent in higher education cannot be studied in isolation but have to be considered as part of a broader pattern of public sector reforming; the State seeks to steer higher education subsystems as it does other publicly funded service delivery subsystems" (Ferlie et al., 2008).

Needless to say, governmental strategies applying to the academic world should be also deeply concerned with one specific characteristic: academic freedom. Academic freedom requires a sufficient degree of independence from government control and from the state in general; this does not mean that academics should never support national strategies, but it also requires that these strategies respect fundamental academic rights. Universities should not oppose their autonomy to the need for accountability, as rights and freedoms carry with them "duties and responsibilities", as stated by article 10 of the European Convention on Human Rights (Vrielink et al., 2010). One of the best arguments for a policy-maker to respect academic freedom is precisely the example of the ERC, an institution where freedom and an unbiased quest for excellence have really paid off! The real question is to find ways to bundle up the initiatives than sprout out from this academic freedom into a coherent and effective package. Jo Ritzen has mentioned that "Universities, as a rule, are just not able to find a consensus of what kind of changes are absolutely necessary (…) So what is needed is strategic thinking about how promising ideas about the university of the future can be put into practice in combination with political pressure to bring that about." (Henningsen et al., 2013, p. 118).

Altogether, we have to beware of a fetishist attitude towards strategies. A fetish can be defined as the belief in something having the power to make our desires come true and protect us from harm. Rajani Naidoo (Naidoo, 2016) wrote recently that higher education can be seen to be trapped in a kind of magical thinking that makes a fetish out of competition. Unfortunately, strategies are very often also presented in the same fetishist way, becoming a goal by themselves, and forgetting that they only serve more fundamental goals. This fetishist attitude can also trigger an "iconoclastic" reaction i.e., that the universities, or the individual scientist, will pretend they know better, and that the strategies are just hampering their creativity. As usual, the truth lies somewhere in the middle. A strategy is only a means, not an end.

In fact I would much prefer to present national strategies the way Chinese generals have been taught to fight a war. I can only cite François Jullien, philosopher and specialist of Chinese culture: "The strategist, like water, bypasses the obstacles and insinuates himself where the path is free before him; like water, he never ceases to marry the line of least resistance and find, at any time, where it is easier to progress" (Jullien, 2016). In other words, a good strategy should remain invisible.

REFERENCES

Brennan, R., Federico, S., & Dyer, M. A. (2010) "The war on cancer: have we won the battle but lost the war?" *Oncotarget* 1(2): 77–83.

Butler, D. (2017). Climate scientists flock to France's call. *Nature news* 18 July 2017. Available from: https://www.nature.com/articles/d41586-017-01713-4 [Accessed: 15 October 2017]

Council for Science, Technology and Innovation Cabinet Office, Government of Japan (2015). "Report on the 5th Science and Technology Basic Plan". Available from: http://www8.cao.go.jp/cstp/kihonkeikaku/5basicplan_en.pdf [Accessed: 15 October 2017]

Dutch National Research Agenda (2016). Available from: https://wetenschapsagenda.nl/approach/?lang=en [Accessed: 15 October 2017]

Economic and Social Research Council (n.d.)., "What is impact?". Available from: http://www.esrc.ac.uk/research/impact-toolkit/what-is-impact/ [Accessed: 15 October 2017]

European Commission (2017). "Commission staff working document — interim evaluation of horizon 2020" Available from: https://ec.europa.eu/research/evaluations/pdf/archive/h2020_evaluations/swd(2017)221-interim_evaluation-h2020.pdf [Accessed: 15 October 2017]

European Commission (2017b). "LAB – FAB – APP — Investing in the European future we want. Report of the independent High Level Group on maximising the impact of EU Research & Innovation Programmes" Available from: http://ec.europa.eu/research/evaluations/pdf/archive/other_reports_studies_and_documents/hlg_2017_report.pdf#view=fit&pagemode=none [Accessed: 15 October 2017]

European Research Council (2016). "Qualitative Evaluation of completed projects funded by the European Research Council". Available from : https://erc.europa.eu/sites/default/files/qualitative_evaluation_of_completed_projects_funded_by_the_erc.pdf [Accessed: 15 October 2017]

Ferlie, E., Musselin, C. & Andresani, G. (2008). "The steering of higher education systems: a public management perspective". *Higher Education*, 56 (3), pp. 325-348.

French Ministry for Higher Education and Research (2015). Stratégie nationale de recherche — France - Europe 2020. Available from : https://cache.media.enseignementsup-recherche.gouv.fr/file/Strategie_Recherche/26/9/strategie_nationale_recherche_397269.pdf [Accessed: 15 October 2017]

Fuchs, A. (ed) (2016). "Recherches sur les radicalisations, les formes de violence qui en résultent et la manière dont les sociétés les préviennent et s'en protègent. Etat des lieux, propositions, actions". *Rapport de l'Alliance Athena*. Available from: https://cache.media.enseignementsup-recherche.gouv.fr/file/Actus/87/9/Rapport_ATHENA_544879.pdf [Accessed: 15 October 2017]

Hazelkorn, E. (2007). "The impact of league tables and ranking systems on higher education decision-making". *Higher Education Management and Policy* 19(2): 87-110.

Hazelkorn, E. (2011). "World-Class Universities or World- Class Systems? Rankings and Higher Education Policy Choices", slides presented at the UNESCO Forum on Rankings and Accountability in Higher Education, Paris, 16-17 May 2011. Available from: http://www.unesco.org/new/fileadmin/MULTIMEDIA/HQ/ED/pdf/RANKINGS/Elllen%20Hazelkorn_.pdf [Accessed: 15 October 2017]

Henningsen, B., Schlaeger, J., & Tenorth, H. E. (2013). *Humboldt's Model: The Future of Universities in the World of Research.* Berlin: BWV Berliner Wissenschafts-Verlag.

Hindi, R. & Janin, J. (eds) (2017), "Anticipating the Economic and Social Impacts of Artificial Intelligence —- Contribution to the National Strategy on Artificial Intelligence" *France Stratégie,* March 2017. Available from: http://www.strategie.gouv.fr/sites/strategie.gouv.fr/files/atoms/files/report-intelligence-artificielle-en.pdf [Accessed: 15 October 2017]

Jullien, F. (2005)., Conférence sur l'efficacité, Paris : *Presses Universitaires de France* (personal translation).

Le Déaut, J. Y. & Sido, B. (2017). "Assessment of the 'France Europe 2020' national research strategy". Available from : http://www2.assemblee-nationale.fr/content/download/57321/570715/version/2/file/4+pages+SNR+EN.pdf [Accessed: 15 October 2017]

Ledford, H. & Tollefson, J., (2016). "Obama proposes cancer "moonshot" in State of the Union address". *Nature News* (13 January 2016). Available from : http://www.nature.com/news/obama-proposes-cancer-moonshot-in-state-of-the-union-address-1.19155 [Accessed: 15 October 2017]

Monthubert, B. (ed.) (2017)., *Livre Blanc de l'enseignement supérieur et de la recherche.* Available from : https://cache.media.enseignementsup-recherche.gouv.fr/file/Actus/04/1/ESR_Livre_Blanc_707041.pdf [Accessed: 15 October 2017]

Naidoo, R. (2016). "Competition as a fetish: why universities need to escape the trap". *The Conversation.* Available from : https://theconversation.com/competition-as-a-fetish-why-universities-need-to-escape-the-trap-58084 [Accessed: 15 October 2017]

Nature Index 2017 Innovation (2017). *Nature,* Vol. 548 No. 7666_supp ppS3-40. Available from: http://www.nature.com/nature/supplements/nature-index-2017-innovation/index.html [Accessed: 15 October 2017]

Van der Zwaan, Bert (2017), *Higher education in 2040.* Amsterdam University Press.

Vrielink, J., Lemmens, P. & Parmentier, S. (eds) (2010). "Academic freedom as a fundamental right". *LERU advice paper N° 6.* Available from: http://www.leru.org/files/publications/AP6_Academic_final_Jan_2011.pdf [Accessed: 15 October 2017]

Weizmann Institute 2017. "Weizmann institute ranked 6th in the world for innovation". Available from: https://www.weizmann.org.uk/news/weizmann-institute-ranked-6th-in-the-world-for-innovation

CHAPTER 18

Beyond Brexit: the Road ahead for UK Universities

Leszek Borysiewicz

At the time of writing this essay, I'm in the final year of my seven-year tenure as Vice-Chancellor at the University of Cambridge, long enough for me to notice when things have turned a full cycle.

I took up the post amid a flurry of government policy proposals affecting British universities. These included the introduction of higher fees, the loosening of the regulatory framework for higher education providers, and a greater emphasis on student experience and widening participation.

The surge in attention from the government caused what I described, back then, as "an existential panic" for the university sector, triggered by the bout of changes in state policy. Some of those changes have, indeed, had a profound impact on British universities.

Almost seven years later, we are in the midst of yet another spate of government policies and — it seems to me — another spell of existential jitters. British universities are prone to regular pangs of paranoia, panic and plunging self-confidence. But I am reminded of that line by Joseph Heller: "Just because you're paranoid doesn't mean they aren't after you."

I am aware of the pitfalls of committing one's forecasts to paper (especially when they won't be published until a much later date). Whatever the political landscape is at the time of publication, there are key issues that will continue to shape and affect the United Kingdom's university sector in years to come — let's call them, to use that ill-fated phrase, the "known unknowns". Among the most salient, to me, are the UK's departure from the EU; the implementation of the new Higher Education and Research Act; and the challenge to all universities presented by growing scepticism about the role of expertise and knowledge. It is these issues I wish to address in the following pages.

LEAVING – BUT GOING WHERE?

After 44 years of a fruitful and occasionally fractious relationship, the UK and the EU are now, in the words of novelist John Irving, "involved in that awkward procedure of getting to unknow each other".

The exact nature of the UK's new relationship with its 27 European partners will not be clear until a couple of years from now. No matter what the results are of the complex negotiations that lie ahead, the implications for British universities cannot be over-stated. They will have an impact on our ability to recruit and retain international students and staff. They will affect our ability to compete for European research funding. And they will reduce our ability to become part of, and lead, networks of collaborative research.

People

British universities' reputation for excellence hinges on having excellent people. Whether it is the brightest undergraduate and postgraduate students, or the best academic and support staff, we rely on the talent of people from all over the world who study, teach, do research or work at our institutions.

The prospect of Brexit has inevitably caused unease and insecurity among EU nationals working and studying at universities in the United Kingdom: 17% of all academic staff in the UK, comprising tenured and postdoctoral researchers, are nationals of other EU countries. At many of the research-intensive Russell Group universities, this number is considerably higher — at the University of Cambridge it is close to 23%.

In fact, at these Russell Group universities over 30% of academics in areas of strategic importance including economics, maths, IT, software engineering, are from other EU countries. The same is true for Modern Languages.

There are around 125,000 students from other EU countries studying at UK universities, representing 5% of the nation's total student population. Almost half of them study at Russell Group universities. At Cambridge, non-UK EU students make up 10% of our undergraduate population and almost one quarter of our postgraduates.

According to one study by Universities UK, students from other EU countries attending UK universities generate £3.7 billion for the UK economy and support more than 34,000 jobs across the country (THE, 2016).

The risk to our ability to continue attracting excellent staff and students is tangible, as suggested by the 14% drop in undergraduate applications from other EU nationals for the academic year beginning in 2017.

The UK government's announcement that non-UK EU students will continue to be eligible for the same financial support as their UK peers for the 2018-2019 academic year is certainly welcome — but it doesn't offer the long-term certitude that families need to make significant life choices such as where to pursue a course of studies.

Meanwhile, the uncertainty surrounding the migratory status of EU nationals working at British universities has had a chilling effect on our reputation as a country that keeps its doors open to talent from around the world.

As the government conducts negotiations to disentangle the UK from the EU, British universities have called for clarity about the future rights of residence of other EU nationals we employ. We have asked that any post-Brexit immigration system should ensure minimal barriers for future staff and students from those other EU countries. Finally, we have recommended that international students should not be classified as long-term migrants for the purposes of public policy — a recommendation that has not, to our regret, been adopted.

Research

European research funding has been a very significant part of the UK's funding portfolio. The UK was awarded €6.9 billion of competitive funding under the Seventh Framework Programme (FP7) — equivalent to over 15% of total EU funding for research.

It has secured €3.3 billion so far under Horizon2020 (close to 16% of total funding), and has the highest levels of participation in H2020-funded projects.

In the year 2015-16 alone, Russell Group universities secured over €700m of EU funding for research that will help to improve health, society and the economy.

Once again, the University of Cambridge has done well in this area: our researchers were awarded €424m under FP7 (2007-13). Under H2020, they have been granted €180m so far.

We especially value the impact of funding from the European Research Council (ERC), which rewards research that is truly innovative and which, by taking big conceptual risks, is able to tackle big questions.

The UK has been the largest recipient of ERC awards — between 2007 and 2015, almost a quarter (24%) of all ERC funding was awarded to UK-based researchers.

Since its foundation in 2007, the ERC has funded more than 1,500 projects by UK-based academics. In practice, this has been equivalent to having an additional Research Council, handing out awards for innovative, risk-taking research.

With 218 of those awards so far, Cambridge is the greatest beneficiary of ERC grants under the current H2020 program. In fact, 14 of our PIs are recipients of a second ERC grant. We have one pair of siblings with one ERC grant each, and at least one married couple with their respective "His" and "Hers" ERC awards.

We consistently hear from our academics that an ERC grant allows them the time and the freedom to innovate and take risks with their research. They are able to pursue their ideas wherever they may lead them. They are able to recruit, build and train teams of PhD students and postdocs who are then likely to move on to their own successful career paths. In the words of one of our grantees, the ERC offers a financial model that "enables us to do work that is 15 or 20 years ahead of the rest of the world".

The issue is not only access to funding, which is essential, but also access to facilities, on which much of the cutting-edge research depends.

All of which raises some inevitable questions: how will the country and its universities make up for the very likely shortfall in funding of excellence-driven research when the UK finally exits the EU? Under what circumstances, and at what cost, will UK-based researchers be allowed to use European facilities when we are no longer full members of European research schemes?

There are some promising signs. The current government seems to be in no doubt about the value that well-funded, research-intensive universities can add to their strategies for growth. Ministers have hinted that, even as we disengage from the EU, there are European programs (including Horizon2020) that we might wish to keep paying into. One suspects, however, that the decision of what European programs we continue to be part of in the future will not be entirely up to our own Ministers. In the meantime, the question of whether there will be a mechanism to replace the ERC's excellence-driven research looms larger than ever.

Collaboration

The challenge to available research funding posed by Brexit is matched by the challenge to Britain's proven capacity to establish, to be part of, and to lead networks of international collaboration. Research is a global endeavour. Tackling some of the most urgent problems — whether it is ageing societies, infectious disease or climate change — demands collaboration across disciplines and across borders.

Even at this stage, where we continue to be part of the EU, and to win very significant European awards, there seems to have been a collective loss of confidence in the UK's ability to lead research consortia — and, among some of our European partners, a loss of appetite for collaborations with the UK. Both are short-sighted and ill-advised reactions, though perhaps understandable.

We know that approximately 60% of papers co-authored by UK-based academics are done in collaboration with European partners. Germany, France and Italy together account for 16% of papers co-authored by UK-based researchers — higher than the US, with 13.7% of the share.

As a member state of the EU, the UK has been able to influence the formulation of European research policies and priorities. It articulated the case for the award of research funding on the basis of excellence, and has been able to influence policy on research ethics, open access and regulatory frameworks.

Switzerland learned, through bitter experience, the implications of being excluded from regular participation in the H2020 framework programme. One question for the UK in years ahead is: will we be able not only to have access to the next Framework Programme (FP9), but also to influence how its priorities are set — and to ensure that it maintains its focus on excellence? The best-case scenario, at the moment, is that we will find a way to participate in future Framework Programmes, but will be mostly unable to shape those discussions or help set the agenda.

A FINE BALANCE: THE HIGHER EDUCATION AND RESEARCH ACT

However one feels about Brexit and its impact on our institutions, there is no doubting that it will happen. And, in time, it will be the new normal. We cannot make the weather — but we can prepare for it.

Alongside the impact of Brexit, we must consider the effect of what one member of the House of Lords called "the most important legislation for the [higher education] sector in 25 years". Indeed, the Higher Education and Research Act (HERA), passed into law at the end of April, is likely to underpin the work of the higher education sector for a long time to come.

Focusing on students

I cited in my introduction the surge in policy proposals affecting universities when I first took up the office of Vice-Chancellor in 2010. The purpose of the reforms back then was, to use the government's words, to "put students at the heart of the system".

This most recent change in higher education legislation has taken those reforms further. It creates a new regulatory and funding body for universities, the Office for Students (OfS), which will have statutory responsibility for quality and standards, approve the creation of new universities, and confer title- and degree-awarding powers.

The HERA makes provision for a Teaching Excellence Framework (TEF), carried out by the OfS, to assess the quality of teaching in universities. The controversial link between TEF results and universities' ability to raise fees above inflation has been put on hold until 2020, following a review of the TEF.

The UK higher education sector has broadly welcomed the developments heralded by the passing of the HERA, in particular the spelling out of a more strategic direction from the government. This is much needed at a time when other external issues like Brexit and increasing competition from universities around the world, are a challenge to our competitiveness.

Maintaining autonomy

One worry for many Universities when the legislation was proposed was that the new provisions would impinge significantly on our autonomy. Misgivings about the power given to the new regulatory bodies have been somewhat mitigated. Institutional autonomy remains one of the salient features of the new Act, which goes some way towards codifying institutional autonomy.

The opening section of the Act explicitly states as one of the OfS's requirements "the need to protect the institutional autonomy of English higher education providers". The Act goes further, and sets out to define institutional autonomy as universities' freedom to manage themselves, to determine the content of their courses and the manner in which they are taught, to determine the criteria for selection or dismissal of staff, to determine the criteria for admission of students, to question and test received wisdom, and to put forward new ideas and controversial or unpopular opinions.

Restructuring research funding

Another significant feature of the Act is the wholesale reform of the research funding structures. This is good news. On the research side, the UK's seven research councils will be reorganized under a single strategic research body called UK Research and Innovation (UKRI).

The creation of UKRI responds to the need to simplify structures and reduce bureaucracy. It will allow a better coordinated and more strategic global approach to research funding. The new body will be able to focus on cross-cutting issues in ways that the various separate funding agencies could not easily do in the past. It will be able to set up mechanisms for sharing expertise and data. Crucially, and perhaps for the first time, the UK's research sector will have in the newly appointed head of UKRI a champion in government.

Marketization or necessary reform?

Critics of the HERA have claimed that it slavishly follows a global trend in the marketization of higher education. I understand this to be a necessary reform in a sector that is already stretched to the point at which it is unable to make the contribution to society that we all expect it to make.

I was the beneficiary of a system that offered a full university education, at no cost to students. But when I went to University, only 7% of the UK's population went to University. Today, that number is closer to 50%. The introduction, and subsequent increase, of student fees was an inevitable result of this trend.

In a system where students (or their families) are expected to contribute to their education, should there not be an expectation that they are offered a good student experience? Should our teachers and researchers not be challenged to raise their standards? Should students not be better informed, and better represented in the governing structures of our universities? Is it not universities' duty to ensure that students whose instruction we are charged with will receive the best possible education we can offer them — so that we are only training people for today's jobs, but educating minds to face tomorrow's challenges? These are some of the questions that the passing of the Higher Education and Research Act confronts us with.

IN PRAISE OF EXPERTISE

To thrive, British universities will have to adapt to new ways of being assessed and funded, even as we adapt to new ways of engaging with our international partners. We will also have to face up to one of the greatest challenges to our credibility, and to the public trust that gives us licence to operate.

At the 2017 World Economic Forum, in Davos, the communications company Edelman published the results of its annual Trust Barometer, revealing the largest-ever drop in public trust in the institutions of government, business, media and NGOs.

Trust in conventional institutions, the survey tells us, is at its lowest. More than half (53%) of respondents across the world believed "the system" had failed them; 59% of them claimed to have more trust in search engines than in human content editors when seeking information. The survey tells us that people are now as likely to believe a "person like themselves" as they are to believe an academic expert.

It may come as no surprise that the trust gap between the informed and uninformed public is growing. That gap is at its widest in the US — followed by the UK. Almost half of all respondents in the Trust Barometer believe that facts don't matter.

A particular worry for many of us ahead of the UK's Brexit referendum was the rhetoric surrounding evidence-based arguments, infamously summarized in the phrase "the people of this country have had enough of experts". The dictionary defines an expert as "a person who is very knowledgeable about, or skilful in, a particular area." How strange, then, that this word has now become a term of abuse.

Another poll carried out by Ipsos Mori just before the referendum suggested that Academics were ranked third in trustworthiness as a source of information on EU issues — after friends and family, and small business owners.

Even the perception that universities cannot be trusted to generate knowledge that is pertinent to most people's lives can be profoundly damaging. It is damaging to our reputation as institutions capable of effecting social change. It is damaging to our reputation as institutions interested in improving lives not just at our doorstep, but wherever in the world that improvement is needed. It is damaging to our reputation as institutions that should take a position of leadership on the most important issues of the day.

So we must ask ourselves: what is the role of universities that pride themselves on educating and recruiting experts? What is our role, as purveyors of expertise, at a time when that very expertise is being dismissed as irrelevant?

There is a long and distinguished tradition of anti-intellectualism in the UK and the US. It can be traced back to at least the 18th century, and the writings of Edmund Burke, who praised the English character as being rooted in "common sense" and empiricism. Writing on the history of anti-intellectualism in the United States, American historian Richard Hofstadter claimed that it was "a part of our English cultural inheritance". In Britain, Leonard Woolf observed: "No people have ever despised and distrusted the intellect and intellectuals more than the British."

Common sense is fine, and underpins many of our best ideas. But common sense alone does not help us cure cancer or eradicate infectious disease. Neither does common sense alone help us fight crop failure or mitigate climate change. Common sense in isolation does not help us make cities smarter and more efficient, or combat extremist ideologies, or interpret ancient civilizations and texts. We need the experts to do that. Universities happen to be full of them.

So my challenge to university leaders everywhere is this: let's be self-confident about our mission. Let's continue to achieve excellence in research and education — and alongside it, let's achieve excellence in outreach and communication. Let's continue to innovate, and to challenge conventional wisdom — and while we do that, let's strive to be more transparent, open and diverse. Let's continue to push the boundaries of knowledge — and work hard to demonstrate the many ways in which this knowledge touches lives everywhere.

We must reclaim the mantle of expertise, and make no apologies about it. As long as we can show that we have society's interest at our heart, we will have the legitimacy and the autonomy to keep on doing what we do best. If we wish to remain relevant, we cannot simply hide behind our reputations.

We have a responsibility to engage in discussion with the public. Doing so will not always make us popular, but it will ultimately strengthen our integrity and build up public trust — which is the most precious commodity. From that public trust we derive the licence to continue with our vital work.

FINAL THOUGHTS: REASONS TO BE CHEERFUL?

I began by referring to the policy proposals affecting higher education when I took up the post of Vice-Chancellor in 2010. We are now seeing some of those reforms being finally put into practice through legislation, and confronting universities with serious questions about their purpose.

At a glance, the combination of Brexit, the HERA's comprehensive shakeup of British higher education, and the challenge to our expertise seem to be a perfect storm for British universities. In fact, for institutions prepared to adapt, there may well be opportunities to enhance our reputation for excellence in all areas.

One of the biggest tests ahead lies in having to adjust to — and plan for — a future that is, at the moment, so opaque. We know we can expect increased competition from universities elsewhere. We can expect a different sort of relationship with our European partners, unmediated by the European Union and its funding mechanisms. We can expect greater pressure to be accountable, transparent and open to assessment.

I'd like to believe that ours is a resilient sector. In the face of the uncertainties ahead, and through close engagement with the UK government, we must continue to push for the right balance between regulation and autonomy. Through close collaboration with our partners in Europe and elsewhere, we must step up our efforts to offset the disadvantages of the UK's exit from the EU with the opportunities — financial, regulatory and otherwise — that it presents. And we must ensure that we dispel, categorically, any reservations about the relevance that our expertise has to local, national and global communities.

Only by doing so can we ensure that British universities remain globally competitive in the years ahead. Only by doing so can we ensure that British universities continue to act as society's critics and conscience. Only by doing so can we ensure that British universities continue to carry out their mission to contribute to society.

REFERENCES

THE (2016). "EU students generate £3.7 billion for UK economy, says UUK", *Times Higher Education*, 8 April 2016.

CHAPTER 19

Preparing the American University for 2030

James J. Duderstadt

Although the university has existed as a social institution for almost a millennium, with each historical epoch it has been transformed in very profound ways. The scholasticism of early medieval universities, first appearing in Bologna and Paris, slowly gave way to the humanism of the Renaissance. The graduate universities appearing in early 19th century Germany (von Humboldt's University of Berlin) were animated by the freedom of the Enlightenment and the rigour of the scientific method. The Industrial Revolution in 19th America stimulated the commitment to education of the working class and the public engagement of the land-grant universities. The impact of campus research on national security during WWII and the ensuing Cold War created the paradigm of the contemporary research university during the late 20th century.

Although the impact of these changes has been assimilated and they now seem natural, at the time they involved a profound reassessment of the mission and structure of the university as an institution. But the pace of change in our world is accelerating, with the impact of rapidly evolving technology and changing demographics, and the impact of humankind on our planet. These will pose great challenges to our universities in the next few decades.

CHALLENGES OF TODAY

Developing a vision for the future of the American university is a challenging exercise, both because of the unusual size, breadth and complexity of our institutions, and because of the important leadership role they are expected to play for our society. Today we are challenged to adapt the university to a post-industrial, knowledge-based society as our economies are steadily shifting from material- and labour-intensive products and processes to knowledge-intensive products and services. In this knowledge economy, where the key assets driving prosperity are intellectual capital, education has become a power political force, both nationally and on a global scale. The key technologies enabling the global knowledge economy, e.g. information technology, biotechnology and nanotechnology, all evolve at an exponential pace, and are also reshaping the learning and scholarship on our campuses.

Our universities are also challenged by the rapidly changing nature of our population as our current population ages, similar to other developed nations in Europe and Asia. Yet here the United States stands apart because of a second and equally profound demographic trend: immigration. As it has been so many times in its past, America is once again becoming a highly diverse nation of immigrants, benefiting immensely from their energy, talents and hope. Yet, while of great value, this increasing diversity of our population is complicated by social and political factors such as prejudice and segregation.

Added to these broad changes in our world and nation are specific challenges currently faced by American higher education. Today much of the earlier commitment of public funds that built our great research universities in the 20th century has eroded. Over the past decade, state support of our public universities has dropped by roughly 35%. After a brief surge in federal support of research during the late 1990s, both federal and corporate support of basic and applied research has fallen significantly in recent years, while fields such as the social sciences have been savaged by conservative political forces. And, perhaps most telling of all, the inequities characterizing educational opportunity have become extraordinary. Today most of those responsible for public policy at both the federal level and among the states have ignored the public good character of higher education. Instead, and in sharp contrast to most of the rest of the world, most Americans view a college education primarily as a private benefit for individuals aimed at providing them with good jobs. Hence it is accepted that their education should be paid for through student fees, and increasingly funded through personal debt, rather than through public investment. (Holliday, 2012)

While most nations are facing — or at least coping with — the ongoing challenges of massification, academic competition and limited public resources, culture, tradition and local politics shape their particular approach. Because of our origin as a federation of independent colonies (and then states), the United States continues to rely on a highly decentralized, market-driven approach to higher education, with little strategic direction from the federal government. In fact, with the recent change in our federal government in 2017, education has not only dropped low on the list of nation priorities, but it has come under attack because of its efforts to sustain the important academic values such as truth, evidence and the scientific method that undergird its learning and scholarship.

THE WORLD OF 2030

Demographics

Demographers project that global population will continue to increase for several more decades, rising to 8.5 billion in 2030, then 9.7 billion in 2050 and 11 billion in 2100. Growth will be limited in developed nations in Europe, Asia and North America where aging populations and depressed fertility rates are likely to lead to declining populations (with the notable exception of the United States with its unusually high immigration rate).

In sharp contrast, developing nations in Asia, Latin America and particularly Africa (where population is likely to double) will be characterized by young and growing populations with exploding needs for education. Unless developed nations step forward and help address this crisis, billions of people in coming generations will be denied the education so necessary to compete and survive in the knowledge economy. The resulting despair and hopelessness among the young will feed the terrorism that so threatens our world today.

But there is another important demographic trend: the lengthening of human lifespan driven by the progress of biomedical science, particularly in developed nations. Those in today's Millennial generation (those born between 1980 and 1995) have an expected lifespan into their 90s, while today's young children have a 50% chance to live to 100 or longer (Gratton, 2016). While certainly encouraging from a public health perspective, the downside is the fact that even prosperous societies will simply be unable to afford supporting decades of retirement beyond the age of 70. Longer lives will require more years of work. Yet it is also clear that an education received in one's youth will likely not be sufficient to sustain employment 50 years later. Hence lifelong education and continually retraining will become essential, and this will pose new challenges to higher education. (*The Economist, Lifelong Education*, 2017)

Technology

The technologies of today — cyberinfrastructure, big data, artificial intelligence, clouds and soon quantum computing — have the disruptive feature that they continue to grow in power at exponential rates, increasing 100 to 1,000-fold each decade (Kelly, 2016). The rapid evolution of digital technology not only accelerates conventional economic activity, but it creates entirely new ventures such as social media, virtual and augmented reality, intelligent agents (Siri and Alexa) and sophisticated data management and access (*The Economist, Technology Quarterly*, 2017). Furthermore, as the technology continues to evolve, so too do the ambitions of those organizations that exploit it such as Google (to make available all the world's knowledge to all people), Facebook (to connect all the people of the world) and Amazon (an everything, everywhere store).

While such technologies have had great positive impact on our lives, they also threaten our current activities. For example, increasing power of AI clouds, the Internet of Things and other automation technologies are transforming our economy (what Schwab calls the Fourth Industrial Revolution) (Schwab, 2016), eliminating more routine jobs in fields such as construction, manufacturing and services. More generally, there is a strong concentration of wealth driven by the new technologies, since the return on capital and technology is greater than for labour, leading to not only jobless economic growth but also increasing income disparities. In fact, some suggest that in a future that may have only 20% of today's jobs, the real challenge will become how to create meaningful lives in a world with rapidly increasing machine intelligence. (*The Economist, On Artificial Intelligence*, 2016) With our current education system, most citizens will not have the skills for the new jobs. Of course, we might argue that there will always likely be some jobs that can be performed better by humans than AI systems, particularly those involving empathy or social interaction. In fact, one might suggest that such "human traits" should be given a much higher priority in learning organizations such as universities.

Today, a rapidly changing world demands a new level of knowledge, skills and abilities on the part of our citizens. Just as in earlier critical moments in history when our prosperity and security were achieved through broadening and enhancing educational opportunity, it is time once again to seek a bold expansion of educational opportunity. But this time we should set as the goal providing all citizens with universal access to lifelong learning opportunities, thereby enabling participation in a world both illuminated and driven by knowledge and learning.

CREATIVITY, COMMUNICATION AND CONVERGENCE

The professions that have dominated the late 20th Century — and, to some degree, the contemporary university — have been those which manipulate and rearrange knowledge and wealth rather than create it, professions such as law, business, accounting and politics. Yet, it is becoming increasingly clear that the driving intellectual activity of the 21st Century will be the act of creation itself.

We now have the capacity to create new objects literally atom by atom. With new methods in molecular biology such as CRISPR/cas9 and gene drive, we can not only precisely modify the DNA code for a living organism, but we can actually cause it to propagate through a species to change future generations (a frightening thought when human gene editing is considered) (Baltimore, 2015). The dramatic pace of evolution of information technology shows no sign of slowing, continuing to advance in power from 100 to 1000-fold a decade, enabling not only new forms of analysis such as augmenting the traditional tools of experiment and theory with the sophisticated tools of data analysis (big data). Indeed, the tools of artificial intelligence not only are rapidly progressing, but they have stimulated fears of eventual sentient behaviour of machines.

Already we are seeing the spontaneous emergence of new forms of creative activities, e.g., the "maker" fairs providing opportunities to showcase forms of artistic, recreational and commercial activity; the use of "additive manufacturing" to build new products and processes atomic layer by atomic layer; and the growing use of the "app" culture to empower an immense marketplace of small software development companies. In fact, some suggest that our civilization may experience a renaissance-like awakening of creative activities in the 21st century similar to that occurring in 16th century Europe.

The determining characteristic of the university of the 21st Century may be a shift in intellectual focus, from the preservation or transmission of knowledge, to the process of creativity itself. If so, then the vision for the university of 2030 should stress characteristics such as creativity, innovation, ingenuity and invention, and entrepreneurial zeal. But here lies a great challenge. While universities are experienced in teaching the skills of analysis, we have far less understanding of the intellectual activities associated with creativity. In fact, the current disciplinary culture of our campuses sometimes discriminates against those who are truly creative and do not fit well into our stereotypes of students and faculty.

Yet another feature of our information-rich society is our capacity for communication. The internet and related technologies such as smartphones and cloud computing make it cheap and easy not only to communicate but also to collect, store and analyse immense quantities of information. But, while facilitating communication and communities, such technology also has its downside. Always on, always used communication consumes the attention of individuals. Indeed, this attention is the valuable commodity needed by advertisers that actually funds these communications networks.

Finally, the very structure of knowledge is continuing to shift as fields such as biology, physics, mathematics and the social sciences are converging. (Sharp, 2014) Today physicists and engineers have as much impact on the evolution of biological science as biologists do on chemistry and computer technology (e.g. the deep learning algorithms derived from neural networks). The emergence of convergence (or consilience, as E. O. Wilson would term it) is challenging the disciplinary fragmentation of the University into departments, schools and colleges.

Any vision proposed for the university in 2030 must consider the extraordinary changes and uncertainties of a future driven by exponentially evolving information and communications technology. The extraordinary connectivity provided by the Internet already links together the majority of the world's population. To this, one can add the emerging capacity to capture and distribute the accumulated knowledge of our civilization in digital form and provide opportunities for learning through new paradigms such as MOOCs and AI cognitive tutors. This suggests the possible emergence of a new global society no longer constrained by space, time, monopoly or archaic laws and, instead, even more dependent upon the generation of new knowledge and the education of world citizens. In such an era of rapid change, it has become the responsibility of democratic societies to provide their citizens with the learning opportunities they need throughout their lives, at costs they can afford, as a right rather than a privilege (Germano, 2010).

SOCIAL AND POLITICAL CHANGE

Even as our world becomes increasingly dependent upon knowledge, the very technology that is key to creating, archiving and making available knowledge is ironically being used to attack and undermine it. In the Trump era, social media not only has become a powerful tool of American politics, but it provides the capacity to distort knowledge and truth, the "alt-truth" phenomenon that allows a tidal wave of anger built on the social media Twitter to not only win a presidential election, but to build a powerful, almost mythological force capable of challenging the evidence-based truth critical to a democracy (Brooks, 2017). While counterforces such as Wikipedia and digital libraries were thought of as power technologies capable of distributing facts and truth, the worry today is that the alt-truth deluge from social media may in fact be eroding American democracy (*The Economist, Technology and Politics*, 2016).

Xenophobic and racist energy creates a hostile electorate that is not only unwilling to accept truth established by evidence, but has largely abandoned the scientific method (with only 25% of Americans now expressing confidence in scientific discovery) (Miller, 2016). Both parents and young people are beginning to question the value of higher education. Indeed, one wealthy billionaire is even trying to bribe students not to go to college.

Policy-makers, determined to serve their "populist" constituencies, are erecting barriers to higher education based on race and class. Nearly two decades into our new century, there are unmistakable signs that America's fabled social mobility is in trouble — perhaps even in serious trouble. "We are faced with a challenge to liberalism by populists who are challenging the ideas of freedom, equality, human rights, representative democracy and globalization with our current post-truth age in which expertise on matters such as climate change is rubbished and institutions are deemed untrustworthy." (Gitlin, 2017)

Broader Challenges

Over the longer term there is compelling evidence that the growing population and invasive activities of humankind are now altering the fragile balance of our planet. The concerns are multiplying in number and intensifying in severity: the destruction of forests, wetlands and other natural habitats by human activity, the extinction of millions of species and the loss of biodiversity; the buildup of greenhouse gases and their impact on global climates; the pollution of our air, water and land. We must find new ways to provide for a human society that presently has outstripped the limits of global sustainability.

Of comparable concern are the widening gaps in prosperity, health and quality of life characterizing developed, developing and underdeveloped regions. To be sure, there are some signs of optimism: a slowing population growth that may stabilize during the 21st century, technological advances such as the "green revolution" that have fed much of the world, and the rapid growth of developing economies in Asia and Latin America. Yet it is estimated that one-sixth of the world's population still live in extreme poverty, suffering from diseases such as malaria, tuberculosis, AIDS, diarrhoea and others that prey on bodies weakened by chronic hunger, claiming more than 20,000 lives daily. These global needs can only be addressed by the commitment of developed nations and the implementation of technology to alleviate poverty and disease.

There are other possibilities that might be considered for the longer-term future. Balancing population growth in some parts of the world might be new pandemics, such as AIDS or an avian flu virus, that appear out of nowhere to ravage our species. The growing divide between rich and poor, the developed nations and the third world, the North and South hemispheres, could drive even more serious social unrest and terrorism, perhaps armed with even more terrifying weapons.

Technology could present new challenges that seem almost taken from the pages of science fiction. Clearly if digital technology continues to evolve at its current pace for the next decade, creating machines a thousand, a million, a billion times more powerful that those which are so dominating our world today, then phenomena such as the emergence of machine consciousness and intelligence become very real possibilities during this century. In fact, some even suggest that we could encounter a "technological singularity", a point at which technology begins to accelerate so rapidly (for example, as intelligent machines develop even more intelligent machines) that we lose not only the ability to control but even to predict the future.

Clearly phenomena such as machine consciousness, contact by extraterrestrial intelligence, or cosmic extinction from a wandering asteroid are possibilities for our civilization, but just as clearly they should neither dominate our attention nor our near-term actions. More generally, it is clear that as the pace of change continues to accelerate, learning organizations and innovation systems will need to become highly adaptive if they are to survive. Here, we might best think of future learning and innovation environments as ecologies that not only adapt but also mutate and evolve to serve an ever-changing world.

We cannot predict these things...but we can make sure that our descendants are equipped with the education and skills to handle them!

HOW DO WE LEAD OUR UNIVERSITIES TO 2030?

As many leaders in higher education have come to realize, our changing environment requires a far more strategic approach to the evolution of our institutions at all levels. It is critical for higher education to give thoughtful attention to the design of institutional processes for planning, management, leadership and governance. The ability of universities to adapt successfully to the profound changes occurring in our society will depend a great deal on their collective ability to develop and execute appropriate strategies. Key is the recognition that in a rapidly changing environment, it is important to develop a planning process that is not only capable of adapting to changing conditions, but to some degree capable of modifying the environment in which the university will find itself in the decades ahead. We must seek a progressive, flexible and adaptive process, capable of responding to a dynamic environment and an uncertain — indeed, unknowable — future.

But, today, incremental change based on traditional, well-understood paradigms may be the most dangerous course of all, because those paradigms may simply not be adequate to adapt to a future of change. If the status quo is no longer an option, if the existing paradigms are no longer viable, then transformation becomes the wisest course. While universities have always successfully managed the balance between preserving and propagating the fundamental knowledge sustaining our cultures and civilizations and not only adapting to but actually creating the paradigm shifts that drive change, the time scales characterizing these roles are becoming ever shorter. The centuries it took for earlier forms of learning as scholasticism to humanism and enlightenment to evolve contracted to decades for the industrial revolution and globalization and now have been compressed to a generation or less for the age of knowledge as the technologies of our times now evolve at an exponential pace. Put another way, during the transition from Generation X to the Millennials, info-, bio- and nano-technology have increased in power a million-fold and will do so yet again with Generation Z.

To succeed, we strive for a more flexible culture, one more accepting of occasional failure as the unavoidable corollary to any ambitious effort. We must learn to adapt quickly while retaining the values and goals that give us a sense of mission and community. Many view the current rigid and hierarchical structure of the university as obsolete. To advance, we must discover ways to draw upon the unique and vibrant creativity of every member of our community. Our challenge is to tap the great source of creativity and energy of outstanding faculty, students and staff, working at the grassroots level of the academic enterprise of the University in a way that preserves our fundamental missions, characteristics, and values.

The American University, Circa 2030...and Beyond

So what might we anticipate over the longer term as possible future forms of American universities? The monastic character of the ivory tower is certainly lost forever. Although there are many important features of the campus environment that suggest that most universities will continue to exist as a place, at least for the near term, as digital technology makes it increasingly possible to emulate human interaction in all the senses with arbitrarily high fidelity, perhaps we should not bind teaching and scholarship too tightly to buildings and grounds. Certainly, both learning and scholarship will continue to depend heavily upon the existence of communities, since they are, after all, high social enterprises. Yet as these communities are increasingly global in extent, detached from the constraints of space and time, we should not assume that the scholarly communities of our times would necessarily dictate the future of our universities.

Imagine the linking together of billions of people with limitless access to knowledge and learning tools enabled by a rapidly evolving scaffolding of cyberinfrastructure, which increases in power one-hundred to one thousand-fold every decade. This hive-like culture will not only challenge existing social institutions such as corporations, universities, nation states, which have depended upon the constraints of space, time, laws and monopoly. But it will enable the spontaneous emergence of new social structures as yet unimagined — just think of the early denizens of the Internet such as Google, Facebook, Amazon...In fact, we may be on the threshold of the emergence of a new form of civilization, as billions of world citizens interact together, unconstrained by today's monopolies on knowledge or learning opportunities.

Perhaps this, then, is the most exciting vision for the future of knowledge and learning organizations such as the university, no longer constrained by space, time, monopoly or archaic laws, but rather responsive to the needs of a global, knowledge society and unleashed by technology to empower and serve all of humankind. And all of this is likely to happen during the lives of today's students. These possibilities must inform and shape the manner in which we view, support and lead higher education. Now is not the time to back into the future.

Yet we also might remember a quote from the 2009 Glion Declaration:
"For a thousand years the university has benefited our civilization as a learning community where both the young and the experienced could acquire not only knowledge and skills but also the values and discipline of the educated mind. It has defended and propagated our cultural and intellectual heritage, while challenging our norms and beliefs. The university of the twenty-first century may be as different from today's institutions as the research university is from the colonial college. But its form and its continued evolution will be a consequence of transformations necessary to provide its ancient values and contributions to a changing world" (Rhodes, 2009).

REFERENCES

Baltimore, D. et al.(2015). "A Prudent Path Forward for Genomic Engineering and Germline Gene Modification", *Science* Vol. 348, 3 April 2015, p. 36.

Brooks, D., "The Enlightenment Project", *New York Times*, February 28, 2017.

Duderstadt, J. J. (2000). *A University for the 21st Century*. Ann Arbor, MI: University of Michigan Press.

Germano, W. (2010). "What Are Books Good For?", *The Key Reporter*, New York, Phi Beta Kappa Society, Winter, 2010.

Gitlin, T. (2017). "Promoting Knowledge in an Age of Unreason", *Chronicle of Higher Education*, 9 March 2017.

Gratton, L. & Scott, A. (2016). *The 100-Year Life: Living and Working in an Age of Longevity*, London, Bloomsbury, 2016.

Holliday, C. (chair) (2012). *Research Universities and the Future of America: Ten Breakthrough Actions Vital to Our Nation's Prosperity and Security*. National Academies Committee on Research Universities. Washington, D.C.: National Academy Press, 2012.

Kelly, K. (2016). *The Inevitable: Understanding the 12 Technological Forces That Will Shape Our Future*, New York, Penguin Publishing Group, 2016.

Miller, J. D. (2016). "Civil Scientific Literacy in the United States in 2016", Institute for Social Research, the University of Michigan, 2016.

Rhodes, F. H. (20010). "Respice, Prospice: Higher Education: A Decennial Review", in Weber L. E. & Duderstadt J. J. (eds) *University Research for Innovation*. Economica, Paris.

Rhodes, F. H. *et al.* (2009). *The Second Glion Declaration: Universities and the Innovative Spirit,* Glion Colloquium, Geneva (June 2009).

Schwab, K. (2016). *The Fourth Industrial Revolution,* World Economic Forum, Geneva.

Scott C. (2016) "When College Was a Public Good", *Chronicle of Higher Education,* November 27, 2016.

Sharp, P. A. (2014). "Meeting Global Challenges: Discovery and Innovation Through Convergence", *Science,* Vol 346, 19 December 2014.

The Economist, Technology Quarterly (2017). "Finding a Voice", 7 January.

The Economist, On Artificial Intelligence (2016). "March of the Machines: The Return of the Machinery Question", Special Report 25 June.

The Economist, Technology and Politics (2016). "The Signal and the Noise", Special Report, 26 March.

The Economist, Lifelong Education (2017). A Special Report, 14 January.

CHAPTER 20

The Story of the Cambridge Taxi Driver and the Future of the University

Bert van der Zwaan

INTRODUCTION

The university is one of the oldest institutions in the world. After 800 years, it is still going strong, where many other institutions have foundered. The university even appears to be flourishing: in the Netherlands, for instance, as elsewhere, student numbers continue to rise, research enjoys a good reputation and Dutch universities' results are impressive — certainly if one takes the size of the country into consideration (Times Higher Education, 2017).

Nevertheless, these are turbulent times. There is criticism from all sides: criticism of the mass nature of education, the focus on efficiency and research output, the lack of collaboration with industry, and the relatively meagre attention that universities are said to pay to societal problems. And that is just criticism from the outside world. Within the university community, the voices of lecturers and students can also be heard. They are often critical of administrators, "who have transformed the university into a factory".

In addition to criticism of the current situation, there are challenges for the future. No doubt Higher Education will change profoundly over the next 25 years; I have recently summarized the main trends (Van der Zwaan, 2017). For example, education will transform due to digitalization, but also due to customizing of teaching programs and the rapidly increasing importance of obtaining course certificates over a degree (see for instance Barber *et al.*, 2013). Research will move more and more towards interdisciplinary questions

(National Academies Press, 2014; Wernli & Darbellay, 2016). Supported by IT, global cooperation will be the norm, also because research facilities will be so costly that they will be out of reach for many universities.

How is the university tackling the existing problems and how is it preparing for the future? Where will the bottlenecks and opportunities lie in the coming 25 years? Or, to put it differently: how can the university best survive? University leaders tend to answer this question by immediately starting the narrative of the need for more funding or by pointing to all the changes that are needed to face the challenges in teaching and research. But by doing so they run the risk of ignoring the tremendous social changes around us. In this essay, of which some parts have been published before (Van der Zwaan, 2017), I will focus on these changes. I will argue that if we continue our present course, we run the risk of ending up doing very well in splendid isolation, but being totally disconnected from society at large.

THE STORY OF THE CAMBRIDGE TAXI DRIVER

In May 2017, a taxi driver brought me from Clare College, where she picked me up, to the Cambridge train station. This was after a meeting with the LERU (League of European Research Universities) rectors, who just had been discussing the threats and challenges to our research universities. The debate had very much focused on Brexit and EU-funding as important items. However, the taxi driver confronted me with a completely different view. In the 20 minutes or so of this drive, she talked non-stop and made comments on the city of Cambridge and the landmarks we passed. But, unintentionally, she very nicely captured the difference between the academic world and her world, in which she was forced to cope with completely different challenges than our universities.

At some point, she commented on the booming business in Cambridge. She told me that the university was instrumental therein: many of the staff and faculty were looking for housing, among them quite a lot of foreigners. That was the reason, she said, that she was forced to live at a one-hour driving distance from Cambridge, because housing in Cambridge was much too expensive due to the high demand. "These people", she said, "complain about housing prices by putting a manifesto in Latin on houses that are being built for a price of £1 million or more, whereas we don't profit at all from the booming business." She further summarized the world of a Cambridge taxi driver in a few words: local, no access to higher education due to high tuition fees. Her "facts" were generated on social media. The feeling which spoke out of her words: "We are not protected in a globalizing world, we are losing out to others, we are not participating in prosperity."

The rectors' conference I just had left behind me had been filled with a completely different world, the one of academia: global, (scientific) fact is truth, with a strong sense of wider cultural perspective and the ability to handle different scenarios. The feeling of the rectors while discussing Brexit and other issues contrasted markedly with that of the taxi driver: "We are global universities, the labour market is ours, globalization is imperative to improve the world."

The changing landscape

The story of the Cambridge taxi driver illustrates that while universities are grappling with all the changes mentioned in the introduction, they should not lose sight of societal undercurrents affecting the very foundation of the university. In 1852, J. H. Newman wrote: "A university is a place…whither students come from every quarter for every kind of knowledge…in which the intellect may safely range and speculate. It is a place where inquiry is pushed forward…discoveries perfected and verified…and error exposed, by the collision of mind with mind, and knowledge with knowledge." For many years, the university has built upon this idealistic mission. On top of that, over the past several decades, it has been forced into the role of innovator, provider of skilled personnel, and attractor of international talent and business investments. But now society increasingly demands more influence on the scientific agenda-setting, requires Open Science, and urges the university to think more about its impact and meaningful contributions rather than about "creation of economic value".

Underlying this trend is the sense of a growing divide in society. Statistics support the emergence of such a social divide, not only in the US, but also in Europe. Education is increasingly becoming a characteristic of social class: worldwide, there is now an educated elite which benefits from rising global prosperity. However, a growing proportion of the population, also in Europe, is faced with a decline in opportunities in the labour market. The negative sentiment of the so-called angry white man who is losing out, or feels he is losing out, to globalization and the open borders that promote international trade, has grown over the past few years. This resulted in the dissatisfaction that coloured the elections in the US, led to the British electorate turning its back against the European Union, and continues to dominate polls, referenda and elections in the Netherlands, Italy, France and Germany.

In this context, Stephen Hawking wrote a letter to the Guardian in 2016 with the meaningful title "This is the most dangerous time for our planet". He starts the letter with: "I have lived my life in an extraordinarily privileged bubble," indicating the way universities still tend to operate in relative isolation. He continues: "…taken together, we are living in a world of widening, not diminishing, financial inequality, in which many people can see not just their standard of living, but their ability to earn a living at all, disappearing". His warning seems right on target: universities run a considerable risk of losing societal support exactly due to this divide.

But perhaps the most disturbing undercurrent is that facts hardly play a role any more, and that societal debate is primarily governed by emotions. This is evident in people's reactions on social media, where facts are no longer recognized as facts, and are instead dismissed as mere opinions. Here, President Trump set a new precedent by stating that "a lot of people feel it wasn't a proper certificate" after President Obama released his birth certificate.

This profoundly changing landscape that surrounds the university demands a considerable re-adjustment, in addition to the challenges already imposed through teaching and research. Therefore, although some mourn the fact that the university has left its ivory tower as described by Newman, in my mind universities should go further in order to become more visible, and play a more significant role in society. This could range from addressing major societal problems to providing knowledge for better informed politics. Rather than withdrawing into its old role, an engaged, civic university should be vocal and take up a position in public debate. This would certainly help to legitimize the university and create new carrying capacity in society to sufficiently fund higher education from public sources, instead of leaving it to private funding through sky-high tuition fees. Access to higher education, now prevented by high costs, is crucial for a future society without a social divide which only spells trouble. Higher education for as many as possible is a key feature of a prosperous and stable future society. But most of all, in this "post-fact era" (see for context also Fukuyama, 2017; Stiglitz, 2017) the university needs to regain its role as a speaker of truth. In an age ruled by the wisdom of the crowd, reliable institutions are crucial. The university should be such an independent authority, showing clear ways out of complex problems.

The change of mindset needed

If the university were to play a more visible role in society, this would certainly be helpful to retain support. The fringe benefit for the university would be that, by doing so, it will become part of a broader system in which knowledge circulates, and therefore brings higher returns. This could even lead to universities forming associations with large organizations such as the United Nations, or parts of them, such as the Food and Agriculture Organization (FAO), or with NGOs, regions and governments, so as to provide their large programs with the essential knowledge.

In order to support this movement towards society, but at the same time to remain truthful to the mission of continuously exploring new knowledge domains, research programs ideally focus on the cutting edge of major societal and fundamental questions. This requires input from many disciplines. Interdisciplinary research will therefore inevitably play a large role. In turn, this demands the opening up of the rather closed academic silos. Teaching needs to shift from solely monodisciplinary education to training of students as "T-shape professionals". Students are thus prepared for their future roles, not only as university graduates in all kinds of professions, but also — for a considerable number of graduates — in their roles as leaders in society.

In short, we need to consider our scientific problems in a wider context. For instance, we should be more aware of the fact that most problems in society and science are not of a strictly disciplinary or technical nature. Climate change is a good example. From the point of view of science, we are very far advanced in understanding and predicting the climate system. We know that if we persist in our present behaviour, we will certainly surpass the critical boundary of 2°C warming of the earth. So the problem is one of governance and social arrangements, more than a technical issue. However, technical solutions such as alternative energy sources can help to implement pathways to sustainability and facilitate in finding a way out. But then again, extremely viable technical solutions, like the use of the deeper underground for storage of heat or carbon dioxide, might immediately run up against societal resistance, which could be mediated and overcome by applying insights from social sciences.

This brief example illustrates that it is absolutely inevitable that engineering and technical disciplines combine forces with disciplines from the sciences and social sciences and humanities, but also vice versa, that comprehensive research universities team up with technical ones, in order to arrive at successful solutions. This brings more than only short-term success: in my view, the combination of disciplines, and recombination in new convergences, facilitated in the future by powerful IT, could lead to a new "renaissance" in the literal meaning of the word. However, this sounds easier than it is: it will require a truly profound change in mindset in order to be successful in breaking down the disciplinary and cultural barriers which are characteristic of the traditional university.

REQUIRED INSTITUTIONAL CHANGE

The 2008 financial crisis and its aftermath have led to a rapid and profound change in the social climate worldwide. In nearly all Western countries, politicians are going back to focusing on national interests. In this climate, universities are facing a difficult period. Following the election of President Trump in 2016, many anticipate a dark spell in the US, in particular in terms of its leading role in higher education, the excellence of this education, but also — and especially — the role of the US as a place where international students are welcomed. This gloomy picture also applies to the agendas of the European populist parties in countries such as France, the UK, Germany, Italy and the Netherlands: the focus on curtailing immigration and the limited attention for higher education that this speaks of, can be viewed as a threat to the academic community.

In all cases, there is a growing fear of the denial of scientific facts. Here, too, President Trump in the US is setting a prominent example that many are hoping will not be followed by others: the prioritization of the economy over the environment, while at the same time denying the existence of major environmental issues, denying climate change, and his lambasting of the National Institutes of Health as being a waste of funds are not reassuring.

The importance of core values

Guzella and Folkers (this volume) argue that traditionally the university is a place of curatorship, of preserving knowledge even in the digital era. This includes education of new generations, making use of the most modern techniques. Of course, this still is a central role of the university. But what has changed since the origin of universities is that research has become an equally important task as teaching and curatorship. Especially since the middle of the previous century, universities have become among the most prominent providers of new knowledge in modern society. This came at a cost, since governments and research funders demanded a say in the universities' agenda, in return for the financial support for research. The good news is that by doing so, universities became better connected to society than maybe ever before. However, the bad news is that to some extent we have sold our soul to the devil since this connection constantly threatens the freedom of research.

Although we now realize that the ideal of value-free research is not realistic (Collins & Evans, 2017), the statements of the Trump government reminded us that freedom of research is not a given, and that universities should continuously fight for it. Marches for Science, as we saw in 2017 in reaction to the Trump administration, are of great value to fuel this fight. Moreover, we should constantly be aware that the freedom of research is not only affected by actions of governments, but that also rankings, funding and demands from the market can steer research along undesirable paths. Therefore, independence of thought, honesty and integrity should always be active core values. In combination with curiosity and inquisitiveness, this remains the heart of the university, needing active attention to let these values circulate through the organization and pass them on to new generations.

Gathering wisdom instead of knowledge

Since the Enlightenment, the ideal of knowledge — the gathering of knowledge for knowledge's sake — has come to lie at the very heart of the university. The idea gradually developed that production of knowledge is always meaningful, even if it results in a huge number of articles that no one reads or cites any more (see San Francisco Declaration, 2013, for some context).

In the coming years, we should step away from the neo-liberal model of the university where production is central, measured with quantitative KPIs. Instead, it is essential that the idea of production of papers evolves into a different concept, namely that the university is concerned with something more like the production of "wisdom". Analogous to the way in which the university's contribution should be measured in terms of meaningful impact, and not only in an economic sense, knowledge should be valued to the extent that it functions in the context of a really pressing question, and the degree to which it provides a broadly applicable answer. An excellent university is not a university that has the highest production in papers, but the university that combines asking really profound questions with contributing to society — in equal measure (see also Barnett, 2011, and Nowotny, 2015, for comparable discussions).

In a critical intellectual environment, words as "meaningful" and "wisdom" soon provoke follow-up questions, for behind such terms lies a whole range of potential implications. Instead of defining them immediately, these concepts should be explored in discussions with the university community and in debate with societal actors. This search is important because it will allow us to identify precisely which pressing questions we are facing, and how knowledge might contribute to solving these. But it will also be a search to discover when knowledge becomes wisdom: thus, when it becomes a solution that really enriches people's lives.

Trying to find answers to such questions will contribute substantially to further legitimize the university in society. It is time well spent to debate our mission. By doing so, we become more aware that science could be a powerful glue that keeps society together, which straddles boundaries in a crumbling political system. Even more, that science is the only way forward to solve many fundamental societal issues. That should be our discourse with society, with open science as an excellent tool of showing what we have to offer.

Institutional change versus society

It is essential that universities clearly establish a position in the societal debate. There will be an increasing need for indisputable facts, and institutions with the authority to provide them. But, in order to do this successfully in the "post-fact" era, universities must be aware of the gap between the higher- and lower-educated. This gap can only be bridged through adequate outreach: not only by stating the facts, but also by putting them in context and interpreting them in a broad range of different ways. This includes directly liaising with the media, but also extends to raising awareness and providing information at various platforms, such as through academic hubs and museums, or by organizing debates. The university must look for ways to successfully approach sections of the population which have long stopped reading the paper or watching television, but which predominantly or exclusively get their information from social media.

The younger generation is essential in this process: Altbach and De Wit (2016) rightly note that, in the referendums and elections of the past few years, the voting behaviour of students in both Europe and the US is markedly different from that of the older generations. They are predominantly proponents of globalization, all the more since they are often part of the educated elite and therefore stand to benefit from it. But that also means that students, who in the US mainly voted for Bernie Sanders and therefore against Clinton's establishment and Trump's populism, and in Europe voted against Brexit and in favour of the European Union, will increasingly protest against the populist concept of "taking care of our own people first". This places universities in the difficult position of having to reconcile conflicting aims: on the one hand, they will have to play a role in bridging the gap in the societal debate with facts and knowledge, but, on the other, they will increasingly be populated by young students who will take a clear stance against anti-globalization and populism. In that sense, universities may once again become centres of protest, but at the same time they must avoid being the isolated ivory towers of the elite. Hopefully, universities will be able to help give shape to these protest movements while at the same time strengthening their connection with the "angry white man".

EDUCATING YOUNG PEOPLE AND CITIZENSHIP

Over the past decades, we have seen an increasing shift away from the provision of a broad college education. A growing number of voices argue in favour of using the university in a more targeted fashion as preparation for the labour market, also in view of the cost. What is certain, however, is that the labour market that we are used to, which has been employing graduates for centuries, is undergoing a truly fundamental transformation. Whereas, for many years, employment could almost be taken for granted, nowadays we see a general contraction of the labour market due to, for instance, competition with an increasing volume of graduates, and robotization (Frey & Osborne, 2013; Susskind & Susskind, 2014). In such a situation, the extent to which a university program is tailored to rapidly changing demands from society is becoming increasingly important. Clearly, employability will be more of an issue than it has been so far.

In many respects, emphasis in academic education today still lies on the acquisition of knowledge. But, in future, knowledge will be available everywhere around us or "in the cloud". Hence, the role of the university graduate will shift from gathering and generating knowledge, to using it, and above all, using it in a truly creative way. Asking good questions is increasingly more important than knowing facts. To compete with digital universities and the growing offer of Lifelong Learning programs, universities need to be more student-centric, more geared towards customized learning, more towards creativity, in order to survive the growing pressure on the traditional university.

University curricula tend to be supply-driven, that is, driven by academic traditions or lecturers' interests. Research universities in particular are not really demand-driven in the sense that they readily respond to needs from society. As a result, often little attention is paid to so-called 21st century skills, like soft skills, leadership-skills. But also to awareness of what is going on in society, general academic skills, Bildung if you like. Yet, these are precisely the skills that should characterize the curriculum of tomorrow, resulting in responsible citizens who will show leadership in the face of tomorrow's challenges. This will form the best bridge between the university and a changing society.

Leadership at all levels

The greatest task for the university of the future is to be constantly willing and able to adapt to all of these different challenges, to local circumstances, and to constantly shifting conditions over time. We therefore need to see university planning based on portfolios, rather than classical planning based on disciplines. For this is the great challenge: on the one hand, to keep traditional, discipline-based scholarship intact, because it is essential to achieve progress in this, while on the other hand allow the results of this scholarship to be used flexibly and often in interdisciplinary ways in social contexts.

This means that also the university will need to be organized in a flexible, readily adaptable way. But, at the same time, it needs to preserve scientific knowledge and disciplinary traditions which have been built over a long span of time. At the heart of all these changes should be a clear view on core values, which constantly need to be discussed and renewed. It falls to university administrators in particular to encourage debate on this within their institutions. This requires strong leadership at all levels. But much too often university leaders see themselves as the agent of change, whereas, in reality, leadership should reside deeply in a professional organization, and not only at the top.

First and foremost, this leadership should be visible in the continuous development of teachers. More than at any other level, authoritative study directors and professors leading the continuous change and improvement of curricula, in view of the challenges imposed by a dynamic labour market, are key. Their essential position should be recognized and supported, in particular because of the traditional slight with which teaching is regarded compared to research.

The research leadership role is traditionally already strong in universities. But now, more than ever, a new type of leadership is required to explore rapidly changing "convergences", combinations of disciplines that collaborate in unexpected configurations. This new leadership demands speaking the "language" of the disciplines involved, and the ability to tear down the disciplinary silos.

Universities have become large, sometimes extremely so, and with the growing size there has been an enormous increase of bureaucracy. This is aggravated by the continuously increasing number of rules imposed by the government. What is needed, however, is an agile organization that supports teachers, scientists and scholars in a dynamic context. Although strong academic leadership is essential in positions like those of vice-chancellor, dean and study director, much too often academics see investment in good managers of increasingly more complex university services as a waste of money. However, in this case their often-heard maxim that all funds should go to academics, is clearly one of myopia: flexible, high-quality services are essential to survive.

CONCLUDING REMARKS

After 800 years, the state of the university should be reconsidered very carefully. In the English-speaking world there is an increasing chorus of voices that comment on the "crisis of the research university", and that predicts a troublesome future based on the sky-high tuition fees, increasing privatization and decreasing government support. The first reflex to this is to react from an inward-looking perspective, and to start the narrative that pleads for increased funding to preserve the university in present state. However, instead of reasoning from within, it seems wise to consider the question whether the university is still well positioned in a changing society. Crucial in this respect is to connect the world of the academia to the world of the taxi driver.

ACKNOWLEDGEMENTS

I thank the organizers of the Glion Colloquium 2017, which was inspirational, and Esther Stiekema and Margreet de Lange for helpful comments and suggestions to improve the manuscript.

REFERENCES

Altbach, P.G. & De Wit, H. (2016). "Will Trump make US HE great again? Not likely," *Times Higher Education*, November 2016.

Barber, M., Donnelly, K. & Rizvi, S. (2013). "An avalanche is coming. Higher education and the revolution ahead". Institute for Public Policy Research.

Barnett, R. (2011). *Being a University*. Routledge.

Bovens, M., Dekker, P. & Tiemeijer, W. (2014). "Gescheiden werelden? Een verkenning van sociaal-culturele tegenstellingen in Nederland", Sociaal Cultureel Planbureau en WRR.

Collins, H., & Evans, R. (2017). *Why democracies need science*, Polity.

Frey, C. B. & Osborne, M. A. (2013). *The future of employment. How susceptible are jobs to computerization?* Oxford Martin Publications.

Fukuyama, F. (2017). "The emergence of a post-fact world", *NewEurope*, 8 January 2017.

Guzella, L. & Folkers, G., (This volume). "Universities as curators of knowledge".

Hawking, S. (2016). "This is the most dangerous time for our planet," *the Guardian*, 1 December 2016.

National Academies Press (2014). "Convergence. Facilitating Transdisciplinary Integration of Life Sciences, Physical Sciences, Engineering, and Beyond". National Research Council.

Newman, J. H. (1852): *The idea of a university*. Newmanreader.org

Nowotny, H. (2015). *The cunning of uncertainty*, Polity.

Stiglitz, J.E. (2017). "The age of Trump", *NewEurope*, 8 January 2017.

San Francisco Declaration on Research Assessment (DORA) (2013). Ascb.org

Susskind, R. & Susskind, D., (2014). *The Future of the Professions. How Technology Will Transform the Work of Human Experts*, Oxford University Press.

Times Higher Education (2017). "The European University Ranking 2017: Power behind the throne". June 2017.

Van der Zwaan, G. J. (2017). *Higher Education in 2040; a global approach*, Amsterdam University Press, 255 pp.

Wernli, D. & Darbellay, F. (2016). "Interdisciplinarity and the 21st century research-intensive university". LERU position paper 2016.

SOME CONCLUDING REMARKS

This was the 11th Glion Colloquium and arguably the most successful, distinguished both by the quality of the papers and the discussion. Unlike in many previous meetings, there was less emphasis on the more familiar themes of research opportunities, financial sustainability, good governance, leadership and educational access and affordability. These topics were by no means absent. And neither were the extraordinary breakthroughs in science and technology which may well define the next generation for the world's leading research universities: artificial intelligence, gene editing, big data and so on.

But there was a palpable sense of a long shadow having been cast across the world of higher education since the previous meeting in 2015 and indeed in the months between the Colloquium being organized and it actually taking place in June 2017. Some presentations were hastily revised; the discussions were more outward-looking than was customary. What was somewhat obliquely referred to as "context" predominated.

The cause of this was of course the tumultuous political events of 2016 in both Europe and the United States. The result of the referendum in the United Kingdom to leave the European Union and the election of Donald Trump as President of the United States, together with the "new populism" which they reflected, demanded a reconsideration of hitherto rather taken-for-granted assumptions of the role of higher education in contemporary society, its direction of travel and the perceived failures of the academy to see it coming.

The sense of threat was more than merely abstract. In a world of "post-truth" and fake news, how was future knowledge to be accepted and legitimated? And what were the implications for academic freedom, curriculum content and educational pedagogy?

There was also some genuine anxiety that perhaps the 18th-century Enlightenment ideal of the growth of knowledge leading to social progress had run its course. How could the astonishing advances in science and technology be accompanied by the economic and social polarization now so manifest? And how far were we, as leading research universities, complicit in this process? There was some sense that we may have failed in our educational role. In the long arc of post-war university expansion, we had rather assumed, though rarely pronounced, that an increasing number of graduates would lead to a world at once more prosperous, more tolerant, more respectful of human rights and more civilized. It would also be more global, or at least more internationalized. We were educating not just national but global citizens to tackle the big issues of the 21st century: climate change, resource sustainability, poverty, health, peace. In time, through our efforts in research and education, the world would become a better place.

And, of course, in so many ways, it has. But there was a sense that in 2016 this world had shifted on its axis. The global financial crisis was frequently referred to as a defining moment. Ten years on, large parts of Europe and North America, at least, were still living in an age of austerity. It was increasingly difficult to persuade those who had seen their local factories or coal mines or shipyards close of the benefits of economic globalization; or to sell the advantages of the new gig economy and its attendant insecurities as a worthwhile substitute. Only one per cent of the population have benefited from the new liberal economy. Meanwhile, whole communities have been hollowed out and left behind. They found their voice in the elections of 2016. It was not lost on the participants at the Colloquium that the key enabling technology of economic liberalization, the Internet, was rooted in the worldwide web and the research endeavours of the physicists and engineers at CERN.

Furthermore, and closer to home, the decade or more of austerity has had a profound effect on inter-generational equity. Unemployment rates among young people, including graduates, have risen sharply. Careers, in the old-fashioned sense, are scarce and less secure. A generation has become more disaffected and pessimistic. Increasingly strident political voices accuse universities of having failed to meet the needs of society. "Is it worth it?" is a question asked increasingly by both potential students and by political paymasters.

If this were not enough, universities are now faced with the vexed issue of migration and multi-culturalism. Universities worldwide have been in the vanguard of internationalism. Student and staff mobility has increased enormously, sometimes, as in Europe, as a result of official policy, but equally often as a result of individual choice. Universities, and indeed whole higher-education systems, have adopted measures of internationalization as key performance indicators. It was a trend viewed not only as benign but highly positive in educating students for an increasingly multicultural and multinational future.

But little of this seems to have rubbed off on the anti-migrant, and sometimes downright racist, discourse of the new populist politics: quite the contrary.

So is the future of the university — the Colloquium's original title — one of continuing crisis, losing both popular and political support? Students, it should be remembered, still flock to universities in increasing numbers; and research in universities is still viewed by governments and industry as a key component of innovation and international competitiveness. Perhaps, though, the changing context of 2016 has provided a reality check for higher education. The wider societal benefits cannot be taken for granted. The communities left behind by decades of globalization need to be embraced and listened to. We must be seen as part of the solution for them and not part of the problem. They, after all, are citizens too.

Howard Newby
University of Liverpool

Luc E. Weber
University of Geneva

www.ingramcontent.com/pod-product-compliance
Lightning Source LLC
Chambersburg PA
CBHW062158080426
42734CB00010B/1747